TRUE STORIES OF COMBAT
FROM THE MEN WHO LIVED THEM . . .

Captain Frank Kaine, USN (Ret.), shares the remarkable story of the first Demolition Units in the South Pacific, their role in MacArthur's campaign, and how an entire army was fed with centuries-old fish.

Lieutenant E. F. "Andy" Andrews, UDT 15, tells of the terrible prices paid by the original UDTs, and of their single greatest loss of World War II.

Lieutenant George Atcheson, UDT 3, remembers the Korean War, when he first took the UDTs onto dry land—and behind enemy lines.

And **Lieutenant Commander Roy Boehm,** who handpicked the men of SEAL Team Two, tells the harrowing true story of how he accomplished one mission, and ended up having his career saved by a president.

The first comprehensive, fully illustrated history of the Navy SEALs' origins, with exclusive eyewitness accounts as well as rarely known facts about the men and their missions.

ALSO BY KEVIN DOCKERY

Navy SEALs: A History Part II
From Vietnam to Desert Storm

NAVY SEALs

A HISTORY OF THE EARLY YEARS

KEVIN DOCKERY

From Interviews by Bud Brutsman

BERKLEY BOOKS, NEW YORK

A Berkley Book
Published by The Berkley Publishing Group
A division of Penguin Putnam Inc.
375 Hudson Street
New York, New York 10014

Copyright © 2001 by Bill Fawcett & Associates
Book design by Tiffany Kukec
Cover design by Steven Ferlauto
Cover photographs courtesy Bettman/Corbis

PRINTING HISTORY
Berkley hardcover edition / August 2001
Berkley trade paperback edition / April 2003

Berkley trade paperback ISBN: 0-425-18851-5

Visit our website at
www.penguinputnam.com

The Library of Congress has catalogued the Berkley hardcover edition as follows:

Dockery, Kevin.
Navy SEALs : a history of the early years / Kevin Dockery—1st ed.
p. cm.
Includes index.
ISBN 0-425-17825-0
1. United States. Navy. SEALs—History—20th century. I. Title.

VG87 .D6297 2001
359.9'84—dc21   2001035935

PRINTED IN THE UNITED STATES OF AMERICA

10 9 8 7 6 5 4 3 2 1

Contents

Foreword

Creating *Navy SEALs: A History of the Early Years* was both an education and an emotional journey. Being born in the year 1970 meant that my notion of war was Vietnam. But for so many of my generation the Vietnam War was a political and highly emotional matter that our parents and their friends hardly ever discussed. Helping to tell the story of the men in the Navy SEALs and the groups that preceded them was a unique opportunity for someone who was not there to learn what really happened in our country's most controversial war. And to hear it told in all its drama by an amazing range of Medal of Honor and Navy Cross recipients, admirals, captains, and chiefs and enlisted men. During the eight months of interviews on which this book is based, everyone who worked with these amazing men, who to a man adamantly decline to be called heroes, heard more about human will and sacrifice than any book or movie could ever portray.

In the years after the war, the whole subject of Vietnam was often simply swept under the carpet. The mid-1970s and early 1980s became a time for the nation to try to regroup emotionally and politically and attempt to comprehend what it had just experienced. In our schools and at public forums, the real story of the Vietnam War seemed much too sensitive and complex to discuss openly with those who had not been there or were too young to understand what had happened both in Vietnam and America while the war was being fought.

Few of those who were not old enough to have known the Vietnam veterans as they returned understood the second battle that had to be fought here—the battle to become reintegrated into society. Comprehending the real face of war is likely impossible for those who have not been there. And for the Vietnam veterans, unlike their grandfathers and fathers upon their return from World War I and II, there were no huge parades for the "war heroes" and little appreciation for the sacrifice of the combat veteran. Unlike my father's generation, which saw three major conflicts in twenty-five years, my generation—"Generation X"—knows no other way of life than the safety and stability made possible by so much bloodshed decades earlier.

The reality of war is brought home to you when you sit listening to recollections of Normandy, Iwo Jima, Korea, and Vietnam told by the men who actually fought in those places. There are few things in life as moving as sitting across from a veteran and watching his eyes stare back across fifty years as he relives stories of triumph, despair, and adversity.

Following are the accounts of these brave men in their own painful and justifiably proud words. It is a privilege to have been part of the effort to bring to you the true accounts of the courage, pain, sense of loss, and pride as they were really experienced by the men who fought for our nation from Normandy's beaches to the jungles of Vietnam.

—Bud W. Brutsman

Chapter 1

THE NAVY SEALS

The United States Navy SEALs are the direct action component of the Navy Special Warfare community. Named for the three environments they operate from—the SEa, Air, and Land—the SEALs are highly trained unconventional warfare troops. There are presently six SEAL Teams and two SEAL Delivery Vehicle Teams (SDV Team), with a roughly equal number of men assigned to each coast of the United States. The SEAL Teams are organized into ten sixteen-man platoons, with an additional headquarters platoon and a twenty-man support element. Though each SEAL Team is identified by a number, even numbers on the East Coast and odd numbers on the West, the men who man these units often choose to refer to themselves simply as "the Teams."

These simple statistics do little to illustrate the nature of the SEAL Teams or the unique individuals who are their members. Only in the closing decade of the twentieth century does the story of the SEALs come into public prominence. Since the late 1980s, the SEALs have been the subject of many popular books, movies, television specials, and magazine articles. Few of these information sources have told the history of these men.

The SEAL Teams of today descended from the Underwater Demolition Teams. The UDTs also derived from an earlier unit, the Navy Combat Demolition Teams. Other specialized units that were created during the war years of World War II had a strong influence on today's teams as well.

The SEAL Teams of today have a reputation for being among the toughest unconventional warfare troops in the world. The following pages tell us where they came from.

Chapter 2

WORLD WAR II: THE ORIGINS

World War II was an event that a number of people throughout the world saw coming well before it arrived. But like a giant avalanche, there seemed to be little these few could do to prevent it.

The First World War ended in November 1918, and its repercussions and echoes were felt and heard through most of the twentieth century. A twenty-nine-year-old Austrian-born German who had been less than a success in the business world, had enlisted in the German army and fought through the war, being wounded in battle and cited for bravery twice. Reaching the rank of lance corporal, Adolf Hitler saw his country defeated and brought to her knees. That army corporal would later use Germany's defeat and her fallen status to boost himself to a position of domination. A domination that Hitler spread over almost all of Europe and beyond.

Japan, who had allied herself with Great Britain during the First World War, was given a mandate over many of the islands of the Central Pacific. The Marshalls, Marianas, and Caroline Islands were all ceded to Japan. This mandate allowed Japan to extend her influence almost unopposed across a third of the Central Pacific by 1920. The results of the Russo-Japanese War at the beginning of the twentieth century had Korea in Japanese hands by 1910. Renamed Chosen, Korea gave the Japanese a shared border with Northern China at Manchuria.

In the early 1920s, Mussolini's Fascists gathered power in Italy, eventually eliminating any effective opposition to their rule. Germany suffered under financial reparations she was ordered to pay for her part in the First World War. Inflation brought the country to near-complete ruin, creating the conditions for Hitler's appeal to the poverty-stricken people of the country. On 23 October 1929, the New York Stock Exchange collapsed, beginning a worldwide economic depression.

Unrest swept through the junior officers of the Japanese military in 1930. A group of young officers assassinated Prime Min-

A UDT naked warrior looking up from the bottom as he swims through clear ocean waters.

U.S. Navy

ister Inukai in part because of his support of limitations put on the strength of the Japanese military through treaties. A sabotage incident at Mukden on the South Manchuria Railroad gives the Japanese army an excuse to send in troops. Military action by the Chinese was weak and ineffectual, and by early 1932, the Japanese army had conquered Manchuria, renaming it Manchukuo and quickly exploiting the area.

The early 1930s saw Hitler gaining power in Germany. Violent actions by Hitler's henchmen destroy any effective opposition to him, even in his own Nazi Party. in August 1934, President Hindenburg of Germany dies and Hitler proclaims himself *führer* (leader) and chancellor of Germany soon after.

By the mid-1930s, Hitler's Germany began a policy of expansion in Europe. The German seizure of the Rhineland in March 1936 went unopposed by the French or British military. The annexation of Austria and the Sudetenland of Czechoslovakia by Germany takes place in 1938. Mussolini's Fascist regime in Italy has extended relations with Germany and is acting aggressively against countries in Northern Africa. Having joined with Germany, Italy established the basis for what would soon be known as the Axis powers.

Japan conducted operations against China throughout much of

the 1930s. Along the Western Pacific rim and deep within Asia, the Japanese Imperial Empire continued enlarging its sphere of influence. In late 1938, Japan announced to the world its establishment of the New Order for East Asia, which firmly placed it as the dominant economic power for the area.

Further expansions by Germany run unopposed by the rest of the world in the late 1930s. On 31 August 1939, the decision is made in Berlin. The next day, 1 September 1939, Germany invades Poland without a formal declaration of war. World War II had begun.

Within a few days of Germany's invasion of Poland, Britain and France declared war against Germany. Within twenty-seven days, Poland surrendered to the new lightning warfare of the German army. The United States tries to remain neutral to the war beginning in Europe while still supporting Great Britain. German submarines begin patrolling the Atlantic, cutting off shipping to the British Isles.

By April 1940, German warships leave their ports for the invasion of Norway. Further actions are taken against the other countries of Europe. Within months, Belgium, the Netherlands, Norway, and eventually France fall. With the exception of a small number of neutral countries, such as Spain, Portugal, Sweden, and Switzerland, Hitler controls or dominates the coastline of Europe along the Atlantic and much of the northern Mediterranean.

Though Germany moved into Northern Africa, Hitler never invaded Britain itself. Instead, the air and sea war against Britain raged hotter throughout 1940. The Japanese move into Indochina in late September 1940, against little argument from the Vichy government of occupied France. By late 1940, the British begin a heavy offensive against the German and Italian Axis forces in North Africa. The United States continues to supply Britain with war material and humanitarian aid, but is not yet at war with Germany. This situation continues through 1941, with Britain leading the active fight against the Axis on the western and southern front. Having attacked the Soviet Union in June, German forces make deep inroads into Russia and the Baltic states.

The diplomatic situation in the Pacific goes heavily against Japan during 1941. By the summer months, Japanese assets are frozen in the United States and Britain. Over three-quarters of Japanese foreign trade is cut off, and the flow of oil to Japan, which has no oil resources of its own within its borders, is cut to 10 percent of what it had been. Restricted to her limited stock of oil already on hand, Japan is being forced to negotiate and change her expansionist policy.

Heavy pressure is brought against the Japanese government by her military forces. War preparations are begun in secret in Japan while minor diplomatic proposals are still put forth by her to the United States. On 7 December 1941, Japanese forces attack the U.S. Navy base at Pearl Harbor in the Territory of Hawaii.

Less than a day had passed after the attack against Pearl Harbor when the Japanese opened their attack on Hong Kong, began landings in Malaya, and initiated air attacks on Luzon in the Philippines. On 8 December 1941, the United States and Britain declare war on Japan. Australia, New Zealand, the Netherlands, Free French, and others do likewise.

Within days of the attack on Pearl Harbor, Germany and Italy declares war on the United States. On December 11, the United States Congress formally declares war against the Axis forces. World War II is now a global conflict. Before the end of the war, more than seventy countries of the world will be directly involved in the conflict.

The Mission: The Target

Prior to World War II, no major amphibious landing had been successfully conducted during the twentieth century. The last time the U.S. had landed on an enemy-held beach was in June 1898, when U.S. forces, including Colonel Teddy Roosevelt and the Rough Riders unit, landed unopposed in Cuba.

The war against the Japanese in the Pacific would require major amphibious landings conducted against all types of fortified island

A huge line of Japanese log obstacles off the beach of a Pacific island. As part of their post-invasion work, these and other obstacles would be demolished by the men of the UDTs.

beaches. In the Atlantic and the European theater, the lack of any land-based facilities from which to mount the war would also require amphibious landings. It was in part the major difficulties in conducting an amphibious landing against strong enemy opposition that kept Hitler and his forces from invading England.

The U.S. Navy and Marine Corps had been practicing and developing amphibious landing techniques and planning in the 1930s and into 1941. Navy–Marine Corps Fleet Landing Exercises (FLEXs) recognized a need for specialized groups of men to mark approaches and guide landing craft to the beach; locate suitable beaches and scout out enemy forces, fortifications, and obstacles (both manmade and natural); and deal with mines and obstacles with demolition or other clearing techniques.

One astonishingly prescient U.S. Marine officer, Lieutenant Colonel Earl Hancock "Pete" Ellis, had studied the Japanese and their possible operating areas in the Pacific in the 1920s. Even prior to World War I, Ellis had lectured at the Navy War College. Beginning in 1913, he predicted that the U.S. would eventually be at war with the

Japanese and that amphibious warfare would have to be developed soon in order to conduct that fight.

When Japan received a mandate over islands in the Pacific that had been under German control after World War I, Ellis and other Marine and Navy officers saw the possibility of interisland warfare in a Pacific conflict become stronger. Before 1920, Marine operations on islands were of a defensive nature. With the changes in the political structure of much of the Central Pacific, plans for attacking an island rather than defending it had to be developed. Continuing his study of the situation, Ellis submitted a complete report of his findings in 1921.

Ellis's detailed report on his researches became "Operational Plan 712H—Advanced Base Operations in Micronesia," the basic doctrine for Marine operations in the Pacific until the end of WWII. Along with a number of other recommendations, one item stands out. Ellis suggested the assignment of trained demolition specialists with wire cutters and explosives. These men would constitute part of the first wave of an amphibious invasion to break up obstacles on the beach and in the shallow waters offshore.

Ellis died within a few years of delivering his report. The war he predicted arrived twenty years later. During the 1920s and 1930s, military planners in Washington, D.C., developed what were called the Orange plans. Modified a number of times, the basic Orange plan had the Navy conducting much of the offensive action against Japan in conjunction with air attacks and the Army's seizure and occupation of islands in the Central Pacific. The major problem with the Orange plan was that it had the United States facing only a single enemy, Japan, in only one theater, the Pacific.

In 1941, it could be seen that the coming war would involve multiple enemies in different theaters. With the final commitment to action in December 1941, the United States was faced for the first time in her history with fighting on two major fronts at the same time. In the Atlantic and across Europe and North Africa against the Axis, and in the Pacific and Asia against the Japanese Imperial Forces.

Japanese forces had been moving rapidly across the Pacific in all directions immediately after the attack on Pearl Harbor: east against the islands of the Central Pacific; south and southwest against the Philippines, Malaya, and the islands of the South China Sea, Burma, Thailand, and Indochina; west farther into China; and even north into the Aleutian Islands that extended out from the Alaskan territory.

In Europe, the target was a little more concentrated than in the Pacific, but it was as well or better fortified. The Mediterranean was almost completely surrounded with Axis-controlled territory. Combat actions would have to drive the Axis forces from Africa as well as Europe. And the only forward base available was beleaguered, isolated England.

World War II was a WAR. And it was fought strategically. It was totally engaging all the military capabilities of this and other countries. It was an all-out war. It went from submarines to the air. And it had a reason to be fought.

CAPTAIN FRANK KAINE, USN (Ret.) NCDU/UDT

Admiral Ernest J. King was the new Chief of Naval Operations (CNO) for the United States Navy. The greatest of his tasks was to guide the strategy of the Navy through the war on both fronts. Amphibious warfare was going to be the means the United States would use to establish a toehold in enemy territory.

Of all of the U.S. military services, amphibious warfare had always been a specialty of the Marine Corps. As implied by the name, an amphibious operation began with a seaborne force being landed for the invasion and occupation of a land area. Once the forces had arrived on the land, the operation became normal land warfare with naval gunfire support available as long as the combat area was within range.

It was the actual getting from the transport ships to the beaches that took extra training as well as specialized small craft and tactics. For the large number of amphibious operations that would be needed to fight in Europe and the Pacific, specially trained Army commands had to be developed. Planning for the upcoming war included invasions of enough forces to occupy whole continents if necessary.

The Navy's mission during an amphibious operation would be to transport and protect the landing forces while at sea, land the forces on the target and protect them from attack by enemy naval forces, and keep a constant flow of supplies, materials, and manpower coming in to the invading forces.

To conduct these landing operations, a new class of naval ship was developed and classified as landing craft. As a general Navy rule, anything over 200 feet in length is referred to as a ship, anything smaller is a craft. The one major feature of all landing craft was their ability to run aground on a beach, unload, and get off the beach under their own power. This was true for all such craft, from the 36-foot, 3-inch LCVP (Landing Craft, Vehicle, Personnel) to the 328-foot LST (Landing Ship, Tank).

The industrial might of the United States turned to the production of war materials, even before war was declared. Landing craft were one of the items produced, and built in tremendous numbers. Invasions involving hundreds of thousands of troops, material, and vehicles would be delayed or abandoned without the many simple, ugly, floating plywood boxes known as LCVPs.

To conduct the operations as efficiently as possible, the Amphibious Force was developed. This force would contain the specialized manpower, ships, and small craft necessary to conduct amphibious operations. Amphibious Forces were assigned to each of the fleets that would need them.

Admiral Chester W. Nimitz had been assigned to the post of commander-in-chief of the Pacific Fleet (CINCPAC) shortly after the Pearl Harbor attack. The initial Allied strategy of the war, known as War Plan Rainbow 5, had been prepared in 1941, prior to Pearl Harbor, and focused the initial efforts of the United States on the defeat of Germany. With the European theater under control, a concentrated effort could then be made against the Japanese in the Pacific.

Admiral Nimitz could easily see the problems that would ensue if the Japanese were allowed even more time to consolidate their positions and reinforce the fortifications of islands, some of which they had already held for years.

The newly established U.S. Joint Chiefs of Staff (JCS) consisting first of the Chiefs of Operations for the Army and Navy, organized the Pacific theater into two major commands, the Southwest Pacific Area and the Pacific Ocean Areas. General Douglas MacArthur would command the forces operating in the Southwest Pacific. His area of responsibility contained Australia, New Guinea, the Bismarck Archipelago, the Dutch East Indies, and the Philippines.

The Pacific Ocean Areas consisted of the North Pacific Area, which was everything north of latitude 42 degrees North, and the South Pacific Area, which was south of the equator and east of the Southwest Pacific at longitude 159 degrees East. Extending from the equator north to the forty-second parallel, and including the main islands of Japan, was the Central Pacific Area.

The Pacific area had been organized and the campaign against the Japanese Imperial Empire outlined. With the decision made to conduct the Pacific campaign concurrently with the Atlantic and European campaign, the buildup of men and materials began in earnest.

Detection of a buildup of Japanese facilities on Guadalcanal in the Solomon Islands caused great concern for the Allies. The capacity to launch land-based long-range bombers would give Japan an edge in cutting off the shortest sea routes between the United States and Australia. To prevent this from happening, the first major U.S. offensive of World War II was planned and conducted.

On 7 August 1942, Operation WATCHTOWER begins and the First Marine Division lands on Guadalcanal. Additional detachments land on Tulagi and Gavutu Islands. The Marines are transported by Admiral Richmond Kelly Turner's Amphibious Force. The landings themselves were made against relatively light resistance and few fortifications and obstacles. The fighting for Guadalcanal itself was considerably different. It took four long months of debilitating jungle warfare before the Japanese were defeated and Guadalcanal taken by the Allied forces.

Only a few weeks after the invasion of Guadalcanal, another amphibious action took place in Europe. Allied planners, especially the British, wanted a major landing in Europe as quickly as possible. Resources for such an operation—manpower and available ships and small craft—simply weren't available in 1942/43. Instead, a large raid or commando sortie was planned for mid-1942.

On 19 August 1942, the first major invasion in the European theater was conducted as a large-scale raid by Canadian troops and British commandos along with a small number of American and Free French forces at Dieppe in northern France. Following a British plan, the primarily Canadian force landed with the intention of destroying a German radio location center as well as a number of gun and other installations. The intention was also to learn how the Germans would fight against such an invasion and the nature and extent of their resistance.

In spite of their fighting with tremendous valor, the troops never reached their objectives. Flaws in the basic plan, its organization and support, caused the tide of battle to turn against the raiders as they fought heavy German resistance.

Lessons were learned on how to conduct future amphibious landings in Europe, but they were learned at a cost. Of 6,000 men in the landing force, 3,369 Canadians alone were casualties or taken prisoner. Additional Allied losses included 106 aircraft, a destroyer, 30 tanks, and 33 landing craft. This against a German loss of about 600 men and 50 aircraft. Included in the Allied casualties was Lieutenant Loustalot of the U.S. Army Rangers, the first American serviceman of World War II to die in combat on European soil.

It was now unequivocally clear that the taking of a defended port such as Dieppe would be too costly in terms of men and material. Another site needed to be chosen for the eventual European landings.

Additional forces were going to be necessary in both the Atlantic and Pacific theaters to properly conduct the amphibious campaigns.

Material was being developed and produced at an increasing rate by the United States' industrial complex. Men were enlisting and the Selective Service was drafting more to fill out the U.S. military forces. Additional specialized units were created as the needs arose, or had been foreseen by military planners.

■ Chapter 3

THE NAVAL CONSTRUCTION BATTALIONS: THE SEABEES

In almost every conflict the U.S. Navy had been involved in, it needed to build, modify, improve, or just repair shore facilities quickly in order to support the fleet. By the early 1930s, the Navy's Bureau of Yards and Docks had started laying the groundwork for the Navy Construction Battalions, but for most of the decade, preparations for the new units never got very far beyond an idea and a name. The beginning of World War II changed that situation drastically.

The international situation at the start of the war forced the U.S. government and military to increase their preparedness. By the end of the 1930s, the U.S. Congress had authorized an expansion of naval shore facilities. In the Caribbean and the Central Pacific, new naval construction projects were begun in 1939. In the Pacific, on Guam, Midway, and Wake Island, as well as at Pearl Harbor in Hawaii, larger naval base construction had begun by the summer of 1941. In the Atlantic, new bases were being built or existing Navy facilities were being enlarged in Iceland, Newfoundland, Bermuda, Trinidad, and a number of other sites.

To aid in the work of these projects, the Navy Bureau of Yards and Docks organized the military Headquarters Construction Companies. Each company consisted of two officers and ninety-nine enlisted men. Instead of their personnel doing the actual construction work, men from the Headquarters Constructions Companies were to supervise the civilian contractors who did the actual work. On 31 October 1941, Rear Admiral Chester W. Nimitz, the Chief of the Bureau of Navigation, authorized the first Headquarters Construction Company. The men were recruited and undergoing Navy boot camp training by the beginning of December 1941.

Four more companies were authorized by 16 December. But by that time the situation had drastically changed after the Japanese attack on Pearl Harbor on 7 December. The men recruited for the Headquarters Construction Companies quickly received another assignment.

With the U.S. having entered a state of war in December 1941, the civilian contractors who had been doing much of the Navy's construction could no longer work overseas. International law kept civilians from fighting an enemy in a combat zone, even in defense of their lives. Any armed civilians who were captured after a fight could be executed as a guerrilla.

In December 1941, Rear Admiral Ben Moreell, then 45 and the youngest man in the Navy to hold that rank, was the chief of the Bureau of Yards and Docks. On 28 December, Admiral Moreell sought the authority to create a new kind of Navy construction unit to meet the wartime demands. On 5 January 1942, that authority was granted. Men were recruited to form the new militarized Naval Construction Battalions. The men who were originally slated to go to the Headquarters Construction Companies found themselves in the new units.

Command of the new units was given to the officers of the Civil Engineer Corps by the authority of the Secretary of the Navy effective 19 March 1942. Admiral Moreell, who had been an officer in the Civil Engineering Corps, gave the new units their official motto: *Construimus Batuimus*—"We Build, We Fight."

Earlier, in January 1942, at the Naval Air Station in Quonset Point, Rhode Island, some 250 recruits were gathered to man the new Construction Battalions. At the request of the officer-in-charge of the new recruits, plan file clerk Frank J. Lafrate designed an insignia for the new unit. The final design showed a sailor-capped bee in flight, holding a stylized Thompson submachine gun in its front arms and tools in its hands. Below the bee were the initials of the Construction Battalions—CB—and thus the name "Seabee" was coined.

The first groups of men recruited specifically for the Seabees were trained and experienced civilian construction workers and engineers. Selection of the new recruits was based on their experience and skills, not their physical condition. The normal Navy physical standards were lowered in order to bring on board capable, otherwise-qualified individuals. During the first year of the Seabees' existence, the average age was thirty-seven, much older than the average sailor or soldier. The range of age for enlistment into the Seabees ran from eighteen to fifty. But a number of over-sixty men had managed to get through the enlistment boards and were serving in their units.

These recruits were construction men who had built bridges, roads, and dams. Men with experience in building skyscrapers, roadways, and tunnels and in working quarries and mines could all be found among the ranks of the Seabees. Quarrymen, hard-rock miners, blasters, powdermen, and others came into the unit, bringing with them years of invaluable experience in explosives handling and demolition. Military discipline, drill, and weapons handling were taught to the recruits so that they could defend themselves in some of the frontline construction sites they would operate at.

Initial Seabee boat training was given over three weeks at Camp Allen, Virginia. Later the training was moved to a much better site at Camp Peary, located northwest of Norfolk, on the shores of the York River near Williamsburg. Camp Peary soon became the basic training camp for most of the Seabees during the early part of the war.

By December 1942, the older volunteers could no longer directly enlist in the Navy and the Seabees. A presidential order required all of the new men entering the Construction Battalions to have come through the Selective Service System. Experience and skill levels lowered as the age of the new Seabee recruits dropped. An additional six weeks of advanced military and technical training was included in the basic training course. This was over and above all the additional training the new Seabees would receive once they arrived at their new units.

The men of the Seabees quickly earned a reputation for toughness and skill. They operated in every theater of the war. Roadways were cut and airfields opened by the Seabees, even while under the direct fire of the enemy. (Some airfields were made operational and U.S. fighter aircraft worked from them while the sounds of battle could still be heard over the roar of the engines.)

During the war, Seabees filled 151 regular construction battalions, 39 special construction battalions, and a host of additional battalions, detachments, regiments, brigades, and forces. By its end, 325,000 men had enlisted in the unit, along with almost 8,000 officers. These men built and fought on six continents and over 300 islands. The majority of their construction efforts took place in the Pacific, where the Seabees built airstrips, bridges, roads, hospitals, oil tank farms, barracks, and buildings.

Following some of the first waves of landing U.S. forces onto enemy beaches, the Seabees would immediately set to work. Some Seabee volunteers would find themselves going in to enemy beaches even before the first landings took place.

■ Chapter 4

SCOUTS AND RAIDERS (JOINT)

To aid the new Amphibious Force in conducting its mission of landing troops on enemy beaches, a number of specialized units were created. Rear Admiral Henry K. Hewitt was assigned to command the Amphibious Force of the Atlantic Fleet in late April 1942. It would be Admiral Hewitt who would first take the Amphibious Force into combat.

To best prepare the force for future operations, Admiral Hewitt was put in charge of all amphibious training for his command. Even the Army units who were to conduct the actual landings were placed temporarily under Hewitt's command for training. The mission was still a new one, but the military situation in the European theater and the diplomatic situation among the Allies was heating up rapidly by the early summer of 1942.

Landing craft of any type were still few in number in all of the Navy fleets in early 1942. Trained personnel who knew how to operate in the surf zone along the shore, and who could teach others the same skill, were in even shorter supply than the landing craft. Experienced rough-water Coast Guard chief petty officers were among the first instructors at the new Amphibious Training Base (ATB) at Solomons Island, Maryland, on the shores of the Chesapeake Bay.

The Coast Guard chiefs and their students made up what was called the Boat Pool at the Solomons ATB. A number of the Boot Pool's chief specialists had been instructors in the Navy's Physical Training Program, nicknamed "Tunney's Fish" after their commander, former world heavyweight boxing champion Gene Tunney.

The very strong and fit chief specialists quickly learned the handling characteristics of a number of landing craft. All of the Boat Pool people would operate the available landing craft at all hours of the day or night, practicing maneuvering, signaling, and assaulting the beach itself.

Just the year before, fleet training exercises had demonstrated the need to do amphibious reconnaissance prior to a landing. A Marine Scout-Observer group assisted in the landing exercises and was instrumental in developing some of the techniques for amphibious reconnaissance. Additionally, an Army group experimented with various small craft, conducting beach examinations and hydrographic soundings at likely training sights along the Maryland coast. The seven-man inflatable rubber boat was a direct result of the Army experiments, the lead NCO of the unit working with engineers and production people from Goodyear to produce the now common small boat.

By the middle of 1942, the Marine Corps was committed to actions in the Pacific at Guadalcanal and elsewhere. Marines who had been assigned to the Amphibious Force were moved to other assignments, leaving the landing force actions to the Army. With the Marines went their Scout-Observer group, leaving a gap in the intelligence-gathering capabilities of the Atlantic Amphibious Force.

The Army NCO who had earlier worked with the Army group conducting amphibious reconnaissance experiments and who had been instrumental in developing the seven-man inflatable rubber boat was now a commissioned lieutenant. Lieutenant Lloyd Peddicord was called in to the headquarters of the Atlantic Fleet Amphibious Force at Norfolk, Virginia, and given the assignment of developing a new reconnaissance school on an immediate basis. The new school was to be located at the nearby Naval Amphibious Base (NAB) being built at Little Creek, to the east and slightly south of Norfolk.

The decision was made to call the new school the Amphibious Scout and Raider School (Joint). Men from the Army's Third and Ninth divisions would be trained in small boat work, including the new rubber boats, physical training, working with and from landing craft, observation and scouting of beaches and shorelines, and raiding techniques against different types of objectives.

The Navy contingent at the Scout and Raider School would take many of the same courses as the Army students, but with much less emphasis on land combat and raiding. Instead, the Navy personnel would be trained to become experts in the small boat handling, including landing craft and rubber boats. The school emphasized the study of navigation and operations in poor conditions and at night, as well as signaling, communications, and gunnery. Small-arms and hand-to-hand combat were taught to all of the Scout and Raider students.

The new school was formed on 25 August 1942 by the order of Admiral Hewitt. The first training classes began 1 September 1942.

Among the first personnel arriving at the new school were forty sailors from the Boat Pool at Solomons, Maryland, as well as ten of the chief specialists. These naval personnel made up ten Scout boat crews of four men and a Scout boat officer. The Navy group was under the command of Ensign John Bell, USNR. Lieutenant Peddicord was the officer-in-charge of the new Scouts and Raider School.

The basic objective of the school was laid out by Lieutenant Peddicord. The Army and Navy men would be trained to scout out and locate landing sites on selected beaches just prior to a planned invasion. The men would go ashore at night, scout the areas, and set up signaling locations. The signals would be used to guide in the waves of landing craft for the invasion.

Both the Army and Navy personnel in the new Scouts and Raiders (S&R) unit conducted a number of exercises and demonstrated their abilities to a number of officers from both services, including Major General George S. Patton Jr. Most of the Navy personnel not only had their own mission to learn, they also had to teach these same skills to the members of the Army contingent. In a very short time the school was closed at Little Creek and all of the S&R personnel assigned to Operation TORCH, the upcoming Allied landings in North Africa.

The doors at the S&R School had hardly been closed when class number two was mustered to begin training. Army troops who were to join the second S&R class were delayed, as was the start-up date of the training. As these events were taking place in the U.S., Operation TORCH was unfolding in North Africa.

Chapter 5

NORTH AFRICA: OPERATION TORCH

Operation TORCH would be the first major U.S. and Allied amphibious landing in the European theater. The mission was to place U.S. troops into North Africa, reinforcing the British there, attacking the Germans on the eastern flank, and preventing the Axis from winning an operational base on the Atlantic shore of Africa.

There were three primary targets for the Allied landing forces. The central target was Fedala near Casablanca and just outside of the city's fixed defenses; Safi, 190 miles to the south, was the second; and Mahdia and Port Lyautey, 65 miles to the north, the third. With newly promoted Vice Admiral Hewitt in command, the Amphibious Force Atlantic Fleet set sail from the United States for Africa in spite of the threat from German submarines. As soon as the force was afloat, it was renamed the Western Naval Task Force, or Task Force 34. The Western Task Force split up into three groups as it approached Africa the morning of 7 November 1942.

The Southern Attack Group would land in Safi. The Central Attack Group would go in at Fedala, and the Northern Attack Group at Mahdia. As the U.S. landings were taking place, task forces of primarily British ships and troops in the Mediterranean would be landing at Oran and Algiers in Algeria.

During the intelligence-gathering phase of the planning for Operation TORCH, sea-level photographs of the coastline at the U.S. landing sites had not been available. Such pictures would have facilitated the identification of the proper landing beaches for the incoming landing craft. Instead, the Scouts and Raider detachments would go in and mark the landing beaches just prior to the invasion.

During the invasions on 8 November, the S&R units made heroic efforts to complete their missions. On enemy beaches, without immediate support, the men scouted their areas, set up their signals, and brought the incoming landing craft to their targets. Resistance to the landings by Vichy French forces was almost nonexistent in some areas, and stronger in others. For their actions during the TORCH landings, eight of the ten Scout boat officers were recommended and later awarded the Navy Cross. The eight chief specialists of the S&Rs were commissioned as ensigns.

The Northern Attack Group also conducted its landings on 8 November. In the attack group, a small group of Navy personnel and several platoons of Army Raiders were assigned a special mission. Mahdia was a small community on the Atlantic shore, near the mouth of the Sebou River, called the Wadi Sebou in the local language. Several miles up the winding Wadi Sebou was Port Lyautey along with its very important airfield. The Allied forces and General Patton wanted the airfield captured intact so that it could be used for U.S. P-40 aircraft as soon as possible. The capture of that airfield was considered the primary objective of Mahdia landings.

Intelligence gathered prior to the invasion revealed that the French had put a cable boom and possibly a net across the Wadi Sebou, blocking the river to any attack force. In September, at Little Creek, a special volunteer unit of Navy personnel had been gathered under the command of Lieutenant Mark Starkweather and Lieutenant James W. Darroch. The fifteen enlisted men of the unit as well as the officers all had experience in salvage work for the Navy. Prior to being sent to Little Creek, ten of the men had worked raising ships sunk at Pearl Harbor. Once at the new ATB, the seventeen-man unit received a quick course in demolition techniques, cable cutting, small boat operation, and other techniques. Extensive training was given by the personnel of the Amphibious Scout and Raider School (Joint) before it was closed for Operation TORCH.

The special net/cable cutting team, called a Navy Demolition Unit by some, was attached to the USS *Clymer* for transport to North Africa. The Navy unit was to cast off from the *Clymer* and board a small landing craft, the type known as a "Higgins boat," for the trip into the mouth of the Wadi Sebou, about 4,000 yards upriver to the blocking boom.

During the landings on 8 November, a S&R boat, manned by Lieutenant Peddicord, was on station at the end of the southernmost of the two jetties that bracketed the mouth of the Wadi Sebou. The commander of the Army Fifteenth Engineers, Lieutenant Colonel Frederick A. Henney was in charge of the net cutting crew as they launched from the *Clymer* in the early morning hours and moved through the dark waters to the mouth of the Wadi Sebou.

The sea was very rough and the small Higgins boat was violently driven into the mouth of the Wadi Sebou. Expert seamanship on the part of the Navy crew kept the small craft on course until it reached the much calmer waters between the two jetties. But once it was on the river itself, the situation turned much worse for the small Navy boat.

Machine guns dug into the cliffs on the south side of the Wadi Sebou opened fire on the Higgins boat as soon as it was within range. The U.S. landings down the beach closer to Madhia had alerted the French crews and they were able to mount a serious defense. Incoming fire on the small craft was so heavy that Lieutenant Colonel Henney ordered the boat's withdrawal before it was sunk. The demolition men returned to the *Clymer* to try again later.

The U.S. forces continued their landings at Madhia and elsewhere along the Moroccan coast. It was the evening of 9 November before the demolition party was able to set out again. Pressure was mounting to capture the upriver airfield, which U.S. ground forces had been unable to reach by land. The USS *Dallas* had tried to steam up the river and ram the boom, but had been driven off by cannon fire from the old Casbah fort near the mouth of the river on the southern shore.

At 2130 hours on the night of 9 November, the demolition unit set off again in the Higgins boat. Lieutenant Starkweather had been unable to find Lieutenant Colonel Henney at a planned rendezvous and went forward with the operation under his own authority. The Higgins boat had been stocked with materials the demolition crew needed for its second attempt at cutting the boom. Besides incendiary devices, two light machine guns had been included, one in each of the two forward gun tubs.

Careful navigation got the small boat into the Wadi Sebou under better control than had been the case during the first attempt. Slipping past the Casbah as quietly as possible, the boat reached the cable boom blocking the river without taking fire. The crew cut the inch-and-a-half-thick steel cable and even put a man into the water to confirm that the blockage was breached. By 0230 in the morning, the mission had been accomplished. The ends of the cable drifted apart on their buoys and broke a small signal wire. The guard forces in the Casbah were alerted and opened fire on Lieutenant Starkweather and his small command.

Returning fire with their own weapons, the crew of the Higgins boat turned and made a dash for the open sea. Incoming gunfire was reinforced by small-caliber cannon fire as it tore downriver at its top speed, zigzagging to avoid the searchlights from the old fort. Fire from one of the boats' two light machine guns put out one of the searchlights and discouraged some of the machine gun crews on shore. But one of the machine guns jammed and couldn't be cleared for operation.

The Higgins boat took a large number of hits and several of the personnel on board were wounded as she made her way back out to sea. Demolitions, materials, even the jammed machine gun were dumped overboard to lighten the small craft as she took on water through the many bullet holes in her hull. But the injured craft made its way back to the fleet and none of the personnel on board were lost in the operation.

The next morning, the USS *Dallas* steamed upriver, ramming through the remainder of the cable boom that was held up by its buoys and anchored to the river bottom. A local river pilot had been spirited out of the area earlier by the new Office of Strategic Services (OSS) personnel and was on board the *Dallas* to pilot her through the dangerous waterway. At 0530 on 10 November, the ship entered the Wadi Sebou. The Raider detachment left the *Dallas* in rubber boats when she finally ran aground in the shallow river, near the desired airfield. By 0800 in the morning, the Port Lyautey airfield was in U.S. hands.

French resistance to the U.S. landing in Morocco ended soon afterward. Many of the men from the Scouts and Raiders and the Special Demolition Unit returned to the United States during the following weeks. Over 107,000 Allied troops were now on shore after the landings. The land battle for North Africa had begun and the major fighting was up to the armies now. Six months after Operation TORCH, the last active German soldier in Africa would surrender.

■ Chapter 6

THE ESTABLISHMENT OF THE NAVAL COMBAT DEMOLITION UNITS

The first inroads against the Axis in Europe had begun with Operation TORCH. Afterward, some Scout and Raider Navy personnel remained in North Africa to train additional units for further operations in Europe and the Mediterranean. Other Scouts and Raiders returned to the United States and their training school at the Little Creek ATB in Virginia. The S&R School was re-formed in December 1942 in preparation for its move to a more southern location.

Review of the battle reports on the actions of the Scout and Raider personnel who took part in Operation TORCH resulted in the decision to continue the school. Naval Scout boat crews and Army Scouts and Raiders were considered essential for preinvasion planning and reconnaissance. These men would hold key positions in upcoming amphibious operations. With winter descending on the Norfolk, Virginia, area, it was decided to move the S&R School south to a more year-round training site. The new school would be located at the new Amphibious Training Base at Fort Pierce, Florida, on the east coast of the state, roughly halfway between Miami and Cape Canaveral.

One of the Navy commodores at the TORCH invasions, Captain Clarence Gulbranson, was ordered to expedite the opening of a year-round amphibious training site soon after the operation was over. Captain Gulbranson chose the reasonably isolated Fort Pierce location. At 10 A.M., 26 January 1943, the USNATB Fort Pierce was officially commissioned. Soon a number of other amphibious support organizations arrived at the Fort Pierce base to set up training programs of their own.

On 14 January 1943, the S&R School was closed in Little Creek, Virginia, and the six officers and seventy-five enlisted men making up the Navy staff and students of class number two moved south to Florida. Originally, the school was going to be set up at Camp Murphy. On 17 January, the convoy of sixteen amphibious DUKW trucks transporting the S&R School received orders to stay in the new USNATB at Fort Pierce overnight. The orders received on 18 January instructed the S&R School to stay where it was and set up training in Fort Pierce. Preparations were to begin immediately so that the first class from the Forty-fifth Infantry Reconnaissance Group could begin training by 24 January.

The DUKW (pronounced "Duck") that the S&R School used for transportation was another invention of World War II. The vehicle was essentially a two-and-a-half-ton truck that could float and drive itself through the water. The DUKW could travel 45 mph on land or 6 mph in the water, all while carrying 5,000 pounds of material or 25 men. A single shaft and propeller drove the DUKW through the water, while its six wheels moved it on land. For the first weeks of training at the new S&R School, the students used the DUKWs as landing craft until more suitable boats were available.

While the Scout and Raider School was running training, additional planning was going forward to prepare the Navy for the next major amphibious operations in Europe. The invasion of Sicily was planned for the early summer of 1943 and major landings on the coast of Europe in 1944.

The building up of the beaches of Europe was known to be under way. Layers of fortifications were being produced that would lead up from the beaches. Prudent planners had to expect beaches thick with obstacles and mines. Heavy weapons would back up machine gun emplacements and mortar pits. Such were just the standard fortifications, already known to exist in other parts of Europe. The specific fortifications of the Atlantic wall portion of Hitler's Festung Europa (Fortress Europe) were not known to the Allies. But there was no question that if it wasn't built now, it would be soon.

A German Tellermine 43 "mushroom" antitank mine mounted on a post driven into the ground at Normandy Beach. The post is angled so that it's pointing out to sea. Any incoming landing craft striking the post would detonate the twelve pounds of TNT contained in the mine. These were one of the targets the NCDUs were intended to destroy.

U.S. Navy

In May 1943, Allied strategic planners had made the decision to open the Western Front in Europe by the next year. Only fourteen months were left to prepare what would be the largest amphibious invasion to date. Admiral Ernest J. King, the U.S. Chief of Naval Operations (CNO), had the tremendous task of preparing his Navy for the upcoming campaigns.

The decision to use explosives to breach obstacles had yet to be made. The demolition operation by the net-cutting party at the Wadi Sebou during TORCH was the extent of the Navy's experience in the Atlantic so far. Though their training had been rushed, the men of that unit had completed their mission, though taking much longer than originally planned.

The only certain method to clear a beach was to hand-place explosives on each obstacle to be destroyed. That method was labor-intensive and would take many men skilled in demolitions and explosives handling. The Seabees had men trained with explosives, but not in the kind of demolitions needed to face the expected target. Instead, men would have to be trained to do the job. A large number of shoreline demolition experts would be needed, and in a relatively short time.

Admiral Ernest J. King signed and issued a two-part directive on 6 May 1943 to address the problem of obstacle clearance. The first part of the directive required men immediately for an "urgent requirement." The second part called for demolition and obstacle clearance techniques and materials to be developed and for the training of permanent "Navy Demolition Units."

Captain Jeffrey C. Metzel of Admiral King's planning staff was an experienced officer who had a reputation for energy and getting a job done quickly. He had been involved with the establishing of a number of other special units in the Navy and may have been the moving force behind the idea of specialized demolition units. Whatever the reason, it was Captain Metzel who would brief and give the orders to the officer who would create the new unit.

Draper L. Kauffman was a graduate of the U.S. Naval Academy and the son of Vice Admiral James Kauffman. At his graduation from the Academy at Annapolis, Draper Kauffman had to resign from the Navy because of his poor eyesight. It was the middle of the Great Depression and the Navy had raised the requirements for acceptance. There just weren't enough openings for the entire graduating class.

Not one to let obstacles stand in his way, Kauffman went to sea with a civilian steamship company and later joined the American Volunteer Ambulance Corps in France in 1940. In June 1940, Draper Kauffman was captured by the Germans and held until August. From France, he made his way to England, where he joined the British navy and took up duties as a bomb disposal officer.

Twice commended by the Admiralty and once by King George VI, Draper Kauffman was known to be an excellent bomb disposal officer, this no small thing in England during the height of the German bombing campaign. Unofficially, Kauffman was considered to hold the record for the hundred-yard dash by his fellows in the bomb and mine disposal business. Kauffman was witnessed leaving the site of an unexploded bomb that was, apparently, changing its mind about its unexploded status. His speed while traversing the distance between the location of the bomb and the protection of a sandbagged area where another officer was watching was considered something of a record, given the short time delay of the activated fuze.

In November 1941, Draper Kauffman resigned from the Royal Navy to return to the United States and take up an appointment as a lieutenant in the U.S. Navy. That same month he was ordered to duty with the Bureau of Ordnance. Within weeks, he was ordered to Hawaii, where he rendered safe an unexploded 500-pound Japanese bomb at Schofield Barracks. His skills allowed the bomb to be recovered for study and resulted in his being awarded the Navy Cross.

In January 1942, Kauffman, now appointed a lieutenant commander, was assigned to organize a U.S. Bomb Disposal School at the Washington Navy Yard. Besides setting up the Navy school, he assisted the Army in setting up the same type of training at Aberdeen Proving Grounds in Maryland.

Draper Kauffman met his future wife in the Washington area. In the late winter of 1943, he married and took one of his few leaves during his nearly three years of action. Only six days after beginning his honeymoon, Kauffman received a telegram ordering him back to Washington and a meeting at the new Pentagon immediately.

His explosives experience had stood him in good stead, as did his setting up of two schools involved in explosives work. Captain Metzel met with Lieutenant Commander Kauffman and gave him his new assignment. He was to set up a training program, organize, and train a Navy unit to eliminate obstacles on enemy-held beaches and clear the way for incoming landing craft.

His orders gave Kauffman the freedom to go anywhere he wanted, get any men he might want, and set up his own organization and training. What he wasn't given was much time to get the program going. The situation was considered an emergency and time was critical. The reasons for this time crunch were classified and not necessary for the completion of the assignment. But it was easy for a man of Draper Kauffman's experience to see what was coming—the major invasion of Europe.

His orders in hand and having received his instructions, Kauffman left the Pentagon to start examining how to assemble and train this new unit. Officers from his Bomb and Mine Disposal School were among his first volunteers. Because of their experience with explosives, Kauffman looked to the Seabees at Camp Peary in Virginia as his primary source of enlisted men. But as he began putting together his new staff and students, the first part of Admiral King's directive, listing an urgent requirement for specially trained men, was being addressed.

Naval Demolition Unit #1

By January 1943, the prelminary plans for Operation HUSKY, the invasion of Sicily in the Mediterranean, had been completed. It would be six months before the operation would take place, a very short time for a major operation. Combat was ongoing in North Africa, but the Axis forces were already being driven back.

As the campaign in North Africa continued, there was a buildup of supplies and materials at the secure ports along the Mediterranean and Atlantic shores of Africa. As the preparations for the invasion of Sicily went forward, further specialized Navy amphibious units were being prepared on a crash basis.

As Draper Kauffman was leaving the Pentagon and beginning on his new assignment, another group of Navy officers and enlisted men were receiving new orders. At the Seabee training base at Camp Peary, Virginia, six Civil Engineering Corps officers and twelve enlisted men received orders to report to the ATB at Solomons Island, Maryland. All eighteen of the men had background experience with explosives prior to their joining the Navy. Some had been mining engineers, oil field workers, powder monkeys, and just general construction blasters.

The orders all of the men received just had them reporting to the ATB with no details as to just what they would do when they got there. An additional officer, Ensign Jack Fagerstal, from the Navy Bomb and Mine Disposal School, joined the group of men at the Solomons ATB. The senior officer among the group was Lieutenant Fred Wise.

A Navy commander, Joe Daniels, came down to the ATB and explained to the men and their officers just what they would be doing. As one man wrote later, the first words from Commander Daniels's mouth were, "You are all volunteers and you will be shipping out to Africa in ten days." This was actually the first at least some if not all of the men had heard about their volunteering.

The briefing on their upcoming training and mission continued. The British had reported that all of the beaches in Northern Europe that could be used for landing invasion troops were being fortified. The fortifications included steel and concrete obstacles placed from the high tide line to below the low tide mark. The obstacles were intended to damage, sink, or impale landing craft, blocking them from getting to the landing beach. The men were to be trained to examine landing beaches and destroy any obstacles.

To complete their training, the group was going to be supplied with an LCPL (Landing Craft, Personnel, Large) and various military explosives. They had all of a week to get themselves familiar with the explosives and the LCPL. They would be moving and blasting along the beaches of Chesapeake Bay.

The men were experienced with explosives, but none was a very experienced sailor. Training with the landing craft wasn't difficult, but making any sense of the buoys and channel markers in the Chesapeake was almost too much for them. Reportedly, they made the acquaintance of every mud bar and obstacle in their portion of the bay.

The men had a variety of explosives to work with, including tetratol, TNT, shaped charges, and primacord. The explosives were fired in various ways, but the team had no obstacles to practice on. Their previous experience prepared them for the new explosives, and their experiments with primacord in simultaneously detonating multiple charges impressed even the experienced explosives men.

Within the stated ten days, the men were sent on to Norfolk, where they boarded a ship for transport to Africa. Now designated Navy Demolition Unit #1, the men found a lavish amount of equipment on board for their use. As the transport ship, the USS *Alcyon,* arrived at the port of Oran in Algeria, the men started examining their equipment.

The gear included the expected demolition materials and tools. Also found was an inflatable rubber boat and a small outboard motor. And a set of shallow water diving equipment.

None of the men was experienced with the diving equipment, which consisted of a weight, belt, harness, two-man air pump, hose, and faceplate/mask. When the first lieutenant of the ship saw the men with the equipment, he asked if they could check the rudder post of the ship for suspected damage. One of the men geared up and went over the side. The dive proved interesting, not only as the first underwater experience of the demolition man, but also because of the extremely polluted water he found himself in. The ship's steering gear was satisfactory, and a very long shower rendered the diver acceptable for regular company as well.

Several times the demolition crew, who had very little experience with Navy customs and courtesies, "bumped" into the ship's crew and officers. This situation was alleviated when the captain of the ship spoke to one of the men about an infraction of the rules and discovered the individual had been in the Navy all of six weeks.

It was a few days later that the transport whip and the demolition unit set out for Sicily. Operation HUSKY would put a large number of American and British troops on shore in Sicily at five different beaches. The American Army contingent was Lieutenant General

George Patton's Seventh Army with seven divisions. The British army contingent was commanded by Lieutenant General Sir Bernard Montgomery. The naval armada had to set out from a number of ports in Africa, gathering at sea, and approaching Sicily in time for the invasion on 10 July 1943.

All of the invasion beaches were on the southeastern section of Sicily, and the U.S. Western Task Force, under Vice Admiral Hewitt, would split up to land at beaches near Licata, Gela, and Scoglitti. The men of the Navy Demolition Unit broke up into three teams; Group 1 was under the command of Lieutenant Wise, Group 2 was commanded by Lieutenant Bob Smith, and Group 3 by Ensign Harold Culver.

Each of the NDU groups had their own LCPL, which they loaded with their explosives and equipment. As the landing boats went in for the invasion, the job of the three NDU groups was to stand by in their LCPL between the transport ship and the shore, ready to be called to any obstacles that had to be destroyed.

For hours, the men of the NDU bobbed about in the water in their LCPLs. And for hours, they had nothing to do. There were no obstacles in the water offshore or on the beach that needed clearing. Though there was fighting on shore, it was not as heavy as was expected. The only target the men of the NDU were called upon to destroy was some rubble walls blocking the streets of Scoglitti.

Moving to the shore and jumping to their task, the men placed shaped charges to blast holes in the rubble mounds. The holes would then be packed with high explosives to blow the walls to pieces. The only trouble was, the shaped charges obliterated the loosely piled rubble walls and cleared the way. Packing up their gear, the men of the NDU returned to the landing beach.

After two days of little activity, the nearly empty transport ship took on a cargo of German POWs and prepared to leave. Some of the sailors handling the prisoners made more than a few comments to the Germans. One of the Germans answered with: "Don't laugh at us; we're going to New York and you are going to Rome."

With the prisoners and the men of the NDU on board, the transport returned to Oran. The NDU men continued on back to Camp Bradford, Virginia, near Little Creek, to wait for further orders. Most of the men and a number of the officers eventually were sent to Fort Pierce, where the NCDU school was established. One of the officers, Ensign Culver, was later assigned as an instructor on explosives at the new demolition school.

While the men of the NDU had been undergoing their training and conducting their mission, Draper Kauffman had been hard at work developing his training program back in the States. Personally going to various units, he asked for volunteers for a secret assignment. The mission of what would soon be the Naval Combat Demolition Units was so secret, Kauffman himself did not know many of the details. And most of even those few details could not be told to the men who were being asked to volunteer. In spite of this limitation, Draper Kauffman was able to fill the ranks of his first groups of student volunteers without a lot of difficulty.

Robert P. Marshall Jr., Commander USN (Ret.)

Our group went down to Fort Pierce from the Seabee training camp in Virginia. The officers were all from the Civil Engineering Corps and the enlisted men were all Seabees or Seabee candidates. As I remember, we were the second group to go down to Fort Pierce for training in the late spring of '43.

The Seabees had been fine organizations, but some of us wanted to get a little closer to combat in those days. The job they had been doing was important and the Seabees were great. But then Draper Kauffman came along.

Kauffman had been given the mission of establishing a demolition group. It was thought at that time that the best source of people who already had that kind of background would be the Seabees. Draper came up to Camp Peary and gave us a remarkable sales pitch about his new unit. The mission of the new organization couldn't be revealed to us because of security considerations. However, Kauffman did say that it was going to be a very challenging and dangerous kind of group. He also said that we weren't going to receive any extra pay, as some other units such as the submariners and parachutists did, but that we would be getting a lot of medals. That was because we would work in a very dangerous situation.

Most of us were taken with the charisma and personality of this man, Draper Kauffman. He was already experienced in combat and it showed.

Even after we had volunteered, Kauffman would come out to our training. We were still working at Camp Peary until another training base was available. Our training program was still being developed a lot. It was known that we would be working in the water, so it was decided to give us some experience with surface-supplied hard-hat diving equipment. One time, we were out on a diving barge and Kauffman came out to join us.

While we were working with the suits out on the barge, Draper insisted that he go down in the gear and try it himself. That was quite an experience, but not due to the diving. While Kauffman was underwater, he started to become very ill with a malady of the stomach. He shouted, "Get me up! Get me up!" over the communicator. We quickly pulled him up to the surface and were able to get him out of the suit before there were any personal disasters.

That was just the kind of guy Draper Kauffman was. And our opinions of him were proven out later when we served with him in combat. It was because of Draper Kauffman personally that a number of us volunteered for the new unit. In spite of the fact that he was constantly running off to Washington or wherever those first few months, when he was with us, he trained right alongside his men. He led by example.

With the basic manpower coming on board, Draper Kauffman now established his new training site for the Naval Combat Demolition Units at the Naval Amphibious Training Base, Fort Pierce, Florida. The base had been chosen by Kauffman for a number of reasons, among these the fact that the water off the east coast of Florida remained warm enough year-round to allow swimming. In addition, the amphibious forces already at the base allowed interaction with the boats and crews to work out problems in the mission of the NCDUs as they came up. Also, the ATB itself was located on South Hutchison Island. North Hutchison Island was just a short distance away by water, reasonably isolated for security purposes, and experimental demolition work could be conducted on its shores in safety.

On the negative side, the facilities at NATB Fort Pierce were just barely beginning to be developed. Few amenities were available for the troops already in place there. The new NCDU School would begin with tents for housing and all other support to be developed. What stood out to the men of the new NCDUs who would soon arrive at Fort Pierce was the amazing number of mosquitoes, sand fleas, gnats, and other insect life that permeated the area. There would soon be more than one occasion when the men undergoing training would prefer to face the enemy than another night crawling though the bug-infested brush of Fort Pierce.

The Navy Combat Demolition Unit started at Fort Pierce in June 1943. The first class arrived and prepared to begin training the first week of July 1943. The first training courses were literally developed as the men went through them. Much of the information on the possible target of the NCDUs, specifically what they would face, where it was, and what they would have to do on arrival, was highly classified and not known to any of the staff, including Kauffman himself.

The basic unit of the NCDU was determined to be a single officer and five enlisted men. This six-man NCDU would work and live together more closely than any other Navy unit officially had before. The six men would operate a single seven-man rubber boat. The space for the seventh man would be taken up by the explosives and equipment the NCDU would need to conduct their mission.

Draper Kauffman well knew the importance of such a small unit working together as a team. To ensure the teamwork aspect of his training, Kauffman had all of his officers, including himself, go through exactly the same training as the men under their command. Officers and gentlemen in the U.S. Navy did not normally work hand in glove with their enlisted men. In the NCDUs, if they didn't, they

Some of the beach obstacles built along the shores of Florida at Fort Pierce. Instead of protecting the beach from invasion craft, these obstacles were built by the Seabees so that they could be destroyed by the NCDUs in training.

soon found themselves going to another assignment. The NCDUs would not swim in to their targets; instead, they would paddle in a rubber boat and walk to their targets once they reached the shore. Uniforms were boots, dungarees, and steel helmets. Crawling through the sand, brush, and mud soon became very familiar to the lowest-ranking seaman as well as his officers and chiefs as they all went through training together.

Since he had a very short timetable to prepare the NCDUs for their mission, Draper Kauffman decided to create an elimination event at the very beginning of training. Going to the personnel at the Scouts and Raiders School also at the ATB, Kauffman studied their physical training techniques and schedules for a week. He took the physical training program of the S&R School and condensed it down to a single week. That week, originally called Indoctrination Week, later renamed Motivation Week, had another more popular name given to it by the thousands of men who have endured its six terrible days. They call it Hell Week.

During that first week, constant on-the-go training, physical activity, and little sleep soon proved whether an individual had the mental and physical toughness to keep going no matter what. With the very small size of an NCDU, a single man giving up could jeopardize the entire unit and their mission. It is interesting to note that a number of men who went through this early training at Fort Pierce didn't think the first week was as tough as the last week of their eight-week training schedule.

The last week of training involved every aspect of the earlier training received by the men of the NCDUs. Their payoff week was a long tactical problem that kept them in the field constantly. They resolved reconnaissance problems, determined demolition attacks against obstacles of one kind or another—and then they carried out those plans.

Captain Frank Kaine, USN (Ret.) NCDU/UDT

I reported for duty with the NCDU on June 6, 1943. Our training began in Fort Pierce with a combination of instructors, including some from the Scouts and Raiders, some Army Rangers, and a British commando type. These were the men who initiated our training.

Several of us, including myself and my buddy Lloyd "Andy" Anderson, also acted as instructors. We taught things like demolitions, swimming, or anything that we could.

Our concentration in training was on explosive demolitions and rubber boat work. But we did have to teach some of our volunteers how to swim much better than they could when they arrived. That included Draper Kauffman, who was not the greatest swimmer in the world at the start.

Lloyd Anderson and I had been working as instructors at the Navy Bomb Disposal School, which Kauffman had recruited us for months earlier. The idea of spending the whole war in Washington as instructors didn't hold a lot of appeal to us. We wanted at least the chance to see some action.

In the spring of 1943, Draper Kauffman had approached a number of us and told us that he was going to start this new unit. We had no idea what the job was going to be exactly, but we had our suspicions. Kauffman was familiar with the coast of France from his earlier wartime experiences. We figured clearing the beaches of obstacles was going to be a part of this mission. So Lloyd Anderson and I volunteered for the new unit and asked Draper if we could go with him to this new duty station.

Draper agreed with our request and told us we were the first people to sign up with his new unit. As a kind of aside to our volunteering, we had an agreement with Draper. He had agreed that we would be the first to also sign out from the school to see action. Neither of us wanted to be permanent instructors again.

When we finished training, everyone was given the chance to pick the fleet they would be sent to. We didn't know a fleet from anything else and had no idea which one operated where. Kauffman gave us a choice of numbers from one through seven. My buddy and I picked seven just as a lucky number. Number seven turned out to be the Seventh Fleet, serving with MacArthur's forces in the Southwest Pacific.

From our start in action until the end of the war, my unit, NCDU 2, served with the Seventh Fleet forces. We were never relieved or rotated. Ultimately, six NCDUs of six men each were assigned in total to the Southwestern Pacific theater. Later, when the rest of the NCDUs were gathered into Underwater Demolition Teams, our groups remained as NCDUs through the whole of the war.

We remained in the same unit configuration throughout our part of the war. When we finally returned home in late 1945, we were still NCDUs, the last in the Navy. We operated, very carefully, in our six-man units conducting reconnaissance of a landing site prior to an invasion. As many NCDUs as would be needed, usually just two, would be used for an operation.

Our normal operating procedure would be to go in from sixteen days to one day prior to D day, and conduct a reconnaissance of the beaches and offshore waters. We would look for reefs, mines, fishnets, whatever obstacles of any kind. Depending on what we found, we would come back on a later date and conduct our demolition swim prior to the invasion. So the greatest part of our work, and the most dangerous portion, was completed before D day. When we finished, the way was open to get the landing going.

The job was kind of neat to do really. And the support we received from the other Navy units was great. If we received any fire from enemy positions on the beach or in the jungles, the destroyers and other ships would come in and just lower their big guns down on target. When those Navy guns fired right over our heads, we could hear the shells whistling through the air right over our heads.

The other NCDUs who had operated in France weren't really swimming units. The beaches the European NCDUs operated on, especially for D day in Normandy, were wide and shallow. It was much more efficient for them to walk or wade through the water to get to their targets. For us, the situation and the mission were different.

The waters were so shallow off most of the beaches we worked on in the Southwestern Pacific that the larger craft weren't able to come in as close to shore as we might have liked. For an operation, we tended to go from a ship to a landing craft, and then from the landing craft to a rubber boat. Finally, we would swim the last distance in. We had masks and swim fins to work with, a round black rubber mask and heavy black fins. The mask was small and round with no way to breathe except to put your head above the surface. And the fins were not the most comfortable. But that was the gear we had to work with right from the start.

We operated with MacArthur's forces through the New Guinea area, the Philippines, the Schouten Islands, and finally Borneo. Out of all of the operations we did, the landings at Biak early on stand out as probably the hardest. At Biak, one of the Schouten Islands, we had a lot of air attacks come at us from the Japanese forces. And these attacks included kamikazes, which were very hard to defend against.

The next-hardest operation was Leyte Gulf in the Philippines. The only reason Leyte was second in difficulty was that the air attacks at Biak came as a surprise. At Leyte, the kamikazes were expected and the Japanese didn't disappoint us. Also the Leyte attacks came over a period of time; at Biak, the attacks came suddenly and were gone almost as fast. Both operations, Biak and Leyte, involved a lot of strafing attacks against us as well as kamikaze crashes into the ships in the fleet around us. It was something that would get your attention fairly quickly.

In spite of all of the action, we didn't take any losses in any of the NCDUs. Out of the thirty-six men who served with the Seventh Fleet, we all went home in one piece at the end of the war. All of the NCDUs did at least ten or eleven landings while with MacArthur's forces. Some did even more. On some ops, we would split up and only two NCDUs would do one beach. Then the next beach would be done by another pair of NCDUs. We kept busy operating most of the time.

At Leyte I had the opportunity to talk to other UDTs from the CENPAC (Central Pacific) and SOUPAC (South Pacific). Some of those men had never even been on an operation. Others were going on their first or maybe their second. For us, Leyte was something like our sixth invasion. We had joined with the NCDUs intending to see whatever action we could. And we were seeing a good deal of it.

Serving with MacArthur's group was the way we were seeing so much action, but we never even really considered ourselves as working for him. Our commander was Rear Admiral Daniel E. Barbey and the Seventh Amphibious Force, which was under his command. That force was, in turn, part of the Seventh Fleet.

The first invasion we went on was in the Admiralties Islands at Los Negros, a small island that was almost part of the much larger Manus Island nearby. What the higher-ups hadn't known was that Los Negros was home to a batch of Japanese Imperial Marines who were known to be hard fighters. The U.S. Army landed a relatively small group, like a reconnaissance battalion, from the Army's Fifth Cavalry Regiment on Los Negros. The fighting got pretty hot and heavy fast, so command wanted to open up a second front and land troops on the far side of the enemy forces. The troops were already on their way and there was a great bay, harbor really, that could be used to land the troops. The trouble was that the mouth of the bay was blocked by a large coral reef.

The coral reef ran across the bay from about eight feet deep on one side to about twenty feet deep on the other. None of the larger ships would be able to get past it the way it stood. So we were ordered to the other side of the island to blast an opening through the reef.

We had a lot of explosives we hadn't used yet, so all the tools we needed were right at hand with us. There were Mark-8 rubber hose charges, two-inch-thick lengths of hose, twenty-five feet long and loaded with two pounds of high explosives for every foot. In addition, we had boxes of bangalore torpedoes, military-issue pipe bombs, each section made up of five-foot lengths of two-and-a-half-inch-diameter steel pipe loaded with ten pounds of high explosive. Along with those items, we had cases of bulk tetrytol charges and anything else we might need.

When we looked at the reef, we found it was about ten or twelve feet thick. We didn't know what to use to blast the reef to start with; we didn't have enough Mark-8 hose to do the job. So instead, we laid out whole boxes of bangalore torpedoes, ten sections to a case, and draped the chains across the reefs. The box chains lay across the reef every few feet or so the width of the channel we wanted to blast. When the charges were finally in place, we must have had twenty-eight or thirty tons of explosives in the shot.

When we fired the shot, it really went, and the reef went with it. What we hadn't known was that the troop ships were holding detachments from the Army's Fifth Cavalry Regiment on board. The ship didn't even wait until we had a chance to recon the blast site. They just sailed through the channel easily, with enough room on either side and plenty of depth under their keel. We did finally recon the shot, but that was well after the troops were ashore. All told, that was a pretty hairy operation as far as our getting the job done was concerned.

When we fired that big shot, the shock wave swept through the waters around the reef. Every place you looked, fish or something were popping up to the surface. We gathered up a number of huge jewfish (groupers) that were absolutely massive. The heads on these fish were several feet wide, the lips around their mouths were six inches or more thick. These fish may have been hundreds of years old and could eat anything they felt like along that reef.

A Seabee battalion was on shore and they came out onto a floating causeway they had put out to unload ships with a wrecker. Using the wrecker, they could haul the big fish out of our landing craft when we put the tow hook under the fish's jaw. After filleting the fish, the Seabees fed their entire unit from just one fish. We had brought almost a dozen of these monsters in from the blast site and gave them to all of the Army units that were around.

The Scouts and Raiders ran a training program at Fort Pierce at the same time as the NCDUs were training there. At the time we were training there with the first NCDU class, the S&R people were completely separate and weren't involved with our training at all. Later, some Scouts and Raider personnel transferred over to the NCDU school and served as instructors. But I don't know of any who served with the UDTs. The S&Rs themselves had been operating for almost a full year in the European Theater of Operations (ETO) before the NCDU reached the field.

The end of the war for those of us in the Southwestern Pacific was great. We were out there a little over two years, but our units had returned to the States just prior to the Japanese surrender. We had been sent back to California to train for cold-water operations as part of the invasion forces for the Japanese main islands. None of us was very impressed with either the idea of landing on Japan itself or swimming around the waters off Japan during the winter months. There was an advantage to having operated only in the Southwestern Pacific: at least the water was warm.

For the invasion of Japan itself, we didn't have any ideas about what to expect. After two years of combat operations, we had all learned not to anticipate anything. You planned for what you knew and then did your job. The situation would get to be a routine as you knew the people you had, what their abilities were, and what materials you had to work with. Everyone in the unit relied on everyone else and you knew what to expect. The unexpected you couldn't plan for, so worrying about it just wore you down.

Worry was something you did on your first landings. You would wonder about what was going to happen, how much gunfire you were going to take from the beach. In general, you were apprehensive about the coming situation because you really didn't know just what a minimal target a swimmer was in the water. If you knew that ahead of time, you wouldn't worry about it nearly as much.

Five or ten swimmers in the water across 800 yards of beach are little more than dots in the water. That's not much of a target. And the swimmers would be spread apart and constantly ducking under the water and coming up someplace else. It would take a very good shot, or a lucky one, for an enemy to even come very close to hitting one of us while we were swimming. And that hard shot would be made even worse by all of the heavy fire coming in to the beach from the ships offshore. The Navy did a very good job of suppressing Japanese positions when they came in firing prior to an invasion.

Enemy fire just wasn't a real problem for us when we were reconning a beach prior to a landing. The only real problem we had was with our own ordnance. When the rocket-armed landing craft came in to pound the beach with a rain of high-explosive rockets, those bothered us a lot. The 4.5-inch barrage rockets were more of a menace to us than anything else during an invasion.

You could be swimming along and happen to look up, or be swimming on your back, you would see these rockets overhead and one of them would twitch its tail or a couple would bump together, and you knew it was coming down. Wherever that rocket was going to hit wasn't where you wanted to be and we were right under them. None of us was ever hurt by friendly fire. But those barrage rockets could make life a lot more exciting sometimes.

When the war finally ended and we returned to the United States, the story of the UDTs was declassified and the public finally learned of the men who led the invasions in. The term frogman was coined by a magazine writer and adopted by both the public and the teams.

Nicknames were always something that made the rounds in the teams, and once you received one, it tended to stick with you. I was called "MacArthur's Frogman" from having served with the Seventh Fleet in the Southwestern Pacific. General Douglas MacArthur was in overall command of the Allied war effort in that part of the Pacific.

So we came under MacArthur's command in general. Directly, we worked for Rear Admiral Daniel E. Barbey and the Seventh Amphibious Force he commanded. The Amphibious Force did the landing operations for the Seventh Fleet. So when I returned to the United States, the team guys demonstrated their love of nicknames by giving me the "MacArthur's Frogman" title.

At the end of the war, the UDTs and the NCDUs were practically wiped out. As the last of the NCDUs, our units didn't exist past 1945. My understanding was that UDT 27 had just been commissioned as the war ended, so there were a lot of UDTs in operation as the war came to an end. I was finally sent home in January of 1946. When I returned to the service in January 1950, there were only five UDTs left, two on the East Coast at Little Creek and three on the West Coast at Coronado. The teams in 1950 were ten officers and eighty men, still good-sized but smaller than the WWII teams.

The Navy reactivated me for duty with the Naval Beach Group at Little Creek, Virginia, in 1950. I stayed there about six months before going back to demolition work with UDT 4. At UDT 4, I spent about two months as the executive officer of the team. Then I was sent over to UDT 2, where I took the position of CO. UDT 2 was a long assignment; I was there from 1951 to 1958, serving both as the CO and also assigned as the commander of UDU 2. Underwater Demolition Unit 2 was the command structure that both the East Coast UDTs operated under.

While I was the CO of UDT 2, we did operations in the Arctic every year. Construction was ongoing for the Distant Early Warning System (DEW line) and the UDT worked in support of that construction. Those weren't the only cold-water ops we did. There were also Antarctic deployments with operations done on an experimental basis. Jack Connelly and Norm Olsen both were in some of the UDT exploratory operations in Antarctic waters.

Though I personally never went on an Arctic or Antarctic deploy-

---

ment, I never felt I had missed anything. I had been plenty cold enough at other times in my life.

Working in the UDTs was much like operating with my old NCDU, only on a much larger scale. Since I was the commander of a UDT during peacetime, the administrative load was much heavier. There were more people to do the job, but unlike the way it was during wartime, you couldn't ignore the paperwork in order to get the mission accomplished.

And we had a wider mission scope in the UDT at that time. Besides conducting operations in support of the fleet, we ran our own training programs. We also were constantly trying to expand our mission capabilities.

At that time in the mid-1950s we were trying to develop on our limited experience with the British and Italian wartime minisubs. In the UDT we had a division known as Sub Ops, which was really most of the diving operations. For our experiments, we had several British Welman midget dry submarines. And we had an Italian two-man midget wet submarine. The Italian sub I always associate with Joe DiMartino; he always seemed to be on that rig no matter where it went. So we had a lot of good developmental stuff going on in the UDT at that time.

We were using the minisubs to try to develop and keep up-to-date on all submersibles. They were a great attack unit for an organization like ours. So we wanted to know their capabilities and limitations. Depending on where you were and what was going on, the small submersibles could allow a small unit of men to successfully attack even a capital ship.

The Italians had used the minisubs quite successfully during WWII at Gibraltar in the Mediterranean. They had taken a sunken ship in the water across from the British base at Gibraltar and converted it into a hidden base. They stowed their minisubs and equipment in the partially sunken ship, where they could slip out unnoticed and attack ships lying at anchor.

The basic idea of the Italian minisub was that the front end could be loaded with explosives. Within the minisub was a gear train that could release the front warhead. The top of the explosive warhead was magnetic and it could be attached, or even just dropped, underneath the keel of a ship. Men would ride the small craft wearing rebreathers and protective suits against the cold. Once they had the warhead in place, they would just set the fuse and then steam away.

This was very much a mission that could be performed by the UDTs. But we had some trouble with the rest of the Navy in some respects. The Submarine Service decided that the Welmans were true dry submarines, and as such, they belonged to them. So our Welmans disappeared. Since the Italian minisub was a wet type, the men rode on it like a torpedo with seats; those we could keep since only a swimmer could use them.

During the Kennedy administration, the Army Special Forces and Air Force's Air Commandos were looked on favorably. The President was financing the new type of units that were needed to fight an unconventional war. The guerrilla war was looking to be the wave of the future and Kennedy wanted the United States to have the capability to fight one.

Someone in Washington decided that if unconventional warfare was good for the Army and the Air Force, it was good enough for the Navy as well. Up to that point, the Navy was, and still is for the most part, concentrating on very large capital ships and aircraft capable of fighting a major conventional conflict. The other main thrust was for the construction and support of the fleet's ballistic missile submarine as part of the nuclear deterrent force.

To meet Kennedy's desires, a small, specialized unit of men would have to be created that could conduct unconventional warfare in a maritime environment. In 1962, ten officers and fifty enlisted men from the UDTs were gathered on each coast and the SEAL Teams established. Outside of gathering the people and running the units, no one who served with the SEAL Teams themselves had very much to do with their creation.

The men who make up the SEAL Teams today are no different from the men who made up the UDTs or the NCDUs back in WWII. Individuals who go into the Teams are a select group who are able to pass the strenuous training program. These men are also extremely loyal and devoted to their teams and their teammates.

The NCDU mission during WWII was to clear the beaches of obstructions and obstacles so that the incoming landing craft and troops could access the beach. Another part of the job was to determine that the beach could be exited and the troops able to access the hinterland. The UDT mission was exactly the same and included a very detailed survey of the offshore waters so that last-minute charts could be made.

The SEAL mission is the result of an evolutionary process. The NCDU of WWII was originally a foot-slogging, hardworking guy in the water with a lot of demolition knowledge and experience. The UDT swimmer took that same know-how into the water. As we progressed after WWII and into Korea, the UDT man had gone completely under the water to do his job.

In Korea, the UDT operator got back out of the water a little bit and went up on land to destroy bridges and tunnels. So that got the teams back up and out of the water. When the SEALs came along, the teams went to offensive operations for the first time. They became hunters and seekers of the enemy, prisoner takers and intelligence gatherers.

In Vietnam, the SEALs were forced to work almost twenty-four-hour days. When the SEALs were first started, there had been very few of them. But to do the jobs that were given the teams in Vietnam, more and more qualified SEALs were needed.

The actions the teams did during the different conflicts varied as much as the wars themselves did. Korea was a so-called police action. It never got finished. There wasn't a final victory that could be pointed to and described as the end of the war. Vietnam was much the same way. They were both wars of politics. The battles were not the same; there had been no opposed amphibious landings in Korea as there had been in WWII. There were major land battles in Korea, fought with the same kind of fire and maneuver tactics as had been used for centuries.

In Vietnam, there were very few major battles, none of which was like the great land engagements of WWII. The fights in Vietnam were conducted almost on a hand-to-hand basis, units engaging within close proximity to each other because of the thick jungles. And the enemy couldn't be pursued to a final confrontation. The guerrillas vanished into the population. Armed groups could not be chased past a certain point, borders were not to be crossed. Vietnam was a war of frustrations.

There were a lot of jobs and different hats I wore during my career in Special Warfare. I was the head of the training business at Little Creek, running the UDTR School where the new men would get qualified to enter the UDT. And there was an assignment to run a SERE School (Survival, Evasion, Resistance, and Escape) for a year. In 1966, I was sent out to the West Coast to take the position of commander of Special Warfare Group One (SpecWarGruOne) in Coronado.

In the SpecWarGruOne was a SEAL Team, the UDTs, and the Special Boat Unit. All of those units were being used in Vietnam at that time with different levels of involvement. As the commander of the group, I was responsible for carrying forward the training, our fleet commitments, and our new combat commitment in Vietnam. So the position managed to keep me pretty busy.

■ Chapter 7

NCDU ASSIGNMENTS

By the fall of 1943, the first NCDU classes were graduating at Fort Pierce. Besides a number—NCDU 2, NCDU 127, etc.—each NCDU received a name based usually on its officer-in-charge, such as Kaine's Killers, Andrews's Avengers, etc. Officially, the training time for each of the first five NCDU classes was six weeks; later this schedule was increased to eight weeks in time for the sixth class.

The NCDUs from the first class of graduates were sent to Kiska, Alaska, the Southwestern Pacific, and the Mediterranean. NCDU 1 was sent under very secret orders to San Francisco, where they were to receive further transportation and assignment. NCDU 1 was to take part in the invasion of Kiska and other possible operations in the Aleutian Islands off Alaska. The NCDU never joined with the U.S. invasion forces prior to their unopposed landings on Kiska. The Japanese had gone. The men of NCDU 1 were later sent to the Central Pacific forces at Pearl Harbor. There, they ended as an NCDU and joined into the new UDTs.

The next two NCDUs left Fort Pierce for duties in the Southwestern Pacific as part of the Seventh Fleet on 8 September 1943. They were not to arrive in Australia until early January 1944. They were later joined by four additional NCDUs, making the NCDU detachment six units strong with thirty-six men total.

The first NCDU to arrive in England was NCDU 11, arriving in October 1943. They were the vanguard of what would be the largest concentration of NCDUs of the war. The frustrated men of the NCDU were assigned jobs such as guard duty, officer of the day, and other general tasks. No one knew who they were at the time, or what to do with them. This situation didn't start to really change until early in 1944. Until then, valuable training time was lost.

William L. Dawson, Gunner's Mate, Second Class

We came down to Fort Pierce in July and August 1943. In the group were forty-two men straight from boot camp in Bainbridge, Maryland, thirty-six Seabees from Camp Peary, and our officers, who came out of the Mine and Bomb Disposal School in Washington, D.C., including Draper Kauffman, who was our commanding officer. In spite of his rank, Commander Kauffman trained right alongside the rest of us when he wasn't in Washington taking care of one thing or another.

Originally, I had intended to be a submariner. I had finished my boot camp at Bainbridge and volunteered for Sub School up in New London, Connecticut. While I was waiting to be sent up to school, a pair of officers came in to Bainbridge and gave a bunch of us a talk about this new outfit they were putting together. The mission wasn't exactly described, but you would learn how to blow things up and generally be some kind of cloak-and-dagger man. Getting out of Bainbridge and leaving boot was what really appealed to me right about then. Another man and I went up to the officers later and asked if we could volunteer.

We were told that there were enough volunteers for the new program and no more men were needed right now. This didn't sit too well with the pair of us, so we slipped around to the back of the building where they were checking out the volunteers. There was an open window that we slipped through and quickly got into the end of the line. Out of all of the volunteers they had that day, forty-two men were picked and the pair of us were two of them.

Shortly after that adventure, the bunch of us were sent by train down to Fort Pierce, Florida, to start training. The two officers we had tried to volunteer with may have been from Bomb Disposal School, but we didn't see that pair for a while. But the officers we did have down at Fort Pierce didn't act quite like the others we had seen up in Bainbridge.

The officers in training with us had to do just exactly the same things we did, Commander Kauffman as well. They crawled through the mud and swatted insects right with the rest of us. Seeing that made me feel more like our officers were with me rather than being above me. And they could do the same things I could do. It made us feel a lot more like we wanted to follow them.

But we all had to lead in one way or another. During training, you could be coming in on a rubber boat and suddenly the surf would toss you and the men one way and dump the explosives the other way. Then some of the training officers might come up and say, "You're dead, and you're dead," while they pointed to members from your boat crew.

Then the "dead" guys would have to lie on the beach and let the sand flies and mosquitoes eat on them for a while. The rest of the guys in the boat crew would have to continue on and carry out the mission we were supposed to have been on. They would gather up the explosives, gear, boat, and do whatever they had to do to get the job done.

Before coming into the service, I had played a lot of football and baseball. And I considered myself to be in pretty good shape. By the time the trainers at Fort Pierce were done with me, I had muscles I never knew I had before. And I was certain about them because they all ached.

The training at Fort Pierce was considered pretty tough at the time by those of us who went through it. There were seven Army instructors, all of them sergeants, who had taken the British commando course over in England. It was these Army NCOs who set up our physical training course, setting up the two- or three-mile runs along the beach, log PT, and the obstacle course along with rubber boat drills, swimming, and a lot of calisthenics. They gave us a little bit of everything.

The workouts put me in much better shape than I had ever been in in my life. The people speak about Hell Week, which back then was the first week of training and officially called Indoctrination Week. For myself, I considered every week to be Hell Week. In spite of the heavy physical and mental demands put on us, we managed to make it through the training; at least a number of us did. Some men were dropped and others just couldn't keep up the pace. There were a lot fewer men at the end of training than first went into it. But we managed to make out.

There were about ten or more six-man NCDUs who completed the course with that first group of students. Some of the NCDUs were sent to the Pacific and others to the European theater. Our officer, Frank Kaine, had our unit, NCDU 2, join those heading to the Southwest Pacific and the Seventh Fleet. There, we found ourselves under the command of General Douglas MacArthur as part of his campaign against the Japanese.

For a long time it seemed no one knew who we were or what we were supposed to do. The upper command knew us and our mission, but we were so secret, no one on the local operational level had any idea about us. We would receive our orders, get on a ship, and go on an invasion. Once everything was done, we went back to our base and waited for the next set of orders. The bases changed quite a bit.

It seemed that we never stayed in any one base for more than a few months before we were on the move again. In about two years, we did twelve invasions—four in New Guinea, six in the Philippines, and two in Borneo.

Some of the operations weren't too bad. The troops just kind of walked ashore and there wasn't too much to worry about. We didn't find much in the way of obstacles and the enemy didn't put up a heavy resistance right on the beach. Other invasions were a little different.

But it was always pretty much the same for us. We swam in to beaches, made our reconnaissance, checked out piers for mines or booby traps, and blew open the way to the beach. It depended on what was needed; we blew coral reefs, sandbars, and anything else that was in the way. Personally, I thought we did a very good job.

Originally, we had been told we would be shipped out for six months and then returned to the States. That time grew a little bit and we stayed out in the Southwestern Pacific with MacArthur's forces until the end of the war. We were the only Navy NCDUs to remain such all through the war. Other NCDUs eventually joined into UDTs, but we stayed the same six-man units for the duration.

We were kept so busy on operations that it didn't seem like two years had gone by when it was all over. We had been very fortunate that none of us were hurt and we all got through the war okay.

Not that what we did was easy at all. Our first invasion was in the Admiralty Islands, and two NCDUs hit the beach right alongside the Army forces. We moved in on an LST along with twelve tons of explosives. We unloaded the explosives on the beach and just waited there. The Army told us to dig in before it got dark and wait until morning. So we dug a good, deep foxhole right there on the beach.

Eleven of us crawled into that hole and spent the night. It started to rain and our hole filled up with a bit of water. But that didn't do much to keep us awake. The noise from the machine gun fire and grenades going off all night long, that kept us from sleeping soundly. But the next morning, we were all there and had all managed to come out of it in one piece.

When we were in the foxhole on the beach that night, the machine guns and grenades just kept going off all night long. And it started to rain pretty hard, filling the hole we were in with water. We could just lie there all night in miserable conditions and listen to what was going on around us. My officer seemed to have a pretty bad cold, and the situation we were in wasn't doing it any good. I was more worried about him than about myself as the night wore on.

When you're lying there like that, under those conditions, a lot of things can run through your mind. It's hard to even say afterward what they were. But eventually, that night ended and we were able to continue our mission the next day.

A couple of days after that long night we were ordered to the harbor on the other side of the island. When we got over there, we found that there was a coral reef about twenty feet down going all the way across the channel into the harbor. The Army wanted the top of the reef knocked off so that the bigger ships could come right up on shore and unload.

It took us about two or three days to lay all of the powder, about four or five tons a day, that was needed to blow that reef down. We used some shallow-water diving gear; the Jack Brown canvas rig, as I remember it, came down over both your shoulders and had a full face mask. The rig was a rebreather and it had baralyme to purify the air you breathed along with an oxygen tank to replace what you used.

We used the diving gear to help us lay all the explosives along the top of the reef. When we fired the shot, we killed a small jewfish (grouper), which we took in to the Army camp up on the beach. They told us that if we could get any more, they would be glad to have them. They were eating combat rations and any kind of fresh food would be a treat.

The next shot we fired to clear the reef, we must have killed a dozen of those jewfish, some of them pretty big ones. It took seven men to pull this one fish into the bow of an LCM, then we dragged in two more. The Army brought a weapons carrier over with an A-frame hoist on the back of it, like a civilian wrecker truck.

The Army dragged the fish out of the boat and hoisted it up to the top of the A-frame. In spite of the nose of that fish being some ten feet in the air, its tail was still dragging on the ground. The next day, we were told the Army fed some 900 men with that one fish, and the two smaller ones fed the Seabee battalion. All told, they were very happy with both our demolition job and our fishing skills.

We were part of invasions at Los Negros, Aitape, Biak, and Numfoor in the New Guinea area. Then there was Leyte Gulf, Mindanao, Lingayen Gulf, Luzon, Zamboanga, and others in the Philippines. And finally Tarakan Island and Bunei Bay in Borneo. Leyte Gulf was one of our big operations. We went in about four days before D day to make our reconnaissance. We checked the depth of the water and made sure that the landing craft could get to the beach.

We were the guys who opened up the way, or made sure the chosen way in was clear. We would swim ashore if we had to and make a reconnaissance of the beach and the offshore waters. We would make notes if there were any obstacles, sandbars, coral reefs, or anything that would be in the way of the incoming landing craft.

Often enough, we didn't have much to do after we had gone in and conducted our recon. There just wouldn't be many obstacles, natural or man-made. The most common things we found were sandbars and coral reefs that were blocking a way in, especially for the bigger boats. Those blockages we had to blow out of the way.

We checked facilities that might already be at a site and that the command wanted to use. Checking piers for mines or booby traps had to be done before the ships could use them to unload.

What we did more than anything else was just to see if the way in to the beach was clear. Fortunately, we never lost anyone on one of our operations. Other teams on other missions in other places had men killed or wounded; we were lucky enough that everyone who was with us also went home.

Prior to one operation we were supposed to go on, we were up in Lingayen Gulf. A PT boat was supposed to pick us up and take us down to Manila, where there was a cable line across the entrance to the bay. Command wanted the cable cut and the buoys holding it up removed. They didn't know if it was a submarine net or what. So the PT that was to transport us would drop us at the cable and pick us up afterward. The only trouble was, the PT that was assigned to us had been shot up pretty badly making a run along the beaches earlier. So our part in that operation was canceled.

When we would be going in to a beach in a small boat, that was when you might think about what might happen. Thoughts of your home and your loved ones would go through your head. But if you think about those things too much, it can get in your mind and work on you. So you have to put such thoughts aside and concentrate on the mission.

We were there to do a job and on the way in to the beach you just had to put the possibilities out of your mind and go do what you had to do. That was the only way to get the whole thing over with.

We didn't have the training to roll over the side of the boats at speed, not like the UDTs did later in the war. What we did was just drop off the side of the boat, usually a small landing craft, and just swim in to the beaches. Depending on the operation we were on, the boat might just drop its bow ramp and we'd go into the water that way. All in all, we were very lucky and we just didn't hit that many places where the invasion beach was a real rough spot.

Later on, when the cast and recovery system had been developed by the UDT, getting in and out of the boat was much faster and safer. For us, we had only the six men in a unit. Two units working together, which was how we often operated, just made ten enlisted men and two officers. We would go in together and keep track of each other, but we didn't operate in assigned pairs or swim buddies. Mostly, we just swam on our own, and tried to keep everyone else in sight.

On one operation, we went in with a rubber boat full of explosives to blast an obstacle clear. On the swim in, a Japanese sniper opened fire on us. You could dive down to escape the fire, but not for very long. Eventually, you had to come back up for air and the sniper was there, ready to open fire. The only place we had to take cover from the sniper was behind the rubber boat and its load of explosives.

We lucked out again during that sniper episode when an Army patrol finally took the shooter out. Once the patrol had heard we were in trouble, they just went on the hunt for that sniper. And we appreciated what they did for us. We now could go back to our job, laying out explosives to blast a coral reef.

Not all of the military units we worked with acted the same. The Australians had their own way of conducting an invasion. They would hit the beach and soon have a fire going. On the fire would go a tin of water and they would brew themselves up some tea. We thought that was a pretty odd way to conduct an invasion. And every now and then, another Jap sniper would open fire and hit a couple of the Aussies. But that never discouraged them from making their tea.

Most of our operations occurred during the day, and we could see everything going on. When we found obstacles on our swims, we could usually see them pretty well. We didn't have the plastic slates and wax markers the UDT had, so we just made note of them being there and continued on.

Anytime we found obstacles that we would have to remove, we would get the explosives we needed to destroy them, usually a tetrytol pack or two, and load the target. If we had to, we would run a primacord main between multiple obstacles so we could fire them all together. The primacord would be set off with a fused cap, though sometimes we used electrical caps and a hell box.

For sandbars and coral reefs, we would lay bangalore torpedoes or Mark-8 rubber hose charges, whatever explosives we had left, and cap them. If we were using electric caps, we would reel out the electric line, clear the area, and blow the charge.

There was one time in the Admiralty Islands when we loaded a coral reef and the charge misfired. We set off the caps and nothing happened. These are not the best times to be a demo man, so we just left the charge until the next day. I made a straight dive down on the

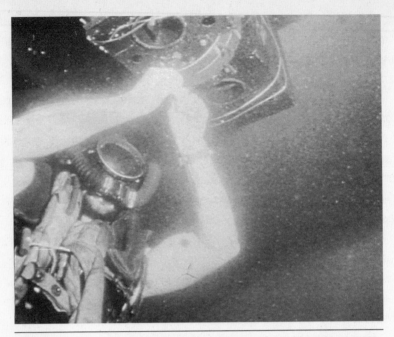

Wearing a closed-circuit rebreathing rig, a UDT operator arms a demolition charge underwater.

charge with a line. Tying the end of the line to the explosive hose charge would let us bring it back up and reprime for firing.

Just before I was to go into the water, a great big sea snake swam by. Sea snakes are among the most poisonous snakes in the world and I wasn't too sure I wanted to share the ocean with him. But after he went out of sight, I had to continue with my job. So I swam down to the charge and tied on my line. We pulled the end of the hose back up, recapped it, and set off the charge. Fortunately, we didn't have many misfires, but that one with the snake was rather memorable.

There was often some rivalry between the Army and the Navy back in the States. Most of that was just in good fun. Out in the field during the war, there just weren't any real problems. We got along pretty well with the Army. When we were on the beach with them, there weren't any problems at all, other than some the Japanese might have tried to throw up at us.

We transferred a lot from one ship to another as we went on different invasions. A lot of things happened over those years. We did our jobs and opened the way for the Army. But there was one transfer to a ship that stands out and that was the one we boarded to go home.

Personally, I think the atomic bomb was a great thing. It saved a lot of American lives, ours in particular. We would have been lined up to go into Japan with the first waves. And there's no telling how many men would have been killed on that operation. My understanding is that the Japanese main islands were very well fortified. And we already knew that they were willing to fight to the bitter end. It's a good thing that never had to be tested; a lot of people would have died on both sides.

Most of the men I trained with were up to par. They did their jobs and they did them well, you could depend on them. And we had a lot of variety in the kind of people in our NCDU. One of the men in our unit was a full-blooded Comanche Indian I thought a lot of. His name was Sam Powderpony and he was a very good man to have alongside you in any situation. After the war he went back to Oklahoma. I had liked serving with him very much.

Our officers were all good officers. Sometimes you might not agree with what they did, but someone had to make the final decisions. All in all, you could describe our unit with the word excellence. We did what we had to do, we got the job done. And I think we did a good job.

Doing the kind of work we did, you didn't have a whole lot of time to think about what might happen. With the job at hand to concentrate on, you were just too busy to think about getting hurt or killed. If you were going to think about such things on the job, then you didn't belong in an outfit like ours. You can get killed anywhere and at any time. Just because we had a more hazardous job than the next guy didn't mean we should worry about it.

There doesn't seem to be a whole lot of difference between the basic man of the SEAL Teams today and what we were back during *our day. The men today are much more highly trained than we were, and they have a very technical job with a lot of things to learn. But the man underneath all that equipment—he's the same.*

■ Chapter 8

TARAWA

The invasion of Tarawa Atoll in late 1943 turned out to be a watershed event in the history of naval special warfare. The operation would remain well known to the Marine Corps and the Navy who took part in its execution. The name "Terrible Tarawa" was remembered through World War II and for some years afterward.

Rear Admiral Richmond Kelly Turner was in overall command of Operation GALVANIC, the invasion of the Gilbert Islands, including Tarawa Atoll. The taking of the Gilberts was planned to be one of the major openings of the Central Pacific campaign against the Japanese. General Douglas MacArthur would conduct his campaign against the Japanese up through New Guinea and the Philippines. The other point of the Allied two-pronged offensive against the Japanese would start with the Operation GALVANIC action. The emphasis on the Central Pacific holding the first major action was placed on Galvanic by the U.S. Joint Chiefs of Staff and the CNO, Admiral King.

Planning for the invasion of Tarawa was based on a number of intelligence sources, including charts, photographs, surveys, and the interrogation of people who were familiar with the area from prewar times. Aerial photographs of Tarawa were taken in September and October 1943. In addition, the submarine USS *Nautilus* conducted surveys of the offshore waters and beach emplacements at Tarawa in late September and early October. These studies filled in a host of missing hydrographic data on the offshore waters at Tarawa. Photographs taken through the submarine's periscope also showed the beaches in great detail.

Plans were made to land the initial waves of troops on Tarawa from tracked amphibious vehicles (LVTs). The limited number of the amphibious vehicles available would require that the follow-up troops be landed in LCVPs. Landings at Makin Atoll in the Gilberts were timed to take place simultaneously with the Tarawa actions.

On 20 November 1943, the landings on Betio, the main island of the Tarawa Atoll began. The first waves of LVTs faced heavy fire from the many Japanese fortifications that survived the preinvasion bombardment. The follow-up waves of LCVPs found a much worse problem than enemy fire. The reefs around Tarawa were covered by much less water than was planned for. An unusual tidal condition left many of the reefs with water far too shallow for the landing craft to cross.

Landing craft ran aground far from the shores of Betio Island. Heavily laden assault troops had to wade in to shore, sometimes hundreds of yards away, in the face of heavy enemy fire. More Marines drowned in the waters off Tarawa during the landings than were killed by enemy fire taking the island itself in over three days of combat. Admiral Turner swore that the mistakes that led to Tarawa earning the nickname "Terrible Tarawa" would not be repeated.

The Creation of the UDTs

In the first week of November 1943, just prior to Operation GALVANIC and the invasion of Tarawa, the Fifth Amphibious Force, under Real Admiral Turner, was directed to begin the organization and specialized training of demolition personnel. The training was to be such that the demolition specialists would be able to clear natural coral formation obstacles as well as man-made obstacles and mines from future invasion beaches. A limited number of men from the Seabees had already been gathered at Waimanolo, Oahu, to form a cadre to train additional demolition personnel. The Seabees were the

A UDT combat swimmer tows a floating demolition charge into the beach during an exercise. On the beach are a pair of UDT swimmers already loading steel rail obstacles with explosives. Additional charges will be used to knock down the log wall farther up the beach.

U.S. Navy

only Pacific naval unit available at that time that had practical coral blasting experience.

The initiative for this training action was reported to have come from the commander-in-chief, Pacific Fleet, Admiral Chester Nimitz's office, in a letter sent to Admiral Turner dated 11 November 1943.

In the aftermath of Operation GALVANIC, in late November, Admiral Turner pushed forward two directives to prevent a repeat of the offshore problems at Tarawa. Turner's first, and most time-constrained, directive required the immediate formation of two Underwater Demolition Teams. The two teams were to be ready for action by the middle of January 1944. The second directive was for the establishment of a secure base in the Hawaiian Islands for the further training of UDTs. This base would later become the Naval Underwater Demolition Training and Experimental Base, Maui.

By the end of November, approximately 30 officers and 150 enlisted men were in training at Waimanolo, Oahu, for underwater demolition work. These men were divided into UDTs 1 and 2. The bulk of the personnel came from NCDUs sent to Hawaii for operations in the Pacific. The balance of the personnel came from the Seabees, Marines (20), and Army (4).

In a letter to Admiral Turner on 9 December, Admiral Nimitz directed that replicas of known Japanese beach obstacles be included in the training going on at Waimanolo. During a 17 December meeting with a joint-force Reef Obstacle and Mine Committee, founded only a few weeks earlier, Admiral Turner discussed the type of unit that would be required to clear coral as well as man-made obstacles from invasion beaches. It was during that meeting that the term *Underwater Demolition Team* was mentioned for the first time to identify the new unit as separate from the existing NCDUs and Seabees.

The new UDTs were formed up and preparing for their first actions by mid December 1943. The new teams consisted of fourteen officers and seventy enlisted men each and were numbered UDTs 1 and 2. UDT 2 was put under the command of Lieutenant Commander J. T. Koehler. On 23 December, UDT 2 was ordered to San Diego. Once in the States, UDT 2 was attached to Task Force 53, under the command of Rear Admiral Richard Conolly, for Operation FLINT-LOCK, the invasion of Roi and Namur in the Marshall Islands. UDT 1 remained in training at Waimanolo, where they were to be assigned to Task Force 52. Admiral Turner was in direct command of Task Force 52, which would attack Kwajalein as part of Operation FLINT-LOCK.

In a message to the CNO on 26 December, Admiral Turner requested the creation of the UDTs as active units. This was several days after Turner directed that UDT 2 be sent on to San Diego to prepare for Operation FLINTLOCK. The breach in military protocol was ignored and permission was issued.

On 29 January 1944, Operation FLINTLOCK began with the invasion of several smaller islands in the Kwajalein Atoll, the largest coral atoll in the world. By 1 February, the invasion of the two islands of Roi and Namur commenced. Under the cover of darkness, UDT 2 moved in to the islands in rubber boats. Testing the depth of the waters over the reef, UDT 2 operators didn't find any mines or other obstacles. The UDT 2 report to the Marines was that the way in was clear. After a very heavy shore bombardment by naval gunfire, the Marines experienced few difficulties or resistance against their late morning landings.

Two UDT combat swimmers place a limpet mine on the keel of a ship during a practice swimmer attack in 1965. The ring of magnets around the base of the mine will hold it securely to the steel hull of the ship.

A further target of Operation FLINTLOCK, the invasion of Kwajalein also started on 1 February. During their offshore reconnaissance of Kwajalein, several members of UDT 1 took to the water, going over the side of their landing craft and swimming in over the reefs to check its depth directly. UDT 1 reported the depth of the water as shallow over large coral heads. Tracked landing vehicles were used to land Marine forces because of the UDT's findings. Postinvasion blasting by the UDTs opened paths in to the beaches at Kwajalein through the coral reefs, allowing faster landing of additional men and material.

In March, after Operation FLINTLOCK had been completed, UDTs 1 and 2 were decommissioned. The men and officers were broken up to supply a training cadre with combat experience for the new Maui training base. They also created an experienced core group for newly

Having been attacked by UDT combat swimmers during a practice live-fire limpet mine operation, this ship splits in half and soon sinks to the bottom.

U.S. Navy

commissioned UDTs 3, 4, 5, 6, and 7 to be assembled around. The new UDTs would soon see action during Operation FORAGER, the upcoming invasion of the Marianas Islands. At this time it was decided that the UDTs would be completely manned with naval personnel except for liaison officers and observers.

On 14 and 15 March 1944, two basic letters covering the organization of the UDT training base in Maui and the UDTs themselves were issued by Vice Admiral Turner as the commander of the Fifth Amphibious Force, Pacific Fleet. The UDT concept was now established and proven. UDTs would continue to be commissioned to the end of the war.

Robert P. Marshall Jr., Commander, USN (Ret.)

The main part of our physical training at Fort Pierce initially came from the Scout and Raider School. Draper Kauffman had come down to examine the Fort Pierce ATB as a possible NCDU training site. He

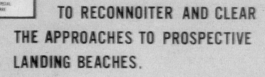

spent a week with the Scouts and Raiders to see what their physical training program consisted of. Then he returned to his own command and instituted a program that paralleled what the S&R people were doing.

Lieutenant Bill Flynn was the training officer for the NCDU School during its first months. He may have brought in some S&R PT instructors for a limited time. But we had Navy personnel running our PT program fairly early on. Captain Gulbranson, the commanding officer of the Fort Pierce Amphibious Base, had good contacts with various athletic teams and other Navy programs. He was also able to help the NCDU School get the qualified people it needed to put together a very rugged and complete physical training program.

Our training at the NCDU School began with a lot of the typical physical training exercises. Included with the usual calisthenics and running were log exercises in which a group of us would move a large chunk of telephone pole through different maneuvers. We would also paddle, drag, and carry our rubber boats through the lagoons and swamps, crossing the whole of North Island.

As training continued, Bill Flynn would add his own special touches, mostly by throwing lit half-sticks of dynamite at us.

We also had an old house that stood on posts some two and a half or three feet above the sand that was used as a form of obstacle. We would have to squat down and duck-waddle underneath that building. That's the exercise I most blame for my bad knees today.

But we also marched or ran through the sand and the water a great deal. We would carry M-1 carbines with us on the marches. Although not the largest rifle in the world, even the M-1 carbine could get heavy over a long distance.

There was very little swimming at that time in our training. Most of our actions were done from rubber boats, also called the LCR or Landing Craft, Rubber. The LCPRs (Landing Craft, Personnel, Ramped) we had would take us out to sea out the inlet between North and South Hutchinson islands. When we launched our rubber boats, we would paddle in to shore until the water was about knee-deep. At that point we would get out of the rubber boats and slip in the rest of the way on foot. Then we would conduct our demolition operations against the obstacles a Seabee detachment had constructed for us.

There was kind of a constant battle between the men of the NCDUs and the Seabee detachment. They were always trying to build obstacles that we couldn't blow up, at least not with the explosives we could carry with us. But they kept building them and we kept blowing them up. With shaped charges and high explosives we could just destroy anything they could make.

At Fort Pierce, we went through training as a group, but hadn't been assigned to a single unit yet. We would work in our rubber boats with a crew picked for that day, normally one officer and four or five men to a crew.

What we called Hell Week then was our final exam, officially called the Jen-Stu-Fu problem. After that weeklong problem, which was the eighth week of training, the next step we took was to join up as an official, numbered Naval Combat Demolition Unit of one officer and five men. The building up of an NCDU was done in a very unique way that was developed and promoted by Draper Kauffman.

All of the group officers who were going to lead an NCDU had the opportunity to interview the people who were going to be available for their units. It was from that pool of qualified people that they would build up their own NCDU. All of the officers, including myself, sat down in front of the stage one afternoon and spoke to the men available.

Each enlisted man would come up and describe himself to us, listing his qualifications and skills. He would tell us where he was from, how old he was, and just what all of his credentials were. We had known these men pretty well already from our earlier training together.

After we had talked to and heard from everyone, we would put down on a list the five men we would like for our boat crew. Then we had to put down five more men that we would accept into our crew. Taking all of our lists with our primary and secondary choices, Draper and his staff would try to give us as many of the specific men we wanted as possible. Not everyone could be satisfied; the best had to be divided up a bit. But it was a good system and it promoted unit integrity.

Usually, an officer would get a couple of the men he really wanted on his crew, and the balance were men who were completely acceptable. But the selection process didn't end there. The enlisted men had the opportunity to turn down their assignment to any particular officer. That was a unique and wonderful way of instilling a team spirit and level of camaraderie right away that no other unit in the service used.

After the men and the officers were selected and the units made up, they were assigned a number and usually made up a name for themselves. The name would be something based on the officer's name followed by a descriptive word such as Kane's Killers, Heideman's Hurricanes, etc. If my NCDU had a name, I just don't remember it. It could have been something like Marshall's Marauders. Our number was NCDU 92.

At the time of our graduation, we had a choice between the European theater or the Pacific. At that time the ETO was considered to be the one that would be the most active. Besides choosing the men that they wanted, Draper also gave each NCDU officer the opportunity to express his preference for which theater he wanted to operate in.

For myself and a great number of other officers, our choice was the ETO. Draper knew a great deal more information than we did as to just what was going on in the war and he knew that the Pacific theater was going to be a very active area. And if he had his way, Draper Kauffman was going to see action in the Pacific with some of the men he trained.

Draper picked and chose a little bit about who would go where. And it was through these machinations of his that I and my NCDU received orders for the Central Pacific area. Looking back at how well things turned out for me in the Pacific, I think I might not be around today if I had gone to the ETO and ended up on the Normandy beaches. When the NCDUs were shipped out, I ended up in the Pacific and my best friend, Ensign George Gallinlock, was sent with his unit to England and eventually Normandy, where he was killed in the landings.

We took a troop train out of Fort Pierce on the first leg of our journey west. The train had something like twelve cars and we were going to be on it all the way across the country. Being resourceful troops, we had secreted about the train a few bottles of beverages to ease the trip for us. But we had forgotten to get any orange juice as a mixer. Warrant Officer "Doc" Barge was the last person to board the train; he was running down the railroad tracks as the train was starting to pull out, a case of oranges on his shoulder.

Doc made it onto the observation deck at the end of the train and we pulled him aboard. It was a long trip, all the way across the country, but we finally made it to our last stop in San Francisco more or less in one piece. There was a layover of some four or five days for us in town while our transportation further west was being arranged. Our party in San Francisco was brought to an abrupt end when it was announced that our ship was ready and we were pulling out.

We left San Francisco Harbor and traveled under the Golden Gate Bridge in fair style. The government had chartered the Matsonia, a civilian cruise ship, to act as a transport for the duration. Not only did we cross the Pacific to Hawaii on a civilian cruise liner, but we had good food and even better company. The living accommodations were crowded, but this was because of all of the troops on board. Included in this crowd was the first contingent of WACs (Women's Army Corps) to serve overseas as well as a thirty-two-woman contingent of Red Cross nurses.

So we spent a very interesting weeklong cruise to Honolulu. For a while we were billeted in one of the great hotels in Hawaii and we managed to conduct some unofficial reconnaissance operations to the area where the Red Cross ladies we had met aboard ship were stationed. After another short week of these adventures, we were placed aboard an LST and taken to Maui, where we would undergo further training.

The invasions at Tarawa had come and gone, but the lessons learned there had not been forgotten. The lack of hydrographic reconnaissance on the offshore waters at Tarawa had been very costly to the U.S. forces. Besides the lack of some very basic information on the reefs off Tarawa, there was no proper way to forecast tides for an unknown shoreline. Between the reefs and the low tides, a lot of landing craft had run aground and a lot of Marines never made it in to the beach.

The high command out in the Pacific, with Admiral Turner in charge of the amphibious operations, told Draper Kauffman that he had to develop the capacity to accurately measure the depths of the water off invasion beaches using swimmers in the water. This information was to be delivered to the high command in the form of accurate charts prior to H hour on D day.

A lot of the reefs that were to be examined could be a mile or more offshore of an island. So the people who were going to do the reconnaissance had to be good swimmers. The plan was to take the men of the NCDUs and reorganize and retrain them into Underwater Demolition Teams or UDTs. The men of the UDTs would have to be good swimmers, and that was the immediate training emphasis at the very new Navy Combat Demolition Training and Experimental Base at Maui.

We found out that we were going to have to do these long off-shore recons of invasion beaches when we arrived at Maui. Now, instead of working from rubber boats as we had at Fort Pierce, we were swimming every day. There were long swims of at least a mile in the bay at Maui. There were swims later in our training where we went halfway to Lanai, the next island and some ten or fifteen miles away, before turning back.

Even though he was a very poor swimmer, Draper Kauffman worked right alongside the rest of us, swimming along in the water. Kauffman had come out from Fort Pierce to see some of the action with the men he had trained, and he wasn't the kind of officer to just sit back in a desk job if there was anything he could do about it. But he just wasn't a very good swimmer. In fact, in the group of us who were undergoing training, there was only one swimmer who was worse than Draper, and that was me.

Draper Kauffman was the designated CO of Underwater Demolition Team 5 when we went through training. UDTs 1 and 2 had already done their operations just a short time earlier and some of the men from those teams were our instructors.

The first two UDTs had proved the concept. Now our mission was being expanded with the requirement to do additional hydrographic reconnaissance. While we were training in Maui, Draper Kauffman developed the string reconnaissance method of measuring the water's depth accurately so that charts could later be made.

The string reconnaissance system was developed and refined late in our training. UDT 5 had been formed and we were getting ready to leave for our first operation when Draper finally perfected the system to his satisfaction. We were still making some of the equipment we needed when we boarded our transport ship, the APD Gilmer.

On board the Gilmer, we had all the strings and lead weights the individual swimmers would use. In addition, we had these galvanized steel drums, one-gallon fruit cans really, that we built into reels to hold the guideline. Boards nailed onto the ends of the fruit cans made up the reels, and the lines were knotted in a pattern that let them be used for measuring distance. All of this material had to be finished before we arrived at our target for Operation FORAGER, the invasion of Saipan in the Marianas Islands.

The string reconnaissance system used a base line of heavy sting or light line, much like twine, that we measured, knotted, and wound on reels. There would be 1,000 feet of line on every reel, knotted in a repeating pattern for measurement. After a given length of the line had been measured and knotted, a colored rag would be tied to the line and the knot pattern repeated. This was done every 100 feet for the length of the line.

The line from the reel would be anchored on the reef at one end, and then swum out and unrolled. Swimmers would then swim out on a line, evenly spaced out at known distances along the main line from the reel. Each swimmer had a small line, like heavy fish line, wrapped around his wrist with a small lead fishing sinker on one end. The lead line was only about 10 feet long and was marked in one-foot increments. Each swimmer would drop his lead line at regular intervals and then write down the depth of the water on a plastic (Plexiglas) slate with a grease pencil. Notes would also be taken about any obstacles and other observations the swimmer might make.

This string reconnaissance system was reasonably simple and no one improved on the basic system for decades. Though they were not used at Fort Pierce at all, we had been introduced to swim fins (flippers) at Maui along with diver's face masks, which were very simple round ones with a small plate of glass in the front. No snorkles, breathing gear, or any sophisticated equipment at all.

Many systems used later by the UDTs hadn't been developed when we did our first operations in the middle of June 1944 at Saipan. Cast and recovery was still very basic. We rolled off in pairs from a rubber boat tied to the port side of our LCPR to get into the water. After our operation was over, we were pulled on board the rubber boat with the LCPR stopped in the water during the pickup.

The LCPR simply sitting there while the swimmers were pulled on board made it very vulnerable to enemy fire. It was a sitting duck really for the people on the shore. That was the reason that the sling pickup method was developed, to give the LCPR a way of picking up the swimmers from the water while remaining under way.

Once at Saipan for the operation, UDT 5 was spread out along about 600 yards of beach. Our beach was one of the ones code-named Green and our mission was to map the offshore waters. We conducted a string reconnaissance, the first one done off an enemy-held beach.

The LCPRs from our APD took us in to about 500 to 600 yards from the offshore reefs. Then we swam in to the reef, deployed our string lines, and then swam in to the beach itself.

The enemy forces on Saipan saw us and opened fire almost immediately. Mostly it was machine guns that were firing at us, along with the occasional mortar. That situation really brought it home to me that this was for keeps; those people on the island wanted nothing better than to kill us all.

Most of the machine gun fire would either ricochet off the water, or dig in and then sink vertically. The bullets would only zip into the water a couple of feet and then just sink to the bottom. A number of them dropped past my face as I was swimming underwater.

At that time I had modified my face mask with a toothbrush holder (tube) glued into the top of the mask. The holder acted a bit like a snorkle, long before they were available. Things leaked a bit, but it did work in a way.

We were operating in plain sight of the enemy, well out in the open. But UDT 5 was lucky right from the start. Our commanding officer was Draper Kauffman, which didn't directly affect us. But Draper's father was Admiral Kauffman and he was not only an admiral, he was COMCRUDESPAC (Commander, Cruisers, Destroyers, Pacific). It could have been normal, paternal concern on the part of Draper's father that resulted in our getting very extensive fire support covering us. Especially since most of the fire seemed to come from cruisers and destroyers.

The heavy guns from the offshore ships kept peppering the Jap positions on Saipan all the time that we were operating in the water. The enemy fire directed at us would surely have been much heavier if the ships hadn't been putting out their all to protect us.

We did have one fatality on our first operation, along with seven wounded. Off of Saipan was the only time we deployed what were called the "flying mattresses." These were inflatable rubber mats maybe eight or nine feet long with a storage battery and an electric motor driving a small propeller. The flying mattresses could each carry two men, one to operate the craft and the other to observe.

The idea of the flying mattresses was that the leadership of the UDT, our officers, would be using them. On the mattress would be one enlisted man, a radio, an M-1 carbine, and whatever else they might need. The officer could stay in communication with support while the enlisted man drove the craft. Then the officers could direct the men of the UDT platoons during their operations. What we found out was that the flying mattresses also made marvelous targets for the enemy.

Draper was on one of the mattresses with his enlisted man also acting as something of a Seeing Eye dog, Kauffman's eyesight being so poor. Ensign Bill Running was also on one of the mattresses with his enlisted man (EM), a man named Christensen. A machine gun bullet killed Christensen while Running never received a scratch. That was our only loss during the whole operation, in spite of four of the mattresses being hit.

For the invasion proper, the first waves were planned to be infantry to move in and hold the beach. Soon after the infantry landing, the plan was for tanks to come in and act as close-in fire support to the troops on shore and begin driving in from the beach. This mobile artillery was limited to the depth of the water it could cross after the landing craft had released them. A lot of the water in the lagoon on the island side of the reefs was going to be a lot deeper than the tanks could accept.

During our reconnaissance, we didn't find any man-made obstacles, only natural ones. We measured and charted out the reef, which also wound through the lagoon a bit as well. What we found was a winding path through the reef that was less than the maximum depth the tanks could cross. The path was plain enough on the chart we made, but the tanks couldn't easily follow the route we would put up on the chart.

An ensign by the name of Jack Adams climbed on board one of the lead tanks during the invasion and led the armored column over the path in the reef. Sitting on the turret, Adams told the driver of the tank how to move and went in all the way to the beach, dropping off buoys behind them to mark the path. In spite of his very exposed position, Jack got through his pathfinding experience without being hurt.

Our post-D-day work involved blowing open a path through the blocking reef to allow landing craft to come in and unload right on shore. By using very large charges of Mark-8 explosive hose on D days plus one, two, and three, we were able to blow open direct channels in the coral reef.

After Saipan was secured and our channels blown, UDT 5 was going to move on to Tinian and work on the planning for operations there. Draper was to assist in picking a possible landing beach. The choice was to be made of a beach that wasn't the most obvious one, read that easiest to land on. Instead, command wanted the beach to be usable, but not one that was blocked either naturally or with man-made obstacles and needing demolition to open the way.

The scouting technique was a fast one. Draper was put up in the nose of a torpedo plane and taken on a flight over parts of Tinian. The plane would dive on likely beaches and Draper would note the likelihood of their being used, along with notes on the amount of antiaircraft fire they took from the surrounding jungle.

The enemy we fought was a hard one. At the time we considered the Japanese a very dangerous enemy, one who would go to any lengths to accomplish their goals. And the Japanese troops were very devoted to their leadership, from the emperor to their officers.

They would, and did, often fight to the death. Outside of that, we didn't really have any other feelings toward the enemy we were fighting.

All of the Teams, not just UDT 5, showed a cohesiveness that was remarkable. Some have said that we depended on our buddies to help us get the job done. But it was more than that, we depended on the Team as a whole, not just any of its parts. Virtually every man of the Team, with few if any exceptions, would work with any other member of the Team. You knew you would get the full support of your Teammate, and he could expect the same of you.

A WWII UDT person was in good shape, and we worked hard to stay that way so we could do our job. Unlike today, we had the stimulation of an ongoing war to help us give everything we had, plus whatever more was needed. We were in for the duration, until we defeated the enemy. Even with our motivations, we never did reach the level of physical fitness of the SEALs today. But they are also young and enthusiastic, just as we were then.

When the war finally came to an end, I had left UDT 5 and been promoted. I was the CO of UDT 3 when the war ended and we arrived at Japan itself. My Team landed at Wakayama, Japan, at the end of the war and conducted a normal combat operation with a string reconnaissance and the whole works.

When we finally got to the beach, there was a whole local delegation of Japanese to meet us. The group was led by some dignitaries—they may have been the mayor and other leaders for all I know, wearing formal dress including top hats. They were quite friendly as a group and there wasn't any sign of a military presence. The group was led by a young Japanese lady who spoke perfect English. When I later asked her where she learned such good English, she told me, "the University of Southern California."

Such was the world before the war. But we were almost welcomed rather than just politely met by this group of civilians. I think they had had just about enough of the war and were as glad to see it end as we were. Some of us were welcomed into the homes of the local people. The war was finally over and we all seemed pretty glad of it.

Chapter 9

NORMANDY AND SOUTHERN FRANCE

The main target of the NCDUs was always planned to be the invasion of Europe and the breaching of Hitler's Atlantic wall. As NCDU units graduated from training at Fort Pierce, they were assigned in increasing numbers to the European theater of operations. Orders regarding the specific mission of the NCDUs were issued in England and the units gathered for training against more specific targets.

One of the targets facing the men of the NCDUs was known as the Belgian Gate or Element C. This massive steel construction was known to be part of the obstacles scattered along the French invasion beaches. Element C was ten feet high, ten feet wide, and fourteen feet long. Built of six-inch-wide steel angle iron that was one-half-inch thick, a single Element C looked like a huge piece of picket fence and weighed close to three tons. And the obstacles could be linked together in long chains, creating a wall of steel posts.

Long experiments with different demolition techniques finally resulted in a way to blast Element C into a pile of steel rubble without turning it into a lot of lethal flying fragmentation. Lieutenant Carl Hagensen was part of the crew that developed a special charge, sixteen of which could be quickly applied to a single Element C and collapse in one blast. The new explosive charge was made up of Composition C-2, a plastic explosive, packaged in a small canvas bag. During development of the charge, old wool socks were used to hold the explosive before the canvas bags were sewn up.

Now called the Hagensen Pack, the new explosive charges held two pounds each of C-2 explosive and could be very quickly attached to many kinds of targets. The primacord used to detonate the

Element C, the Belgian Gate of Normandy Beach. This replica was used by the NCDUs to train in how to demolish the huge steel obstacles. Demolition techniques and materials first designed to knock down this target in 1944 are still in use in the Teams today.

Hagensen Pack could be quickly tied to another long main line of primacord and an unlimited number of charges set off simultaneously. Prior to their operations during the Normandy invasions, men of the NCDUs would spend days assembling thousands of Hagensen Packs for use against the known beach obstacles.

On June 6, 1944, the largest amphibious operation in history began. The target of the huge Allied armada was the beaches of Normandy, France. The U.S. targets were the beaches code-named Utah and Omaha. The initial plan called for waves of infantry and then tank armored support to land first. Under the cover of these units, the men of the NCDUs, reinforced with Army Engineer troops and Navy volunteers, would blast gaps through the beach obstacles. The plan didn't quite go the way it was intended. On Utah beach, the NCDUs and their Army counterparts were able to blast the majority of their assigned obstacles out of the way quickly. On Omaha Beach, the situation was different.

At Omaha, the German resistance was very heavy and losses among the U.S. troops built up quickly. In spite of the inferno of steel and explosions all around them, the men of the NCDUs worked feverishly to blast open gaps through the beach obstacles. The armored support in the form of tanks never made it to the beach, most either sinking on launch or quickly being destroyed by German fire.

In the first day of the landings, a thousand U.S. soldiers were killed, the large majority on a piece of beach now known as "Bloody Omaha." On that blood-soaked ground, 31 NCDU men were killed and 60

From the troop well of an LCVP can be seen the first waves of troops going to shore on Normandy Beach. On the shore ahead of the troops are the men of the NCDUs charging obstacles with explosives.

National Archives/U.S. Coast Guard

wounded. Over 50 percent of the NCDUs assigned to Omaha were casualties. On Utah Beach, six men were killed and 11 wounded.

In the months after D day at Normandy, the NCDUs from Utah Beach were transferred to the Mediterranean theater to join in Operation DRAGOON, the invasion of southern France. On 15 August 1944, the men of the Utah Beach NCDUs joined with the NCDUs who had already been sent to the Mediterranean. The thirty NCDUs joined with the Allied forces in the landings on the French Riviera. These operations went smoothly, for which the veteran NCDU men were thankful.

No losses were taken by the NCDU personnel as they completed clearing the landing beaches of obstacles. Soon after some post-invasion demolition, the men of the NCDUs were sent back to the United States. There, a number of the men returned to their original units or remained with the NCDUs and moved on to the Pacific and the UDTs.

Some of the NCDU men who survived the D day invasion at Normandy. Two of the men on the left in the front row have obtained M1 Thompson submachine guns. The two-inch-wide gray band on their helmets identified them as Navy personnel during the invasion.

National Archives

Myron F. Walsh, Chief Shipfitter

Up in Camp Peary, Lieutenant Kauffman and another officer came by one day recruiting for a new unit. When he asked me if I would like to be in it, I said yes. Then there were some other questions; What's your name? What's your age? Can you swim? Are you single?

It was that last question I had a problem with. At that time I wasn't single and they told me that I couldn't be used. That got me mad a bit and after some argument I was told that they would get back to me. They did contact me to tell me that I was accepted. It may be that I was the first married NCDU man with a small child at home.

We arrived at Fort Pierce in late July–early August 1943. When we arrived at South Hutchinson Island, where the base was located, there were just a few tents and not much else. Groups of up to ten of us were assigned to a tent and we quickly settled in. The next morning we had another introduction to Fort Pierce when we arrived at breakfast. Breakfast wasn't fancy, just a bowl of cereal served on a table that was just a board nailed on some upright posts.

Before you could even eat your food, the sand fleas would get into it and almost turn the cereal black. That was okay, we could skip the cereal. But after a couple of days you were hungry enough that the bugs didn't matter.

In training, I didn't have a lot of trouble or pain. I figured if someone else had done it, so could I. Some of the workouts could be hard. One day of training they might have a three-mile run along the beach. The end of that run could be a 200-yard sprint to see if you could beat the guy next to you. That kind of thing could tire you out. But so could the log PT and the obstacle course. But none of it really got to me very badly.

Training was rough enough with the PT, the work we had to do, and just the local environment. But the hardest part of training was the mental end. You had to keep yourself going. I was pretty lucky in that my wife had come down to Fort Pierce. During some of our free time, I had her to talk to and get back to my senses. The other guys could only lie in their bunks and think over the events of the day.

During our training, I don't remember ever working with the Scouts and Raiders. We were told that we had to be vigilant at night. The S&R people were known to sneak into our camp and wreak a little havoc as infiltration practice. Personally, I never had any trouble with them at all. Other than their being at the ATB, there just didn't seem to be a lot of contact between the Scouts and Raiders and the NCDU.

I was all of twenty years old when I became involved with the Navy and the NCDU. Like many around me, I was gung ho, ready to do anything and to fight for my country. Most of us couldn't wait to get into combat; we feared nothing. Looking back on it now, I think we were more or less just ignorant about the whole thing.

After we landed in Normandy and saw everything that happened there, and then went on to southern France, well, we weren't ignorant anymore.

All of us in our group, or any of the NCDUs, were like a band of five or six brothers. There wasn't any rank between the officers and the men when it came to doing the job; Commander Kauffman wouldn't tolerate that. The officers had to stand in line for chow just like the rest of us. You double-timed to the chow line, and if you were slow, you were at the end of the line no matter what your rank. Demolition was kind of equal opportunity that way.

On graduation from training, NCDU 127, myself included, was assigned to what they called the JANET board. JANET for Joint Army Navy Experimental Test. The JANET board had their officers off post in the Peacock building in Fort Pierce itself. Lieutenant Padgett, our officer, along with our crew would do the fieldwork for the board. The JANET office would call our officer in and explain whatever experiment it wanted done. Then we would go to North Hutchinson Island and do it.

The board might have some new beach mines in from the Pacific they wanted tested. They might be looking for a certain way that we might be able to get rid of them safely. That was our first assignment with JANET and there were all kinds of other projects following that.

There were other NCDU units assigned to JANET along with us. There was Lieutenant Jeeter's unit, along with Lieutenant Frank Hunds's and Lieutenant Hunt's NCDUs. All told, there were four NCDUs assigned to the JANET board while I was there. After a month or two of working with the JANET board, we were reassigned to the new Demolition Research Unit (DRU). JANET had been a joint Army–Navy project while the DRU was mostly a Navy matter.

While the DRU mostly worked on Navy projects, we did work on some Army jobs. A lot of these jobs involved rockets. We put rocket launchers on tanks and on boats. We fit LCMs (Landing Craft, Mechanized) with 120 launchers for 7.2-inch TNT-filled rockets for close-in fire support at landings. These LCMs full of rockets we called "Woofus" boats.

In March 1944, our NCDU (127) received orders to immediately fly out of Fort Pierce and head to Europe. We flew down to Miami, from there to New York, and then boarded a ship for England. We landed in Wales and were moved through England up to Scotland. We were finally stationed at what was supposedly one of the king's retreats up there.

After several weeks in Scotland, we were transferred to Salcombe way down near the southern end of England. There, we met up with the other NCDUs who had been sent over well before us. At Salcombe, we started our specific training for Normandy, though we didn't know that name yet.

A lot of the experience we had developed at Fort Pierce with the JANET board and the DRU came in handy now. We had worked a lot with the new Composition C and C2 plastic explosive and that's what we were going to use in a new packaged charge.

A Lieutenant Toomey had originally come up with the idea of using Composition C2 explosive in a canvas pack as a demolition charge. Lieutenant Carl Hagensen had taken the original idea and developed it into a quickly attached charge that was primed with primacord. That charge was soon called a Hagensen Pack and adopted as the Mark-20 demolition charge. We used a lot of Hagensen Packs at Normandy. In the small world of demolition, I had previously worked with Lieutenant Carl Hagensen in training at Fort Pierce, and even earlier while with the Seabees up at Camp Peary.

The Hagensen charge was developed from chunks of C2 rolled out into lengths. A couple of folds of primacord would be buried in the center of a two-pound chunk of C2 to prime it for detonation. Then you would stuff the whole charge into a flexible container. We used old socks to start with, then sewed canvas containers were made up for the charges. A length of line would close off the sock or container, with the long primacord lead hanging out of the charge. Some extra length of the tie-off line was left on to quickly attach the charge to the target.

We experimented with tying blocks of wood to the primacord leads on the Hagensen Packs. You'd dive down on a target, tie the charge to it, and let the block of wood float up with the primacord behind it. Then another man with a big roll of primacord would trail it along and attach all of the leads to it. Then all of the charges could be detonated together.

Finally, sometime in late May, we were all moved into a marshaling area. No one could come or go once they were in the area without being on official business. There, we were told that we were all getting ready to go into France. They still didn't tell us about Normandy. We didn't learn that name until the invasion was under way.

But we still had a lot of work to do before leaving for the invasion. There were thousands of Hagensen Packs to be made up to use against the beach obstacles. They let us out of the town, to a farmer's field, about six or eight miles outside of Salcombe. In the field, we set up these long tables with piles of explosive, containers, lines, and primacords. There we spent days making up Hagensen Packs.

One day, the person in charge of the detail gave us a break and told us we were all going into town for lunch. This sounded pretty good to us and there wasn't anyone around to bother our gear. So we just left the explosives and everything and went in to eat. There was this big pile of Composition C2 on the table, just sitting there like a big lump of brown clay.

When we got back from lunch, all of that bulk Comp C was gone. No one could figure out what had happened; the area was secure, so no one had just come up and stolen it. We were puzzled for a time until someone figured out that the local farmer's cows had eaten the sweetish-tasting explosive. That made for an interesting little while as we stayed in the field working, wondering if a cow was going to blow up at any moment.

We not only needed a lot of Hagensen Packs to open the beaches, it had been decided earlier that we also needed more men. So the Army engineers worked with us to get the job done. The Army was going to help us so far, and then we would do our part of the operation. The Army guys would also be a big help just moving all of the explosives we needed.

We were transported to within range of Normandy on an LST (Landing Ship, Tank). About 0130 or 0230 hours the morning of the invasion, we went over the side of the LST and climbed down cargo nets to board our waiting LCVP (Landing Craft, Vehicle/Personnel).

There was only one unit to a VP, as we called that type of landing craft. Our whole unit was called a GAT for Gap Assault Team and consisted of our NCDU of five enlisted and one officer, three Navy seamen volunteers, and five Army engineers, fourteen men total. With all of our explosives and rubber boat on board the VP, we pretty much had a full load.

At the very front of the landing craft, we had hundreds of Hagensen Packs stuffed into knapsacks and carriers. Each knapsack, much like a child's schoolbook bag today, held ten packs. Each of us also slung a full M-2 ammunition bag that fit over your head and hung down at the front and back. The M-2 bags had a pouch on the front and back, each of which would hold ten Hagensen Packs. That gave each man forty pounds of ready explosives right on him.

As we hit the water, we circled the landing craft until all of the other units had been able to board their boats. When all of the boats were ready, a signal was given and we all started for the shore. We went in under the covering fire of the battleships first. The fire from the big guns was great for keeping the enemy down, but the muzzle blasts from those guns just about knocked us on our butts.

The covering fire from the cruisers that were closer in to shore wasn't quite so bad. As we approached the shore, the ships were getting smaller and their guns were something we could better stand to be near. We had started in from quite a ways out, so the whole trip took a while. Finally getting in close to the beach, there were Landing Craft, Tank (Rockets) (LCT(R)) launching barrages of five-inch high-explosive rockets right over our heads.

One of the things I remember most from those rocket boats was that you could see the rockets flying through the air overhead. Every now and then, some of the rockets would bump together and then start to fall. We had to maneuver our boat around so that we wouldn't get hit by our own falling rockets.

Finally, we got in close enough to shore that the coxswain, one of the two-man landing craft crew, called out: "Okay, this is where you guys get out."

So we threw our rubber boat over the side and filled it up with our explosives. Then each of us went over the side with our own loads. Of course, the rubber boat wasn't big enough to hold us all. So most of us were hanging on to the side of the boat and swimming or walking in. The water was only about five or five and a half feet deep where we started in. But the tide was coming in and the water was rising pretty fast.

As we got closer to shore, the water was shallower and we could start moving faster. German artillery shells were landing all around us and machine gun bullets would snap past and stitch across the water.

As we got about 100 yards from the landing craft that had brought us in, I looked back just as it took a burst of machine gunfire across the bow. It seemed to be okay and was able to back out and return to sea.

As we moved in to shore, we didn't all remain so lucky. One of our men was hit. We helped him into the boat and continued on to shore. Once we finally reached the beach, we pulled the boat up on the sand and pebbles. Then the 88s started hitting all around us. The shells were being fired in salvos, so we would wait until one salvo had landed and then move before the next one came in.

Our target was Utah Beach and we landed in the first wave. When I looked to my right and left, as far as I could see, there wasn't anyone else on the beach. Nothing seemed to be moving at all for the moment.

When one shell landed close to where a seaman and I were, I quickly dove into the hole it left to take cover. As I waited in the hole, the seaman jumped in next to me. When he asked me what we were going to do, I told him that I was waiting for the next shell to land. Then we would move on to that hole.

"Why are you moving from hole to hole?" he asked.

"They always told me while I was in training," I answered, "that the shells never land in the same hole again. So if you get in one that's just been hit, you're on pretty safe ground."

So that was how we moved up the beach, jumping from one shell hole to another. The tide was coming in pretty fast behind us. Once we reached the seawall area at the high-water mark, we sent back a couple of the Army guys and seamen to bring up the boat and explosives. That was how we finally got the bulk of our explosives on the beach.

Then we started loading all of the obstacles we could reach. Our specific job was to blow a 50-yard-wide gap through about 200 yards of obstacles. The length of the gap really depended on the tide coming in and how deep the water was. Where we were working, the water was about four feet deep at the most as we loaded up the obstacles. We didn't have to swim at all as we got everything we could loaded and set.

The tide was coming in so fast and raising the water level so high that we probably only blasted about half the obstacles in our area. As we moved up to the seawall, our GAT spread out in both directions. Once we were under whatever cover was available, we fired our charges.

A group of men move ashore on Normandy Beach during the invasion on June 6, 1944. The heavy strain of fierce combat already shows in their faces as they struggle to pull a rubber boat loaded with their equipment and wounded comrades ashore.

National Archives

Normandy and Southern France

The group to our left was Lieutenant Jeeter's group, called "Jeeter's Skeeters" back during training at Fort Pierce. They cleared their gap at about the same time as we did ours. A couple more groups to our right also blew their gaps. I'd say that out of the fourteen or fifteen units we had on the beach, nine or so of them completed their mission and blew their gaps on schedule.

We had cleared a gap maybe twenty or thirty yards wide in our fifty-yard-wide assigned channel with our initial blast. Some of the obstacles were the big steel "Belgian Gates" we had worked on during training. Most of the rest of the obstacles were a long log braced up like a ramp with the low end pointing out to sea. There was a Tellermine (land mine) on the high end of the log. The incoming landing craft were expected to slide up these ramps and either be tipped on their sides or go up to where they would set off the twelve pounds of TNT in the mine.

Other obstacles included concrete tetrahedrons with steel bars sticking out of the tops of the blocks. All we could do with those was blow the bars off them. Once we had blown the obstacles and opened a gap, the major part of our mission was over.

Taking cover at the seawall, we stayed there for some two or three hours as a number of waves of troops came in and landed. There was still some incoming fire in terms of 88s and machine guns. But it wasn't near as heavy as it had been earlier. After another few hours under cover, we started to move out and attack more obstacles on the beach as we could with the tide in.

We gathered up unexploded ordnance (shells, bombs, mines, etc.) as we found it. Many of the obstacles we were examining didn't have mines on them. So we could just direct landing craft past those obstacles without a lot of danger. For a while there, we acted as kind of traffic cops along the beach as much as we could. When the incoming fire got heavy again, we moved back to the cover of the seawall.

During all of this, so much was happening that you didn't really have time to think about what you were doing and where you were. We were all cold, wet, and miserable. But it was just that kind of day.

We did wonder about just how badly our wounded man was hurt.

It was just about that time that another of our men was hit. Now we thought about both of them. By that time the medics had set up an aid station, so we were able to take our wounded man to them and get him help.

Eventually, we were taken off the beach and sent back to England. Some weeks later it was decided to use some of the NCDUs from Utah Beach for the invasion of southern France. Of course, they didn't tell us where we were being sent. But before long, we were being shipped out to Italy.

The camp we finally arrived at in Italy was at Salerno, south of Naples. During our first briefing on the upcoming invasion, they told us that we wouldn't be in the first waves this time. The NCDUs that were already in Italy and had been training for a while would be the ones in the first waves. We would be in the fifth or sixth wave as backups.

We all figured that this was a pretty good thing for us. Back on Utah Beach in Normandy, we had noticed that by the time the fifth wave had landed, the enemy fire had died down a lot. So going in with a later wave sounded just fine to me.

The night before the invasion was to take place, we received our last briefing on our assignment. It seemed that a bunch of equipment on shore had been moved about by the Germans and that there might be a lot more obstacles than were originally expected. So the basic plan for us was changed.

The target was estimated to be bigger than the command felt they wanted to assign to the new NCDU men. So now it was the veterans from Normandy who would be going in first. As one of those "old vets," I didn't care for the change a whole lot.

This was about the only time I really got scared. We pretty much had it made when we were going to be in the later waves. Going in on the first wave again was pushing our luck. But those were the orders and that's how we went in.

During the invasion, we were right up front with the first troops on the beach and cleared the beaches on schedule. The obstacles we ran into in southern France were pretty much all posts or pilings driven down into the seabed about twenty to thirty feet from shore. There in the Mediterranean, the offshore ground sloped down quickly, not like the long, shallow slopes at Normandy. Just twenty feet from shore you were already in pretty deep water. The pilings were in double rows running parallel to the beach, and now staggered in relation to the rows beside it. Sitting on top of each piling was an armed Tellermine.

For this demolition op, we swam down the rows of pilings, the water being too deep for walking, and dove down on each one. About eight or ten feet down from the surface, we would tie a Hagensen Pack to the post, letting the primacord lead float up to the surface on a wooden block. Another swimmer went along laying out a long primacord main line between the posts. We tied all our charge leads to the main line for multiple detonation.

Bringing all of the primacord mains to the beach, we detonated all of the charges from there. The blast cut away all of our obstacles at once, opening our portion of the beach. As we finished with our specific assignment, we would move along to the next section of beach and help the demolition crew there.

After the invasion was over, we spent additional time in the area clearing wrecks, blasting additional obstacles, and destroying unexploded ordnance. Some of the blasts were pretty large as a bunch of HE (High Explosive) would all go up at once. But we didn't pay much attention to explosions we hadn't set off.

Demolition had been experimenting with Apex boats back at Fort Pierce and the southern France invasion was one of the first attempts in Europe to use them to clear obstacles. The Apex boat was something we had developed back at Fort Pierce with the JANET board and DRU. An unmanned, radio-controlled landing craft, the Apex boat was loaded with 8,000 pounds of explosives. Once driven onto the obstacles by a remote operator, the Apex charge could be detonated by radio. Whenever we heard a really big blast, we just figured another Apex boat had gone up.

Though they looked like a good idea, the boats just didn't work right in the field and were quickly dropped. Instead, demolition men would go in and hand-place charges on obstacles, a technique we had used successfully both at Normandy and southern France.

The landings in southern France weren't as heavily defended as they had been at Normandy. It was like a Sunday in the park in comparison to that June morning in Utah. There were hardly any problems at all, it seemed to me. From one of the tall buildings in town, maybe a church steeple, well back from the beach, someone opened fire on us a couple of times. And we did have some machine guns rake across our bow as we were coming in.

A destroyer escort pulled in very close to shore, so close I thought he was going to run aground for sure. Then the DE turned parallel to the shore and opened fire a few times with his guns. That was just about the end of any enemy fire coming at us except for a few strafings later in the day. But there was nothing in comparison to what we ran into at Normandy Beach.

After the invasion, the Navy sent us back to our camp in Salerno. We stayed in Italy until sometime in September, when we were loaded onto transports and shipped back to the States. The Navy gave us a thirty-day leave back home before we all had to report in to Fort Pierce again.

After our leave, my unit, NCDU 127, was immediately asked if we would go back to working with the Demolition Research Unit. Some of the guys had gotten their fill of demolition work and went back to the Seabee battalions. Our officer, Lieutenant Padgett, was one of those men who went back to the Seabees. Lieutenant Hund asked me to join with his NCDU and go over to the DRU on North Island. Agreeing, I went over with them. I stayed with the DRU until my discharge from the Navy at the end of the war.

Chapter 10

THE GAP ASSAULT TEAMS AT NORMANDY

Once information on the specific targets at Normandy Beach began to be available to the planners of the beach demolition operation, it became obvious that the numbers of NCDUs available wouldn't be up to the task ahead of them. Because the landing plan called for the beach obstacle demolition operation to be conducted at low tide, on exposed land, the Army Engineers were put in overall command. The NCDUs would work with and under the direction of the Engineers.

Once photographs and intelligence on the landing beaches themselves were revealed to the NCDU planners in late April–early May 1944, a fast reorganization of the demolition teams was required. Each six-man NCDU was reinforced with five Army Engineers. Later an additional three seamen from a personnel pool in Scotland were attached to each NCDU. The seamen were mostly all brand-new to the Navy, being fresh from boot camp in the States. The new men were to be boat handlers for the rubber boats filled with explosives. The boat handlers would free up additional NCDU men to work on obstacle demolition.

The combined Army/NDCU/Navy units were referred to as Gap Assault Teams or GATs. The GATs were part of the Special Engineer Task Force for Operation NEPTUNE, the amphibious portion of Operation OVERLORD, the D-day landings. For Omaha Beach, there were 16 GATs assigned to the landings with an additional 11 support teams acting as backup. In the GATS were NCDUs 11, 22, 23, 24, 27, 41, 42, 43, 44, 45, 46, 137, 138, 140, 141, and 142. Among the support teams were NCDUs 128, 129, 130, 131, and 133. So for Omaha Beach, there were a total of 105 Fort Pierce graduates opening the way through the obstacles.

Each GAT was assigned to blow a fifty-yard-wide gap through the obstacles within twenty minutes of landing. In the horrible conditions at Omaha Beach, only five of sixteen channels through the obstacles were blown clear, with an additional two channels partially cleared. In spite of not getting all of the channels blown clear in the very short time they were given, the Navy recognized the herculean task accomplished by the Omaha Beach NCDUs during the landings. They were awarded a Presidential Units Citation for their actions that day. And a number of NCDU personnel received the Navy Cross for their individual acts that day.

Joseph D. DiMartino, Lieutenant, USN (Ret.)

I wasn't in one of the early NCDU classes. Instead, I was in Navy boot camp at Sampson, New York. In March 1944, 2,000 of us boots were sent to Pier 92 in New York. On Easter Sunday, all 2,000 of us were put on board the Queen Elizabeth *and sailed to Rosneath, Scotland. Rosneath was a U.S. Navy base northwest of Glasgow, and we were all scheduled to be assigned as gun crews and boat crews on landing craft for the invasion against Europe.*

This dashing, handsome, Hollywood-type U.S. Navy ensign came to the base and announced to us all that he needed 100 volunteers for a demolition outfit. What was explained to us was that after the main force of the invasion had landed, there would be debris on the beaches and roadways that would have to be destroyed. This was what the volunteer outfit would be doing. So I volunteered, even though that isn't what a soldier or sailor is supposed to do; it tends to get you in trouble.

We were packed up and sent to southern England to a training base. The first thing we learned to do was to prime explosives with blasting caps, primacord, and time fuse. Then we were shown how to place the explosives on obstacles. And that was the first time we saw obstacles. But it was far from the last.

Through March, April, and May, every day except Sunday, we practiced destroying obstacles. On June 4, we loaded up our rubber boat with 1,000 pounds of explosives for the upcoming operation. There were also Army Corps of Engineers troops with us. They would attack the obstacles up to the high-water mark and beyond. They also had 1,000 pounds of explosives.

All of our gear, rubber boat, and explosives were loaded on board an LCM, Landing Craft, Mechanized. For ourselves, we boarded an LCT, Landing Craft, Tank, for the trip over to the invasion site. So on June 4 we set off for the invasion, which was promptly called off due to bad weather. When June 5 came up, Ike (General Eisenhower) said go.

Halfway across the English Channel, our LCT broke down. In the middle of the night, in rough weather and choppy seas, we transferred from the LCT to the LCM.

At about 6:30 or 7:00 the next morning, June 6, 1,000 yards off of the beach, it looked like we were kicking the pants off the Germans on the beach. As we moved in closer to 500 yards or so, I could see and hear that the situation was a lot different. The Germans were putting out heavy fire on the beach and our guys were being killed.

Once we got to the beach, Lieutenant Culver told us all to immediately take cover. So there I was, on this pebble beach with the occasional big rock, digging a foxhole for myself.

"Joe," I said to myself, "you're seventeen years old. What are you doing here? You were working in a shipyard making a hundred bucks a week, and now you're going to get killed."

That was probably when I was the most afraid of any time in my life. I experienced combat again later, but never in the same way as those first few hours on Normandy Beach. The unknown was what got to you, when the bomb or the bullet or the shell would get you. You just knew it was coming sometime, so you did a lot of praying. And the big hope was that the Army would go up and get the Germans before they had a chance to get me. Lying there in a shallow hole on a pebble beach was not the best place to be in the world.

Anyway, I managed to survive that morning as we conducted our mission to blast obstacles off the beach. The next day we started clearing obstacles. The Army had moved in and taken control of the situation. We stayed on the beach for three weeks, in that time clearing the beaches and roadways of obstacles and rubble. Then we were returned to England.

We stayed in England for another several weeks before being sent on to Liverpool for transportation back to the United States. The USS Wakefield, a Coast Guard troop transport, took us back to Boston. Boarding a train, we were taken down to New York, where we were all given leave. For me, that meant getting back on the train and heading back to Boston, to get to my hometown of Dedham, Massachusetts.

When September had rolled around, I was told to report to Fort Pierce, Florida, to the NCDU training base. Commander Kauffman said, "All you seamen can either go to a UDT Team or go back to the fleet."

Remaining at Fort Pierce, I went through some of the training they were still giving the NCDUs who were going on to UDTs. The one thing I never did in training was go through Hell Week. Whenever I'm asked, "What class were you in?" and "How was your Hell Week?" my answer is that my Hell Week was June 6, 1944. In the early days, that answer was comprehensible, but today the young SEALs and others sometimes ask, "June 6, '44? What is that?"

"You ever hear of D day?"

That was good enough for Commander Kauffman to accept a number of us from Omaha Beach directly into the UDTs. As far as he was concerned, we could go right into the teams.

I was assigned to UDT 25 as one of the three officers and thirty men who had all been on Omaha that June day. The team began training in October 1944. In February 1945, UDT 25 had completed its training at Fort Pierce and was on its way to Maui, Hawaii, for advanced training. In UDT 25, I was assigned as a boat coxswain. We were working on perfecting the pickup of swimmers from the water. Additional techniques were experimented with and the double-loop snare was retained as the best available system.

In June, our Maui training was completed. Now we had to report back to the United States to Oceanside, California, to undergo cold-water training. The purpose of that was to get us ready for the invasion of Japan later in the year.

On August 15, six UDTs left Oceanside for Japan. This wasn't going to be for the invasion since we already knew the war was over because of the atomic bombs. We arrived in Japan in the first weeks of September. There wasn't any work for us to do, as several other UDT were already doing recons in the same area as we were. We just didn't have a mission and command had more than enough UDTs available to them.

We never even got to the shore really. As a boat coxswain, I got to the docks at Yokosuka and Yokohama, but I didn't get a chance to go ashore the whole time we were there. Some of the guys from the team did get a chance to go ashore, but not many. We were never called upon to perform any operations. So about three weeks later, we shipped out for Guam, and then back to the States.

Even though I had never fought against the Japanese in the Pacific, I had enough of a taste of active war on the beaches at Normandy. Personally, I felt that the dropping of the atomic bomb was okay. The use of that weapon not only demonstrated it to the world, it proved that perhaps it should never be used again. It also prevented the invasion of Japan from ever being necessary, and the projected U.S. casualties alone for that operation were over one million. Having been through one major invasion, I was glad that President Truman said, "Let's end this."

When we were sent back to the States, we arrived in San Diego and were sent on to the Coronado Amphibious Base. The Navy gave us all leave prior to reporting back to Coronado. UDT 25 was decommissioned on 13 November 1945. We remained at Coronado, decommissioning UDTs and helping to set up the postwar UDTs with Commander Kauffman, who had made the trip back from Japan with us.

In June 1946, the Navy split up the four postwar UDTs, sending half to Little Creek, Virginia, and keeping the other half in Coronado. I went on with UDT 4 to Little Creek. In 1946/47, UDT 4 went on a deployment to Antarctica and the South Pole as part of Operation HIGH JUMP.

Training with scuba gear started about that same time. We didn't have the aqualung, open-circuit system that became so common later. Instead, we started with the Lambertsen Amphibious Respiratory Unit (LARU), which is a pure oxygen, closed-circuit rebreather. The LARU is what we used off of Saint Thomas in the Virgin Islands and from submarines in experiments in locking in and locking out while submerged. Prior to this time I had always acted as a boat coxswain; now I was starting to get into the swimming with the new underwater gear.

By 1949, we had started using the aqualung, which released bubbles into the water but was much safer and easier to use than the LARU. For the next ten to fifteen years, I was training primarily with scuba gear, conducting underwater swimming, underwater obstacle clearance, and underwater reconnaissance.

A UDT underwater swimmer wears the 1952 model Lambertsen Underwater Respiratory Unit (LARU) during a demonstration in the early 1950s. This was an improved model over the 1940 WWII design.

National Archives

In those days the UDT mission was primarily hydrographic reconnaissance and the destruction of obstacles. The secondary UDT missions were in the marine hinterland, the wetlands, and attacking shipping by placing limpet mines on boats, as the Italians had done during WWII. We also perfected our techniques for locking in and out of submarines while both submerged and under way.

During the Korean War, in the early 1950s, the West Coast teams said that they could handle the UDT commitment to the effort. Our

COs volunteered to augment the West Coast teams with platoons from the East Coast. But the command said no and we never took part in that conflict.

In the late 1950s, we started parachuting, using this as another method of infiltrating into a target area. In previous years officers and individual men had gone to parachute jump training as an experiment. Now, under Captain Olsen and some other officers, a group of UDT enlisted men, myself included, became the first UDT "stick," the line of men who jump from a plane, to go to Jump School together as a group. That was about June 1956, as I remember.

As a bunch of fit, qualified Navy frogmen, we found the Army Jump School at Fort Benning to be nothing but three weeks of repetition. All we did from the morning until late afternoon was practice how to jump out of the airplane and how to hit the ground in a parachute landing fall (PLF). After three weeks of that, we were ready to jump out of that plane just to finish with this constant repetition. It was all right, but nothing in comparison to the way you jump today in the Teams with free-falling.

On that first jump, your adrenaline goes and it is exhilarating. Jumping from the old Bumblebee, the C-119 Flying Boxcar, it was loud and noisy while on board. When you leaped out, suddenly it was quiet while you were in the air.

Now I was both a qualified parachutist and a frogman. In 1960, I took another step and received my commission as a limited-duty officer. After 15 years as an enlisted man, I had finally decided to become an officer, since I was going to do at least my 20 years and retire. As an officer, I could do 25 years and retire at a better rate of pay. If I went for the whole 30 years, I could retire at 75 percent of my base pay. And the duty was good, I enjoyed the work with the Teams. Being happy in my career is why I stayed in.

It was in the early 1960s that the Navy found that it needed a maritime environment organization to combat guerrillas and conduct other commando-type operations.

The new organization, the SEAL Teams, had the order of their mission priorities changed from that of the UDTs. Hydrographic reconnaissance and obstacle demolition was now a secondary mission. The primary mission was to conduct operations in the marine hinterland and beyond. The SEALs would go behind the beaches to infiltrate and gather intelligence.

When the new unit came along, I didn't know much about it, but I was ready to join up immediately. One of the reasons I had stayed in the Teams so long was that I loved to operate and stay busy. Roy Boehm was the officer on the East Coast who was putting SEAL Team Two together. I always had a high regard for Roy; he's a great leader and a good boss, altogether an excellent man.

In general, Roy Boehm is the best deep-sea diver, bosun's mate, limited-duty officer lieutenant commander I have ever known. He hails originally from Brooklyn, New York, I believe. He was, and still is, hell on wheels; he can do it all. Roy was probably one of the best men to be among the first SEALs, as he has initiative, integrity, farsightedness, and knows what to do and when to do it. He is a very versatile sailor and has been since his deep-sea diving days as an enlisted man during World War II. He's just a fish in the water.

The first muster for SEAL Team Two was on January 8, 1962. I was on assignment at Great Lakes Naval Training Station in Illinois when the Team was formed up, so I missed the first days. A letter came to me notifying me of the new unit, so I didn't see anything until I returned to Little Creek. The unit had a nucleus of ten officers and fifty men, a tight group of top-notch sailors and operators.

For fifteen years I had been in the Underwater Demolition Teams. I had seen the beginnings of scuba diving, parachuting, and helicopter operations. Everything you see today as a polished skill of the SEALs, we started out back in those formative years. After I had received my commission, I was made aware of SEAL Team Two and the planning that was going into it. That's when I decided that this was something new and that I wanted to be part of it. Just as I had been for all of my Navy career, I always wanted to be part of something new and operational.

The name of the new team came from the acronym for the three environments it would work in, the SEa, Air, and Land. But the hard-

The Airborne platoon of SEAL Team Two rigged out for an air insertion during the first years of the SEALs. The men are equipped with a mix of equipment, including police ammunition holders for the S&W Model 15 revolvers. Over their shoulders, they have slung the first AR-15 rifles used in the Navy. The platoon is facing their officer, Lieutenant Roy Boehm.

UDT-SEAL Museum

charging bunch of operators Roy Boehm picked to fill out its first ranks soon had determined the true meaning of the SEAL name— Sleep, Eat, and Live it up.

The SEALs were new, but they were a Team from day one, in the bigger meaning of the term. The Team as we had known it in the UDTs and now in the SEALs meant that we were a cohesive group. We always worked as a Team. The ideal of the Team, and the idea of teamwork, is instilled in all of us from day one in training. The SEALs were made up of high-quality, skilled, knowledgeable individuals, but its strength came from them all working together.

You can see the teamwork mentality of the SEALs and the UDT in the smallest working unit of the Teams, the swimmer pair, an operator and his swim buddy. A swim buddy is the man you look after, and that man looks after you. No matter where you go or what you do on an operation or exercise, out of the water or in, that swim buddy is with you. You never, ever, leave your swim buddy. That rule is number one in the Teams.

The swim buddy rule especially holds true when you're operating in the field. If you're in the water or in enemy territory, whatever you're in, wherever you are, you take care of each other. You make sure nothing happens to him and he makes sure nothing happens to you. And that basic integrity goes through the whole group. You always take care of your swim buddy.

It was integrity that made the Teams work. Each man had his own personal integrity and would not break from his stand of staying with his buddy and his Team. And you tried to build further unit integrity as an officer, to have the men work together, and play together in both their on- and off-duty time. But no matter what each man did, he had to maintain that personal integrity to always do the right thing no matter what the cost.

The first duties in the new SEAL Team consisted mostly of going out to different training schools. One of the early schools that stands out the most was the E&E School (Escape and Evasion) run by the Marine Corps at their cold-water training center in Bridgeport, California. The first and last lesson every one of us came away from that school with was don't ever be captured.

At the E&E School, they put you in a prison camp where Marine instructors play the part of Communists. At that camp, they put you through the grinder for twenty-four to forty-eight hours. That taste of prison camp life is enough to instill in you the determination that you will never allow yourself to be captured. And to my knowledge, no SEAL has ever been taken captive by anyone.

It was pain that they inflicted on us during E&E School. But it wasn't a long-lasting pain. We knew that there would be an end to it. But what they exposed us to was what could be expected in a prison camp, where you would never know when the pain would end.

After several years of deployments and training, SEAL Team Two had its first chance at direct combat in 1965, when there was a crisis in the Dominican Republic. Along with two Army colonels and other staff from the commander-in-chief, Atlantic's staff, we flew in to Santo Domingo on a C-7 Army aircraft. By the time we got there, things had already quieted down and there were no operations being conducted.

SEAL Team Two already had a platoon in the area prior to my coming down. They had seen some shooting against the Communist rebels down there, but there were no casualties taken on our side. They had conducted some operations and intelligence-gathering missions, so SEAL Team Two had demonstrated their value in the limited action that took place. The SEAL Team wasn't going to see direct action again for several years, until we sent platoons in to Vietnam in 1967.

By 1966, we were preparing to send direct action platoons against the enemy. That year I was the executive officer of SEAL Team Two and was even the commanding officer of the Team from August to September 1966, while we were transitioning from Lieutenant Commander Tom Tarbox to Lieutenant Commander William Earley. Between Commander Earley and myself, we chose and formed up the platoons that would be the first from SEAL Team Two to go into action in Vietnam the next year. SEAL Team One had platoons in combat in Vietnam in 1966, so we would be working with them initially.

When I went over to Vietnam in June 1967, it was for a yearlong tour as a member of the U.S. Naval Advisory Group, Vietnam. We supported the South Vietnamese UDT/SEALs in both training and in an advisory capacity among other missions.

The Vietnamese I was working with made up a good force. But it was hard to keep them motivated and to get them to work with the U.S. Navy SEALs on operations. They would go to briefings and afterward were supposed to stay in the area. They wouldn't do that and went into town or whatever. That could be a very serious security breach and would compromise the operation they had been briefed on.

By this time we knew very well how the enemy, the Viet Cong and the North Vietnamese Army (NVA), were very ingenious in their methods of operating and gathering intelligence. They inflicted a lot of casualties on the U.S. forces and even the SEALs, but we inflicted casualties on them as well.

In late January 1968, I was up in Saigon. That was when the '68 Tet offensive began and the Viet Cong and NVA rose up all through South Vietnam. The action in Saigon got hot and heavy quickly, but I wasn't able to take much part in it. Those of us at the Navy command were restricted to the building during the fighting.

We weren't too far from the U.S. embassy but just couldn't leave the building when the Viet Cong arrived on the grounds of the embassy itself. The building we were in was only a couple of blocks away from the U.S. embassy and I hadn't even realized that it had been attacked. That situation had been pretty rough for the embassy personnel, but we didn't know about it until several days after.

The VC and NVA forces had infiltrated the whole of South Vietnam, stockpiling weapons and munitions, for their Tet offensive. Infiltration was something they were very good at. Direct fighting in the cities and towns was something else again.

We had been ordered by the Army to stay in our building during the first stages of the offensive. After a couple of days we were told it was all right for us to go to our work areas. Mine was down at the Saigon shipyard, where the Naval Advisory Group had its headquarters.

Then I got together with the Vietnamese Navy lieutenant who was my counterpart with their SEALs. We patrolled the Cho Long area to the north of Saigon. So we did that for a couple of weeks as everything quieted down again throughout South Vietnam. Everywhere the VC had captured territory, cities, towns, or hamlets, it was taken back from them by the U.S. and South Vietnamese forces.

In June 1968, I finished my tour in Vietnam and returned to Little Creek and SEAL Team Two.

In World War II, we had carried little more than swim fins, a face mask, a knife, belt, and explosives. In the Pacific, the water wasn't too cold for the most part, so there wasn't a need for suits or things of that nature at that time. The LCPR boats had a couple of machine guns on them. That was about it in the way of gear for the UDTs.

The SEALs in Vietnam, though, had a world of equipment. There were ammunition vests, M-16 rifles, Stoner machine guns, grenade launchers, claymore mines, and all types of sophisticated weapons. The main idea in equipping the SEALs was to give them the most firepower they could carry in a small package.

The change in the enemy from WWII to today is what forced the SEALs to change the way they fought. Now the Teams have to have the equipment and the technical knowledge to use it in order to fight battles.

In spite of all of the differences between the way the UDTs were equipped and the way the SEAL Teams are equipped, and the differences in the missions, the basic men who do the ops are the same today as they were in World War II. There does seem to have to be a bit more intelligence in today's SEALs; they go through a lot more formal schooling than we did. In the early days it seemed to be mostly brawn that was needed; today it's both brains and brawn.

It takes a person who is strong-willed and has a strong mind as well as being physically fit to get into the Teams. To stay in the Teams, he also has to have a good heart and a sense of value. This lets that person become part of a unique fighting force. What makes the SEALs unique is that they can get into a country or target area by all different methods. They can come in by sea, over land, or down through the air. Acting as peasants or generals, they can infiltrate an area, accomplish their mission, and leave without anyone ever knowing they were there.

Back during WWII, we fought a war for patriotic reasons. We were U.S. citizens fighting a war to stop both Hitler and Japan. The war was fought with big numbers, huge forces; the U.S. Army and Marines had more gear and better equipment than any of the enemy forces. We could just overpower them with bombs and bullets. It was putting force against force and seeing who had the most and the greatest will to use it.

Vietnam was unique in that it was jungle, wetlands, and rice paddies with a people with whom you couldn't tell who was who. There were no solid battle lines. In Europe during WWII, there were the enemy lines and our lines on one side or the other of a battle line. In the Pacific, the battle took place on an island for the most part. In Vietnam, the enemy could be in front of you, in back of you, or right in your camp area with you. They all looked the same and the Viet Cong guerrillas just blended in with the population.

To fight the Viet Cong you would have to go out into the jungle and the bushes and fight their kind of war. And you might think you were killing the enemy, but when you went and looked, they might not be the enemy at all.

The SEALs were effective during the Vietnam War mostly because they had a good intelligence net. They knew exactly where they were going, who they were after, and where to find them whenever possible. This was due to the intelligence net that the Teams had developed themselves and matched up with information coming in from other official sources. Fighting as the enemy did allow the SEALs to do their job where no one else could; knowing who the enemy was gave them their target.

■ Chapter 11

THE UDTS' ORGANIZATION AND LEGENDS

Almost all of the World War II UDTs were known by simple number designations. One single team, however, had a different designation. This was UDT Able. Among the first NCDUs sent to the Pacific area, several were sent to Admiral Wilkinson's Task Force 31 in the South Pacific. As part of the Third Amphibious Force, these NCDUs took part in a few operations in the Solomons, blasting on Guadalcanal, and landings on Green Island and Emirau Island in February 1944.

The South Pacific NCDUs were brought together and reinforced with additional personnel to form a UDT. This new UDT was UDT Able. There is no available explanation for the unusual designation except for the fact that the base NCDUs used in that UDT were among the first graduates from Fort Pierce. But UDT Able completed its training at Maui in time to be included in the planning for the invasion of Peleliu.

In the early morning hours of September 12, 1944, the APD *Noa* with UDT Able aboard was struck by a U.S. destroyer. The crew and UDT personnel were able to abandon the stricken APD before she sank, but without saving any of the UDT's equipment of explosives. Without the material means to conduct its part in the invasion, UDT Able was sent back to Pearl Harbor. UDT Able was broken up at Maui and the personnel from the unit assigned to UDTs 11, 12, 13, 14, 15, and 16 as they were being formed.

UDTs 6 and 7 continued on to the Peleliu operations, conducting the beach reconnaissance and later demolition swims. Instead of doing a single beach operation, UDT 6 was also assigned the operations that would have been done by UDT Able. Initial recon swims were conducted on 12 September, with the needed demolition swims carried out on the thirteenth and fourteenth. The invasion of Peleliu was successfully begun on 15 September 1944.

An Underwater Demolition Team now consisted of sixteen officers and eighty enlisted men. The personnel were organized into four operating platoons and a headquarters platoon. The operating platoons consisted of three officers and fifteen men each. The Headquarters Platoon had the remaining four officers and twenty enlisted men. The commanding officer, executive officer, technical officer, and mine disposal officer were all in the Headquarters Platoon. The HQ enlisted men included signalmen, boat technicians and operators, motor machinist's mates, coxswains, and seamen. The HQ Platoon handled all of the needs for the UDT, including medical, supply, repair, and maintenance.

The officers in the operating platoons were assigned as the platoon leader, assistant platoon leader, a boat officer, and a loading officer. This allowed three officers to operate as leaders of rubber boat crews, each with four of the enlisted men of the platoon. The remaining officer and three enlisted men would remain on the LCPR assigned to the platoon, the men being the coxswain and crew.

UDTs were later reorganized in units of thirteen officers and eighty-five enlisted men. Only two officers and fifteen enlisted men were in the four operational platoons. The Headquarters Platoon now held five officers and twenty-five enlisted men. This UDT organization would last for most of World War II.

The UDTs were normally assigned to APDs (Assault Personnel Destroyers) for transportation and basing. The APDs were high-speed troop transports, early versions being converted "four-stacker" destroyers of WWI vintage, remodeled for troop transport by remov-

Mounted on their davits over the central deck of an APD are the four LCPRs used by a deployed UDT. Each UDT platoon would use a single LCPR for an operation. The two smokestacks between and forward of the LCPRs are the remainders from the APDs conversion from a "four-stacker" WWI destroyer.

U.S. Navy

ing two smokestacks and other machinery. The APD had her own crew and the UDTs rarely took part in ship's duties. Instead, the APD was to transport the UDTs, their explosives, equipment, rubber boats, and four LCPRs to and from target beaches.

Stories quickly grew among the forces that operated with the UDTs on invasions. The UDTs were known to go onto the beach well ahead of any troops, armed with nothing but a knife and a bag of explosives. The UDTs would conduct their operations and return, and often lead in the first waves of landing craft to the cleared beaches during the invasion.

Some Marines landing on Saipan on 15 June 1944 crossed paths with Draper Kauffman, then the commanding officer of UDT 5. When they passed Kauffman, who was wearing only his swim trunks and other minimum gear, the Marines were said to comment on the summer tourists arriving before the beachhead was secured!

But the most memorable story of the UDTs centers around operations at Guam in July 1944. On 18 July, several UDT operators from Team Four crawled up on White Beach at Guam and left behind a sign. When the Marines landed on Guam near the small town of Agat only a short while later, they were met by the astonishing sight of a sign stating:

WELCOME MARINES

AGAT USO TWO BLOCKS

COURTESY UDT 4

The story of this sign soon made its way through the fleet and the Marine Corps. Additional markers were planted by the UDTs for years to come, including a large one placed on Japan to greet the incoming occupation troops. What isn't widely known is the existence of another sign that may have been planted first. It could be that the signs were a result of a bet or some other challenge between UDTs 3 and 4. But on Asan Beach four days before UDT 4 conducted their operations off of White Beach, a smaller sign was left by UDT 3. This sign stated:

Carrying forward a tradition begun by UDT 4, this is the last of the beach greeting signs put up by the WWII UDTs. It was part of the UDTs' answer to just who was first on the beach during an invasion.

Barry G. McCabe Collection

```
               WELCOME

             U.S. MARINES

                  BY

               SEABEE

             DEMOLITION

           7.14.44  U.D.T.3
```

But it was the later sign by UDT 4 that has received the lion's share of the publicity.

Edwin R. Ashby, Boatswain's Mate, Second Class

My Team during WWII was UDT 7, considered the last of the full Seabee Teams. The Seabees were the construction battalions, units full of special rates (jobs) that were really something that we were used to every day. The Seabees rates were what they gave the car-

penters, tin knockers, and other workers who had joined the Navy from civilian life. These men brought their abilities and skills with them and didn't have to go through much training to be put to use.

There were people in the Seabees who had built roads, tunnels, and railways. So these men already had some knowledge of explosives. These men were considered a good source of manpower for the NCDUs and later the UDTs.

After I got out of Boot Camp, I was sent down to Gulfport, Mississippi, for further training at Gunnery School. I had wanted to be a gunner's mate in the Navy and that was what I managed to do. After being sent to New York, a bunch of us ended up in Little Creek, Virginia. There, we were going to crew landing craft, what they called attack boats.

This wasn't what most of us wanted, but then a group of us were sent down to the ATB at Fort Pierce, where they also had attack boat training. We went down to Fort Pierce by train along with a bunch of Seabees from Camp Peary. The Seabees were going down for other training, something I was soon to learn a lot more about.

We were all called in to this big auditorium one day and asked if we would like to volunteer for a new unit training at Fort Pierce. I wanted out of the attack boat business and this new unit sounded like a good deal. So it wasn't long before I was undergoing NCDU and then UDT training.

It was quite extensive and really forced you to put out your best. We talk about Hell Week and the roughness of it all, but we were young then and had high spirits. We felt like we were going to beat the Japanese all by ourselves.

So we took to our training pretty well. For myself, I never had any idea of quitting. And it was an all-volunteer outfit. You could quit at any time. All you had to say was, "I want out!" and you would be gone with no prejudice or bad mark on your record. But I never had any personal doubt that I was going to make it.

At Fort Pierce, we trained as an NCDU, five enlisted men and an officer. The seventh "man" in our unit was a rubber boat. That thing went everywhere with us. We dragged that boat over the beaches, carried it over the rocks, and pulled it through the swamps. And swamps are something Fort Pierce had a lot of back then. Swamps and bugs. There were sand fleas and little biters everywhere.

For our final exercise during Payoff Week, what they called the Jen-Stu-Fu problem, we took our rubber boat for miles. Over the islands, through the rivers and inlets we went. With our rubber boat right along with us.

The demolition part of the exercise centered around blowing the channel open down in Saint Lucie, south of Fort Pierce. During that last week, rations were pretty light. Something like a can of C rations per man per day or whatever. Pretty lean cuisine. When we set off our explosives, the fish came up to the surface after the blast and we went out and gathered them up.

Some guy down near the channel had some potatoes, so we "borrowed" them to include in our seafood menu. We had no salt or anything, but that was some of the best fish I ever tasted in my life.

When we got to Maui in Hawaii, the small NCDU groups were reorganized into much larger Underwater Demolition Teams. Several UDTs had already run through the training at Maui, so the idea was pretty well established. When our group arrived from Fort Pierce, we were broken down and rearranged as UDTs 5, 6, and 7.

The NCDUs hadn't really been big enough to tackle the job they were handed during the Normandy invasion. Casualties were high and the command didn't want any mistakes to be repeated. In Normandy, the NCDU men had carried some weapons in to the beach, carbines and pistols mostly. Out in the Pacific, we weren't going to carry any weapons at all except for a sheath knife on our belts.

The new UDTs were supposed to be organized as hundred-man teams with four operational platoons and a headquarters platoon. The reality was Teams of eighty and ninety men each. We had to do all of the work for an operation, handle the boats, do the swim, handle the explosives, ourselves. And the jobs rotated among the platoons.

Say on one operation, Platoon One would be the swimming platoon and they would go in and do the recon. Then Platoon Two would go in and do the demolition work the next day. Platoon Three would be back on the APD making up the explosive packs for the operation. And Platoon Four would remain in reserve.

If a whole platoon was lost during an operation, the reserve platoon would be sent in. It was our good luck that we never had so many casualties that the reserve platoon was ever sent in. Then, on the next invasion or operation, the platoons would rotate their positions: Platoon One would be reserve, Platoon Two swimming, and so on.

The operating situation had changed a lot for us since we had left Fort Pierce. There, we had dressed generally like Army soldiers, in combat boots, fatigues, and steel helmets. In Maui, the working uniform tended to be a pair of trunks or shorts, a K-bar knife, and a plastic pad and wax pencil. At the beginning we didn't wear any life preservers or inflatable belts. By later in the war we were wearing inflatable life belts so that if a man was hurt, he could be floated a bit more easily. The belt was this canvas and rubber affair what went around your waist and you blew it up with a CO_2 cartridge.

The uniform changes had come because at Fort Pierce we had walked, or waded, in to do our job of demolition. In Maui, we were swimming everywhere. They used to take us out of sight of land and practice being picked up and dropped off for something like six or seven hours. That kept us in the water pretty much all day. On one of the pickups, I hit the CO_2 release on my life preserver just as I was being picked up by the boat. The belt inflated just as I grabbed the snare to get into the boat and the sudden drag just about dislocated my shoulder.

If you did the sling pickup right, and your belt didn't inflate, you would be picked up and rolled into the runner boat without any trouble. Then you would scramble into the LCPR to make room for the next swimmer being picked up.

The cast and recovery system using the double-loop snare worked great for us. A man could be snatched up out of the water without the pickup boat slowing down. To the best of my knowledge, a man named Joe B. Davis actually made the first double-loop snare as the pickup system was being developed. Prior to that, the pickup boat actually had to stop and the swimmer was pulled onto the rubber boat for recovery. That made the pickup boat a much easier target for enemy fire. This was found to be pretty disastrous when done during the first couple of UDT operations.

On the fourteenth of June 1944, we started the Marianas operation along with UDTs 3, 4, 5, and 6. Because the Normandy invasion took place on 6 June that same month, it always kind of overshadowed the start of the Marianas campaign. The targets of the operation included Saipan, Guam, and Tinian. It was a big, important operation, but it just never got the press it should have because of what was going on over in Europe.

During Operation SPRINGBOARD off of Vieques, Puerto Rico, in 1972, the snare man hauls in a recovered UDT swimmer. This technique of recovering UDT swimmers from the water while the boat is moving at speed was first developed during WWII in the Pacific. It is still trained with today.

U.S. Navy

But Saipan was our first operation. It was a Team effort throughout, each of us did our job, but it was drilled into us that we did everything as a Team. That, and your swimming partner is the best friend you could ever have. Those were the two greatest lessons and strengths of the UDT, everyone always worked together, and Teamwork got the job done.

There was a lot of resistance to the Team's going in to the beaches at Saipan. The enemy put out a lot of fire against both the fleet and us.

In spite of that, the operation went very well; we gathered the information that we were supposed to, and got back to the fleet with it. So we had conducted our first combat operation successfully.

The invasion of Guam took place a few weeks later and that used UDTs 3, 4, and 6. Our next operation was at Tinian on July 24. There was more enemy fire at Tinian, which made it harder than Saipan had been. But we were learning and we still got the job done. People at fleet level were happy with what we had been able to do.

Ours was still a very new operation. The Teams had been built up because of what had happened the year before at Tarawa. The Marines took heavy losses just getting in to the beach. They had gotten hung up on the reefs and hundreds never even made it to the island.

So our mission was to clear the way for the landing craft to get in to the beach. We had worked with UDTs 3 and 5 and done very well; everyone did their job and it showed. Lieutenant Commander Kauffman was out there with us, but he had very little power when it came to how to use us. All of this was still very new and we were learning parts of our jobs as we went along. We didn't look very much like any sailors that had been seen before and that rankled some people in command.

Some admiral made a comment to Kauffman that he considered us "the most unruly bunch of Navy men" he'd ever seen in his life and he didn't know what he would ever do with us.

And Kauffman answered that officer with, "Yes, sir, but they got the job done."

"Yes," the admiral said, "I hate to admit it, but they did."

So even in those early days we were not accepted well by the regular Navy. When we went on board our ships, the APDs, we went around in our shorts. The regular crew had to keep their uniforms and hats on as per regulations. We just didn't comply with that sort of thing very much. That did raise some resentment among the rest of the Navy. And after the war, it wasn't long before they broke us up back in the States.

After having served in the UDT, it was pretty hard to go back to being regular sailors. There was more than one base commander who didn't really want us in his area. Putting what was left of the Teams kind of out of the way may have added a lot to our ending up in Coronado and Little Creek.

But after the Tinian operation, we went on to Peleliu in September. After that operation, we finally returned to Maui. We had been told that we would be sent stateside and given a leave on our return. The UDTs had gone on a number of ops during the invasions. Between all of the Teams involved, the men had gone on ten or more swims into the enemy beaches.

So the Team had been promised a stateside leave, but that was just one of those things that never happened. Instead, we got a ten-day island leave and most of the guys went over to the main island. Afterward, when the Team got back together, they made instructors out of many of us for the new Teams going through training. The Navy kept us in Hawaii for months, running, training, and various other jobs.

Finally, in February 1944, we left Maui for the Western Pacific along with five or so other UDTs. A number of the Teams were heading for Iwo Jima and the operations there. UDT 7 passed Iwo and went on to the Philippines. The invasion of the Philippines had already been completed. We went in to Lingayen Gulf and the straits around there and worked in that area. We did a few recons, but they weren't under hot combat conditions. The Japanese were there, but we weren't facing the enemy as such. It was practice for what was coming later.

From the Philippines, we went on to Okinawa, where we took part in the invasion. As I remember, we came in to Okinawa on the thirtieth of March. The invasion was planned for April 1. You think about what's coming when you're still on the ship. You get hyped up about the upcoming op, you wonder about what you're going to find in the water, what might be waiting on the beach for you, or even if you're going to make it. All of those kinds of things run through your mind.

As soon as I could get off the ship and out of the boat, things were better. The ship wasn't my blanket, the water was my blanket. As soon as I got into the water, things were all right. Everything seemed to calm down and I could concentrate much better on what I was supposed to do.

We dropped the LCPRs into the water from the APD to start the op. A UDT platoon would get into one LCPR to go in on the op. The rubber boat would be tied to the side of the LCPR and we would load up and head in.

Near the target, the man who would signal us to drop off the rubber boat would climb down off the LCPR and take up his position. Then we would go in and make our drop run off of the beach. At whatever distance from the beach had been decided by our mission planners, say 1,000 yards, we would start dropping into the water.

All of us would have lined up in the boat with our swimming partner for the drop into the water. The LCPR would be traveling along at flank speed, paralleling the beach, as we left the boat. The man giving the signal would drop his arm, and a pair of us would roll off the side of the rubber boat. As soon as one pair was gone, the next would scramble up and into place. We dropped off in pairs spaced about fifty feet apart.

The first thing you would notice, especially off of Okinawa, was that the water was more than a little cool. That shock brought you to your senses pretty quick. Then you and your swim partner would take a look and make sure everyone was in line before striking out for the beach.

Moving on to the beach, we would take our soundings and make notes on our pads. We would also keep a lookout for man-made obstacles, coral heads, and whatever we could see. We would take bearings on landmarks on the beaches to show where obstacles were or whatever.

Enemy fire was very light at Okinawa. We drew some small-arms and sniper fire, but it just wasn't much. There was plenty of fire going overhead. Our cruisers, battleships, and whatever were still pounding targets on the island. But there was only light enemy fire directed at us, at least it seemed so to me. No one was in trouble as we formed up our line and moved back out to sea.

Our LCPR moved along and recovered each of us with the double-

---

Navy SEALs

loop snare. Then we returned to the ship, where we were all immediately debriefed by the old man and several other officers. Our notes and soundings were taken and compiled together. Then all of the information was taken up to higher headquarters. Then the day was basically over for the time being.

We went in during the early morning, and it seemed we were done by 10 A.M. If we had to make a demolition swim, it would be done later that afternoon, the next day, or whenever. It depended on what the higher command decided from the information we gave them.

Each time we went in on an operation, it was a little harder than the time before to get yourself up for the mission. The first time was the easiest. You hadn't been through it before and you didn't really know what to expect, even though you had heard all of the stories from other guys who had already been there. You always had to get yourself in the right state of mind so you were sure you would have the strength and not fall apart when you had to do your job.

As soon as the stuff started flying, the whole situation started to seem a little like a dream. It was happening all around you, but it didn't seem real. You would psych yourself up and even the sound of the shells and rifle fire seemed to get less. They were kind of muffled, though you could still hear everything.

But you just kept going, did your job, and turned back out to sea for pickup. It wasn't until you got back aboard ship and everything was over that maybe your hand would start to shake a bit, or you got the funny feelings in your stomach.

During our second operation on Okinawa, on our swim in to the beach, I remember seeing a white flag up on the seawall on the beach. I used that flag as my marker for the swim in. The invasion had already been going on, but we didn't take any fire at all. It was as if we could just swim right up to the beach and no one cared. We were taking no fire or anything. Then, just as I reached the beach and could look up and see that white flag—kaboom!

Falling back into the water, I was sure I had been shot and killed. What the noise had been was an American tank, on the far side of the seawall where I couldn't see it, that had chosen that moment to fire its main gun. Right after that little noise, I was scared; everything, all the bravery and psyching up, were gone. All I could hear or feel for a moment was the beating of my own heart.

It seems that for just about everybody, until the situation arises where you've been hit or are in trouble, you stay relatively calm. After something serious happens, though, the shock sets in. Many people do a lot of things when they're in shock that they don't remember afterward. Guys will do things, real acts of bravery, and when you ask them about it afterward, they just don't remember.

On any of the operations we had done, we went in anywhere from four days to just the day before the landings. That was how we could get the last-minute information to the planners on the staffs. It was also how we were able to leave a sign now and then for the Marines when they came in to the beach.

The signs were just a joke and I don't want to run down the Marine Corps. Those are a fine bunch of men who did one hell of a job. We did have the "pleasure" of leading the first Marine landing boats in to the beaches on the mornings of the invasion. At Okinawa, I was one of the men from the UDTs who went in with them.

That first boatload of Marines talked a bit with us on our way in to Okinawa. They considered all of us as crazy as they had even seen. They thought the idea of swimming in to the beaches almost naked was insane and they wouldn't have our jobs for anything. I looked at those men and thought about the fact that we only had to go in to the beaches for two or three hours. Then we were able to go back out to our ships. They had to go in and either take the island or die. I couldn't see their logic in thinking we were so much crazier than they were.

Okinawa was going to be our last combat operation, not that we knew it at the time. In a way, it was probably our worst operation. It wasn't that we had high casualties; only one man was killed, but others were wounded. One good friend of mine, Frank Brittain, was working on one of the obstacles near the beach, and one of our own shells landed near him. The blast nearly deafened him for quite a while afterward.

Frank wasn't one to let things slow him down much. After he left UDT, he joined the Army and became an Airborne Ranger. Later he calmed down a bit, and today he's an ordained minister.

Frank's near miss wasn't the bad action for UDT 7 off of Okinawa.

The serious incident happened to UDT 7 and our APD about 4:30 in the afternoon on April 9. A week or so after the invasion of the main island, we had conducted recons off of Tsugen Shima, a small island off the east coast of Okinawa. We were pulling screening duty off the island when a hidden Japanese shore battery opened up on us and our APD took eight hits from armor-piercing shells.

When the UDTs weren't preparing for or on a mission, we had other jobs we did aboard ship. I had been assigned as head count in one of the mess decks. They woke me up one afternoon to get ready to pull my shift. The nap I had been taking made me a bit groggy, so I went out on the fantail of the ship to get a little air. Standing there, I had one foot up on the depth charge rack and was smoking one of my very rare cigars. That was when I saw the first shell splash into the water behind us.

Even though I had seen enough incoming shells to recognize what had happened, I said, "What was that?" to anyone who could hear me. It didn't matter if anyone had heard me at all, as the second round came in right about then and struck one of the stern 40mm guns tubs right behind me.

I had gone through enough of Gunnery School to know where I could be of the most use right then and I headed toward the bow five-inch gun. From that gun, we would be best able to put some fire back out at the Jap guns that were shooting at us. As I headed up the passageway, more rounds impacted on the ship.

Two or three more rounds had hit, one of them close behind me as I was moving in the passageway. The explosion felt just like a big hand had picked me up and threw me right up the passageway. It didn't hurt or anything, it was just like I was floating through the air. But I was one of the lucky ones.

Other men had been badly hurt in the shelling. Guys were lying all over on the deck, hurt and bleeding. The way forward to the five-incher had been blocked, so there wasn't any way I was going to make it to that gun to be of any use. But the men right there on the deck all around me were able to use any help they could get. So I set to trying to give any first aid that I could to the injured men.

UDT 7 and the ship had twenty-three casualties from the shelling, but only one UDT man was killed, a young man name of Buck. Some of the other injuries were very bad; one UDT man lost his leg.

One of the guys in the Team found a Jap shell that hadn't detonated onboard ship. The round was close enough to our forward explosives stores that if it had gone off, we would probably still be going up into the air. There had been something like twenty-five tons of explosives on board in the forward hold near that shell. That guy grabbed up that dud shell and carried it over to the side and dropped it into the sea. He never received a medal for it.

A lot of guys never were recognized for different things they did. The Team as a whole was decorated for our actions; most of us were put in for Silver Star at one time. But the awarding of medals followed Navy traditions and the officers received the Silver Star and the enlisted got the Bronze Star. But that was just Navy protocol. We had a fine bunch of officers in the Team, leading a great unit of men.

We had stopped off in Manu Bay in the Admiralty Islands on our way back to Maui after Peleliu. We had been transferring powder from our ship to the APD Clemson and UDT 6. Early in the evening a fire broke out on the fantail of the Clemson and spread to our ship. The tetrytol explosives that were still out on deck had caught fire and were burning.

A good buddy of mine, Eddie Remeika, was one of the guys who tossed burning explosive charges off of the ship, probably saving both it and us. But he never received the recognition a number of us felt he should have for doing that. It seems to me that it was much harder to be recognized for heroism back then. Not that we were out looking for medals.

Finally, we were sent back to the States. About the first of August, we reported to Oceanside, California, after our leave. The Team was going to take cold-water training for the upcoming invasion of

Japan. But President Truman changed those plans when he had the bomb dropped. The war was over at last.

We did end up going to Japan anyway, but as part of the occupation forces rather than invaders. Our first area of operations in Japan was in the Yokohama area. Then they sent us up to Sendai, where we reconned the beaches prior to landing U.S. forces.

Going up to Sendai turned out to be quite a deal for us. I was one of the guys in the boats who went in that day. We showed no weapons but just went in to where we could see a crowd on the beach. There were hundreds of people there to greet us. One old, gray-haired Japanese in his ceremonial robes came down to meet us directly. Our lieutenant went up to the old man and returned his bow.

There were so many people on the beach, we didn't know what to do. That crowd could have done anything they wanted with us, but instead of anything we might have expected, they picked us up, rubber boat and all, and paraded us up and down the beach. This was something I could hardly believe; they were treating us like arriving heroes rather than the enemy. It may have been that they were just as glad the war was over as we were.

On that particular beach, we didn't find anything in the way of obstacles or fortifications. Our Team wasn't like the UDTs further south in Japan. There, the guys found lots of obstacles and weapons. Boats filled with explosives, mines, suicide weapons, all kinds of materials had been built up by the Japanese and made ready for their final defense of the islands. Any Allied invasion would have been a disaster, for both sides.

The plans for the invasion of Japan called for thirty UDTs. Eventually, I got a chance to see the plans for some of the invasions and what our part would have been in them. One of the sites looked like it was just south of Tokyo, in an area full of mudflats and impenetrable terrain. It wasn't very fortified, so maybe the Japanese thought no one would be crazy enough to try a landing there. But it looked like we would have.

But the Japanese would have fought to the bitter end. There were going to be a number of invasions, one after the other. That mudflat

Japanese officers prepare to lead members of UDT 21 into a storage cave on the coast of the Japanese main islands just after WWII. The officers were expected to show the UDT men if there were any boobytraps in the caves, which had been used to store weapons and munitions for the last-ditch defense of Japan.

Barry G. McCabe Collection

action may even have been a diversion, for all I know. But that wouldn't have mattered much. The Japanese people would have kept fighting until they were all gone, and they would have taken an awful lot of us with them. The cost of those invasions would have been astronomical, on both sides.

Back then we were all really gung ho to do our part and win the war. Patriotism ran really high and Roosevelt was God. I experienced three wars—WWII, Korea, and I was still in the service during Vietnam. Older now, I can look back on what we did and why we did it with a different view. And the only question I still have is just why can't mankind settle their differences without violence. Wars have always been such a waste. In spite of bringing out the best in some men, they also show the worst.

The young guys in the Teams had come from most every walk of life prior to joining the Navy. That was one of the fantastic things about them: they had come from everywhere. We had farmers, schoolteachers, people from the city and the country. In UDT 7, we had a number of older guys, all of around twenty-five years old, who had already started life. They were married, some even had kids. All nationalities, all types. One of the really great fighters we had in the team later in the war was a full-blooded American Indian, and he was one hell of a fighter.

Some of the guys had come from very poor backgrounds, a few had come from wealth, some with little education, others with degrees. They were all the same type of people in that they wanted the adventure and challenge of being in the Teams. Other than that, they were all different, there was no one kind of person you could point to and say, "That one would be a UDT man."

There was a strong feeling of team spirit among us all. But our job was secret and we couldn't talk about it to anyone except each other. It was a dangerous job and a difficult one. If you were just there for the glory and all, you weren't going to stay very long. What we did wasn't for the kind of person who gets emotional about things. That kind of person who goes out for the glory and all of that, he just wasn't going to stay long.

Our job depended a lot on what the individual could push himself to do. And not just once but over and over again. We didn't have any underwater breathing gear when we went out on an operation. When you dove under the water, what mattered was how long could you hold your breath. We all had to dive down a fair ways, something like twenty-five feet maybe, and tie a certain kind of knot to attach two lines. The knots were the kind we used to attach primacord lines together. If you couldn't do this knot tying, it didn't mean they would wash you out completely. But you would probably be assigned to a boat crew and not be one of the swimmers in the water.

Everyone was important in the Team, and it took everyone working together to get the job done. But the basic job was to get the swimmers within range of the beach. They were the men who went in and got the information and were the spearhead of the invasion force.

It was from in the water that we got our job done. That's why they kept us there for hours at a time during training. And we made mistakes, both during training and on operations. But it was from these mistakes that we learned how to do the job better. Operations changed from day to day; every island was a little different and every invasion had its own problems. When we came up with a better way of doing something that worked, it would eventually get back to Maui and become part of the training.

Friendship isn't really a good enough word for what we felt for each other in our Team back then. What we did and how we did it was *a real bond between us. There was a relationship between the members of my UDT that seems to have been even stronger than the bond between a married couple.*

It takes a special type of person to have wanted to be in the UDTs back then, and the SEAL Teams now. The training and equipment these guys have is so far above what we had that there's no comparison. Many of us couldn't have passed today's SEAL training; we just didn't have the education.

Despite everything that the SEALs have today, it seems that the man underneath all of the equipment and training is the same as we were. It's hard to say for sure about the differences between now and then. Our birth, the UDTs, was under wartime conditions; we had to learn hard and fast how to do our job. The SEALs were created in peacetime. They had the time to learn what their duties were; we went into things pretty fast and made mistakes. But then, we were expendable.

■ Chapter 12

THE OSS MARITIME UNIT

One of the more unusual forces fielded by the U.S. during World War II involved the unconventional combat units of the office of Strategic Services (OSS). The Office of Coordinator of Information (OCI) was started on 11 July 1941 to collect and analyze information for the U.S. government. In June 1942, the Office of Strategic Services took over the mission of the OCI. Both of these organizations were under the direction of General William J. "Wild Bill" Donovan, a colorful individual who put together his organizations at the request of the President of the United States, Franklin Roosevelt.

The OSS soon became known for its clandestine work in gathering information by espionage. The OSS also created and supported guerrilla groups and other unconventional forces. Among these forces was the Maritime Unit, the first underwater combat and sabotage forces in the U.S. military.

The Maritime Unit (MU) evolved from earlier training activities of the OSS. The activities were conducted at a training site known as Area D, near the present Marine Base at Quantico, Virginia. Training centered around the clandestine infiltration and exfiltration of agents by sea but soon expanded to include attacking ships at anchor and other underwater missions.

The OSS Maritime Unit used kayaks and folding boats for overwater operations. Also used were inflatable rubber boats and inflatable two-man "surfboards" that included an electric motor for propulsion. On 20 December 1943, the OSS purchased 30 Lambertsen Diving Units, the first of almost 350 such units purchased.

The Lambertsen Diving Units were closed-circuit pure-oxygen rebreathers designed by Dr. Christian J. Lambertsen. This device, also called the Lambertsen Amphibious Respiratory Unit (LARU) allowed a swimmer to move underwater at up to thirty feet down without leaving a trail of bubbles behind him. With the LARU, the Maritime Units also used swim fins, waterproof compasses and watches, and a variety of explosive devices.

Donovan's OSS was not looked on with favor by a number of leaders in the military. Admiral Nimitz would not allow the OSS to operate in his areas of responsibility. General MacArthur was even more adamant about allowing OSS activities in his command area. The Maritime Unit saw few active combat operations during WWII under OSS direction. So to put his MU to good use, and to try to get a toehold in a new operational area, Donovan offered some of his MU personnel to the UDT school at Maui.

At Maui, the OSS men were able to help the UDTs use swim fins much more efficiently than they had before. Swim fins were reportedly used prior to the OSS MU personnel arriving at Maui, but the MU had different types of fins than those used by the UDTs. The commander of the OSS Maritime Unit, Navy Lieutenant Arthur Choat Jr., was one of five officers and twenty-one men to be assigned to Maui by the OSS. With the arrival of a contingent of men from class 6A from Fort Pierce, UDT 10 was formed around the Fort Pierce men and the OSS personnel. Arthur Choat was made the commanding officer of UDT 10.

The close cooperation between the OSS and the UDTs of World War II would survive the end of the war and continue in the years afterward. When the CIA, the postwar successor to the OSS, needed special personnel during the Korean War, they turned to the UDTs. The same held true in the late 1960s and well into the Vietnam War with the Navy SEALs.

Charles Q. Lewis, Motorman First Class

A man came around the Seabee training base at Camp Peary in 1943 asking for volunteers for a new unit. The guy was just an enlisted man like us, as I remember, and he couldn't tell us a lot about the unit. What he did tell us was that it was a completely volunteer organization and that there were liberties and freedoms you would receive that you couldn't get in the regular service. I liked that last part and volunteered along with a group of my fellow Seabees.

We knew the unit would involve demolition and that was about all. When we arrived at Fort Pierce, we were already in top physical condition. The Seabee training had given us a lot of PT to build us up. So when we got into the program at Fort Pierce, most of it was a snap.

Swimming was something we did a good deal of, several miles a day, two or three times a week. But when I arrived at Pierce, I wasn't much of a swimmer. The instructors changed that. They took a bunch of us over to North Island, threw us into a tank of water, and told us to swim. That was the rough-and-ready Navy way then.

At Fort Pierce training, a boat crew included six men, five enlisted and an officer. If we had an officer who didn't work with us, we could complain to the CO and we would get a new officer. We didn't have to salute, even on liberty, and the officers pulled their own KP and cleaned their own latrines.

One of the best parts of demolition, and what pounded the meaning of teamwork into us, was that our officers had to work right alongside each of us. And if they didn't do it, they were just gone. It made a lot of difference that our outfit was all-volunteer. We had a number of older men, and a number of young kids. But we were a close-knit outfit and morale was high.

Commander Kauffman was down at Fort Pierce and he had an office near the beach. If we marched, or ran, by and didn't make some noise, even at 2:30 in the morning, he wanted to know why. There was a spirit in us, and Kauffman wanted to hear it. We had a love for each other and a love for the job we had to do.

After the Fort Pierce training, I could swim well enough. During the UDT at Maui, I didn't have any trouble. And swimming in the open ocean didn't bother me. I had my trusty knife in case of sharks.

At Maui with UDT 12, we developed the cast and recovery sling system for getting swimmers out of the water fast. There wasn't any one person who came up with the final idea. It was another of our Team efforts.

With a rubber boat tied to the side pickup boat, an LCPR, we put a man in the front of the boat to pick up the swimmers and swing them on board. We found out fast that you couldn't just grab a swimmer and swing him into the rubber boat—your hands would slip.

First, we came up with a sling that was just a length of rope tied to the LCPL with a knot at the loose end. But the swimmers couldn't always hang on to the knot as they swung aboard. Then we tried a loop of rope. That turned into the double-loop (figure-eight) snare that worked. A swimmer could put his arm through the loop and be swung aboard. This was almost a surefire fast pickup system. During our first combat trials, we only missed one swimmer we had to go back for.

UDT 12's first combat operation was the invasion of Iwo Jima. We had a job to do and that was how we had to look at it. I don't think I thought of anything in particular before we went in to the beach. I even had a wife and kid back home. But for two days off Iwo Jima, I didn't have a thought for anything but the job we had to do.

There was a lot at stake if we didn't do our jobs. If we didn't find the mines, blow the clear channels, and destroy the scullies that would impale the incoming boats, we would have lost a lot of friends and good men. We were proud of the mission we were assigned and what we accomplished, that every man accomplished.

It was great to be in demolition. We had no beef against the Marines, though we would leave them a sign now and then. But I never envied them having to land on those islands.

The hardest part of the job for me came after the invasion. We had to go up on the beach and clear wrecked and breached boats. Blasting the wrecks back into the water quickly cleared the way for more troops and materials to come in and be landed. Up there on the sand wasn't any place that I wanted to be. There wasn't any envy of the Marines for me; they could have that place. I didn't want any part of it.

During the operations, I was not classified as a swimmer. I could swim and work along with my Team in the water blowing obstacles. But my job was as a member of the boat crew of Platoon Three. Along with myself as the motorman, we had Browning as my coxswain and Reese as the signalman. The three of us were responsible for running the boat (LCPL) for Platoon One and getting the men to and from the water.

Considering how cold the water was off Iwo, staying in the boat wasn't as bad as it could have been. We had covered the swimmers with a thick coating of water-pump grease to try to give some protection from the cold. There weren't any cold-water suits for swimmers then. At least not any that we had.

But I still spent my share of time in the water. When my ensign told me it was my turn to get wet, I just put on my mask and fins and rolled into the water. Of course, I managed a little payback. On the pickup, my ensign was the man on the sling. Now, he was a pretty good-sized lad. But that was before we started tying the sling off to the boat. When it was my turn to be picked up, I set my fins against the water and braced myself. It was my ensign who was pulled from the boat instead of me from the water.

UDT 12 also was at Okinawa, but we didn't operate off the main island. Instead, we were one of the UDTs who went in to the Kerama Islands near Okinawa. We had gone in to investigate some of the small island beaches when we saw something suspicious. There were natives on some of the islands, and there were Japanese in there as well. But they stayed quiet. The Japanese acted respectably toward us, or at least they never opened fire.

We were looking for Japanese suicide boats and gun emplacements in the Keramas. We went on land at a few of the islands, but never ran into any trouble. In fact, one of the island natives gave me a big pocket watch that I still have today.

Okinawa was the last combat operation for UDT 12. We went back to the States for cold-water training. Twenty-two of us were picked from the Team to do the training. We were going to be part of the invasion forces for Japan itself, the next planned operation of the war. But the bomb was dropped and the war was over.

As far as the dropping of the A-bomb goes, all I can say is "Amen." For myself, I was glad it happened. I was sorry for the people who were bombed, especially after seeing the pictures sometime later. But it was time to end that war and the bomb was the fastest way. I

A line of Japanese Type 1/Improved 4 Shinyo explosive suicide boats being towed out to sea for scuttling just after WWII.

Barry G. McCabe Collection

*have no qualms or bad feelings about using the A-bomb today. If I'd
had to give the order to use it, I would have.*

*The A-bomb ended the war suddenly. The bunch of us were on a
five-day leave that was suddenly canceled. We were scooped up and
shipped out fast. Within a day we found ourselves on a ship for Korea.*

*The Teams were a great bunch of people. We had our differences
among ourselves now and then. But that never added up to anything
much and it didn't last long. We had a lot of respect for each other.
Each of us had his job to do and that job supported each of our Teammates.*

■ Chapter 13

KAMIKAZE

The UDTs were part of almost every amphibious operation conducted in the Pacific from January 1944 onward. Those landings that
did not use the UDTs either went in unopposed or were led in by the
NCDUs working in the Southwestern Pacific. Each operation that led
the Allied forces close to Japan met fiercer and fiercer resistance. The
Japanese brought out weapons that were unheard of in the rest of the
civilized world.

The kamikaze, or "Divine Wind," were generally aircraft pilots
who had sworn their lives to their emperor and country. They lifted
off in their aircraft with no intention of returning. If an Allied ship or
target presented itself, the kamikaze would direct their planes to dive
into the target. Only heavy antiaircraft fire could defeat the kamikaze
attacks, and not all of the time.

It wasn't just aircraft that were delivered to their target by Japanese suicide pilots, explosive-laden boats and midget submarines

Japanese midget suicide submarines are dragged seaward for destruction by U.S. sailors. Locating and disposing of these weapons found along the shores of Japan after WWII was one of the primary missions of the immediate postwar UDTs.

Barry G. McCabe Collection

were also used. The men of the UDTs felt safest when they were in the water, even when that water was just off a Japanese-held beach. They had relatively few losses on operations, but there were exceptions.

E. F. "Andy" Andrews, Lieutenant

When I first heard about Navy demolition, I was an officer in the Navy taking some special classes at Cornell University. There were about two hundred of us in the class and all of us had already put in requests for our preferred assignments. I had asked for and received orders for PT boats. Before I left for the PT boat base up in New England, an officer by the name of Draper Kauffman came to the university and asked to address our class.

During his address, Draper told us about his extra-hazardous-duty unit. The one initial requirement, that we be able to swim, was all he could tell us about the unit. Everything else was classified confidential. Out of those two hundred officers, six of us volunteered to join

For the Apollo 11 recovery operation, there was thought to be a real danger of contamination from the moon's surface. These UDT and SEAL recovery swimmers are all wearing protective masks and coveralls while securing the Apollo capsule. The capsule was later moved unopened to a secure laboratory structure onboard a Navy ship. The recovery swimmers had to go through decontamination procedures after the pickup.

U.S. Navy

the new unit. Within twenty-four hours, my orders for the PT boat base in New England were changed to Fort Pierce, Florida.

It was Draper Kauffman himself whose demeanor and bearing convinced me to volunteer. He was a great guy and a terrific leader, the kind of man you would be willing to follow. He seemed to me to be one of those people who are just impervious to danger. From his background in bomb disposal, and the fact that he had all of his arms. legs, and fingers, my opinion may have been close to the truth.

Prior to Fort Pierce, I had been an officer in the Navy for all of maybe six months. So I had a little experience in the traditional Navy service and the distance that exists between the officers and the enlisted men in most situations. Fort Pierce and NCDU training was not one of those situations.

We had our own officers' tents at the training base, but they were just tents and nothing better than what the enlisted men had. Our tents were located a little off to the side and there weren't as many men assigned to the same tent as the enlisted. But once you left that tent and got into the day's activities, you couldn't tell the difference between the officers and the enlisted men.

About the only difference there was during training was that the officers always sat in the back of the rubber boat as the coxswain. Kauffman never knew exactly what our assignment would be, so training was kind of being made up as we all went along. Until the Tarawa invasion, and later, until we received the intelligence on the obstacles off of Normandy, we didn't have a specific target. Training was in some ways trial and error until we knew exactly what it was we had to attack.

But the basis of training centered around the seven-man rubber boat. That boat would be taken in to shore as our basic transportation. On board would be a unit of men and the explosives they would need to accomplish their mission. To this end, the Naval Combat Demolition Unit was six men, five enlisted and one officer and the rubber boat. The space and weight of the seventh man would be taken up by the unit's load of explosives.

The preferred manning of an NCDU was an officer, up to a senior lieutenant, a chief petty officer, and four men, usually a first class and several seamen. How Draper came up with that lineup, I was never really sure. But the idea was for the seventh "man" to be the powder or gear or whatever else you had to haul along.

For a short while after I had completed training at Fort Pierce, I was placed on the staff for the NCDU School. Then a group of NCDUs, including one I was in charge of, were sent out to Maui. Very quickly in Maui, our NCDU organization was dissolved and we were formed up as UDTs, my unit being UDT 15. That was when the word really came back for us to increase our swimming.

Though swimming had been a requirement prior to being accepted into NCDU training, Kauffman never envisioned the NCDUs as a swim-

"Andrews' Avengers": the six-man Naval Combat Demolition Unit under the command of Ensign Andy Andrews (on the left). This was the basic unit of men that trained at Fort Pierce even though these men went on to be part of UDT 15 in the Pacific. They are armed with M1 carbines, the man at the lower left having an M1 Thompson submachine gun. Around the waist of their uniforms are the inflatable canvas and rubber life belts used during WWII.

UDT-SEAL Museum

ming unit during operations. When the requirement was put out that the men in Hawaii might have to swim up to a mile, Kauffman initially didn't believe it. He wasn't sure a man would be able to swim that far, but his judgment may have been colored by the fact that he wasn't a very good swimmer at the time.

But at Maui, swimming was heavily emphasized. Every day the distances swum and the time spent in the water was increased. This was in addition to time spent paddling the rubber boats. Special training was also given in demolition of coral and lava rock. And we learned reconnaissance techniques for offshore waters and enemy beaches.

When we finished training, UDT 15 was ordered to board APD 48, the USS Blessman, a high-speed troop transport converted from a WWI "four-stacker" destroyer. Prior to our departure, we had to load all of our equipment on board. There were thirty tons of powder (high explosive), all the rubber boats, and all of the other gear that a UDT travels with. We didn't know where we were going or how long we would be gone. So we packed for any eventuality.

My chief petty officer came up to me and asked if the men could have liberty and go into town at least one more time. I explained that we had to have all of our gear on board and properly stowed away by sailing time the next morning. The chief assured me that if I allowed the men to have liberty, he'd see to it that the materials were loaded by the deadline. So I let the men go.

It turned out that day was some kind of holiday in Hawaii and all of the bars were closed up solid. My men, being the resourceful types they were, didn't let that stop them from having a good time. They found a source of native "kanakee juice," which was really just fermented coconut milk. It may have been their last liberty for a while, so they certainly made the best of it.

The next morning I had never seen as drunk a bunch of sailors as my men. But true to his word, the chief got them together and they finished loading on time. The UDTs always got the mission done.

APD 48: the USS *Blessman* with UDT 15 aboard at D-1, the day before the invasion of Iwo Jima.

UDT-SEAL Museum

On board the Blessman, we didn't have the opportunity to exercise and stay in shape as well as we might have. Swimming was impossible while the ship was under way. Spending a week or two under way wouldn't sap the men's abilities too much, but we needed to stay in shape for any mission that might come up. So when we stopped at an anchorage, we would take the opportunity to get into the water and swim at least a bit.

We were at anchor in Ulithi in the Carolina Islands, a volcanic atoll that had a safe harbor from submarines in its center lagoon. The rim of the volcano was only six feet below the surface, while the center of the volcano, the lagoon of the atoll, was hundreds of feet deep. Outside the rim of the atoll, it was thousands of feet deep as it dropped down into the depths of the Pacific.

So we decided to swim across the reef and do some work on the outside rim of the atoll where there was some surf action. Inside of the lagoon, the waters were protected and there was very little wave action and no surf. Swimming across the rim of the atoll was interesting. Just a few feet below us, we could see maybe a hundred sharks sunning themselves in the shallow water. They just looked at us as we swam overhead.

We went outside the reef and conducted our exercise. Then it was time to swim back across the reef and to the ship. Going over the rim of the volcano again, we saw that about half of the sharks were still there. We didn't know what happened to the rest of the sharks, but we left them alone and they didn't bother us. There may have been kind of a mutual respect sort of thing going on there.

Our first landing operation swimming in the water was at Lingayen Gulf on the west coast of Luzon in the Philippines. Our job of swimming in the water and doing the beach reconnaissance was not as hard as just staying on the ship turned out to be. For at least three or four days the Japanese conducted kamikaze attacks against all the ships of the invasion fleet.

Every day Japanese planes would come up over the hills of Luzon and dive down on the ships. The area was called Kamikaze Alley because of all the attacks. The men of UDT 15 were not part of the ship's crew for the Blessman, *but some of our men jumped in to help when the Japanese threatened.*

The kamikazes were coming at the ships from all directions as we floated in the gulf waters. All of the fleet ships put out as much anti-aircraft fire as they possibly could to try to hold off the planes. It was just by luck that the Blessman wasn't hit. We had several near misses with planes falling just short of us and passing overhead to fall beyond the ship.

One particular kamikaze pilot stands out as the plane came in very close. He was aiming at our ship and I could see the expression on his face as he approached our ship. He passed over us by just a few feet and impacted on the water on the other side.

In spite of the nearness of that incident, it was such a big theater of war that the actions just didn't seem personal. Without that direct aspect, and the fact that we were usually pretty busy, you just didn't get as scared of the situation as you might think.

It was when you got into the water and swam up onto the beach to gather a sample of sand that things got personal. The Japanese would be firing and you knew they were firing at you, you were the only target on the beach. In a kamikaze attack, it was almost like being just a spectator at an event. The plane would be after everyone including you. But when you'd gone in to the beach with your swim buddy to gather the sand sample, and the mortars and the machine guns opened up, there wasn't much question what the target was.

To aid in the defense of the ship, the guns from our LCPRs, 50-caliber machine guns, were taken and added to mounts on the fantail of the ship. The gunners from the UDT added our firepower to the overall umbrella of steel that was helping to keep the kamikazes off of us. Other UDT men helped in passing ammunition and doing whatever other tasks could aid the ship. We may not have been a direct part of the ship's company, but for the time being, it was our home too.

We survived the attacks off of Luzon and moved on to our next target, the invasion of Iwo Jima. That island was the most godforsaken place I had ever seen in my life up to that point, with the black volcanic ash beach and dingy, foreboding appearance of the land. Our mission was to perform two operations in one day, one in the morning and one in the afternoon. There were only two beaches on Iwo Jima that were suitable for landing, and the Japanese knew that as well as we did.

It had been pretty well decided that we would be going in on the east beach, which put Mount Suribachi down to our left flank and the cliffs on our right flank. That was the swim we did that morning. That afternoon we conducted the same operation on the west beach of the island. But that last swim was strictly diversionary. The intent was to try to keep the Japanese confused as to which beach we would actually land on.

The Japanese gun position opened fire on us as we conducted our recon swims. Another part of our mission was to try to draw the fire of the Japanese to get them to expose their gun positions. The sites would be noted and the big guns of the fleet would then target them for destruction. This was all well and good in the planning stage. But the actuality of drawing Japanese fire was not the best mission we ever had.

The Japanese guns were in the hills near Mount Suribachi and dug into the cliffside overlooking the beaches. Finding them was well worth the effort. They were so well camouflaged and emplaced that we never would have found them if they hadn't started firing at us. The next day, the big sixteen-inch guns of the battleships made short work of those gun installations well before the Marines hit the beach.

I was one of the platoon officers in the water for Team 15 during that operation. It was my platoon that was up under the cliffs on the right flank at Blue Beach on Iwo, where we were supposed to try and draw fire. UDTs 12, 13, 14, and 15 were working on the Iwo Jima invasion and it was just the luck of the draw that we were assigned the cliffs area. It was in those cliffs that command suspected the Japanese had placed their guns, and it turned out they were right.

Fear is something everyone feels. Anyone who has ever been in war has been afraid at one time or another, and anyone who says he has never been afraid is a fool. A hero is not somebody who does something he isn't afraid to do. A hero is someone who does something he is afraid to do. And I don't know anyone who isn't afraid of being shot at. So in wartime, of course you feel fear. Somebody is out there trying to kill you, and they aren't trying to kill anyone else at that time. Just like off those beaches at Iwo Jima, it gets very personal then.

The operations off of Iwo Jima were expensive in terms of men and material. I give great credit to the LCI(G) gunboats who gave us close-in fire support. We had refined our operations to the point that we knew the heavy, concentrated fire put in right over the heads of the swimmers in the water was what it took to keep the enemy from wiping us out. The gunboats put in 20mm and 40mm shells into the beach not twelve feet over our heads. You could actually feel the shock waves of the bigger cannon rounds as they passed overhead.

The idea was to keep the fire on the beach as the swimmers approached the shore. As we got closer, the gunboats would walk their fire up from the beach and into the jungle beyond. Then, when our mission was done, as we swam out, the gunboats would again concentrate their fire on the beaches to keep the enemy from firing directly at us.

The LCI(G) gunboats were converted infantry landing craft with a number of rapid-fire antiaircraft weapons installed on them. They could come in to the shallow water and put their fire in at point-blank range. And it was those same gunboats that protected us that drew the fire of the Japanese. The fire coming from the boats made the Japanese think our operation was the invasion, so they uncovered their guns.

On the swim in, I was getting to within 200 to 150 yards of the beach and the return fire from the enemy emplacements was getting heavy. I could see that the gunboats just weren't putting the amount of fire we expected in on the beach to keep the enemies' heads down. When I turned and looked back out to sea, I could see why.

There had been twelve gunboats coming in behind us to cover our operation. All of the boats had been disabled or sunk during our swim in. Not one of the LCI(G) boats escaped destruction. Destroyers were ordered in close to pick up the first support for us. But those ships were further out and just didn't have the range needed for the job. For a while we were receiving as much friendly fire as enemy fire.

In spite of the heavy fire from both sides, UDT casualties were very light during that operation. We were able to return to our pickup points and were snared up and on board our LCPRs. Returning to the Blessman, we made our reports and settled in. The Blessman was moved out for screening duty well away from Iwo as night fell.

What came later, on February 18, 1945, was the most expensive situation, not only for UDT 15 but for any UDT or SEAL Team, on any single mission before or since. It was the heaviest casualty count for a single team ever.

Our commanding officer and a few other officers from UDT 15 had left the ship earlier. They had taken our charts and notes on the beach conditions and were briefing the Marine officers on the conditions they could expect in the upcoming landings. Those of us who remained on board had little to do and were able to relax a bit as the Blessman moved into her assigned position in the antisubmarine screen around the fleet.

The captain may have made a mistake as he moved the Blessman out at flank speed to take up her post. The waters off Iwo Jima were heavily phosphorescent and the bow wave the Blessman threw off glowed in the night. Right about nine o'clock, things had eased down and it was time to wait for the next day when the invasion would take place.

A Japanese Betty, their Type-1 2EB twin-engine bombers, spotted the Blessman and targeted her with two 500-pound bombs. One of the bombs was a near miss to the ship and caused relatively little damage. The other bomb was very different.

The Japanese bomb went right down the middle of the ship and detonated level with the mess deck. The blast almost immediately set the ship on fire from stem to stern. On board the Blessman were not only her own ammunition lockers, but 30 tons of high explosives for the demolition teams stored in the aft explosive magazine.

In spite of the fire, the first order of business for the survivors of the blast was to get to the casualties belowdecks. The bomb had detonated in the enlisted men's mess hall. The majority of the men of UDT 15 had been relaxing, playing cards, reading, and writing home in the mess hall when the bomb went off. The carnage was terrible.

The ship was on fire and there was no power whatsoever. With the Blessman *dead in the water,* we found that none of the "handy billies," a self-powered water pump, would start. Without the pumps, we had no active fire hoses. In desperation, since we knew the explosives were there in the fantail locker, we formed a bucket brigade. When the buckets were thrown over the side attached to lines, they wouldn't fill quickly and just floated on the surface. A Jacob's ladder was tossed over the side and I went down to the water. As the buckets hit, I would push them down with my foot to help fill them. Even helmets were tied to lines that were thrown over the side to gather water to fight the fire.

We were trying to keep the fire away from the fantail, on the deck of which were our wounded. For some reason, I started singing "Anchors Aweigh" as I pushed the buckets down. Pretty soon we had all picked up the song. That story about the UDT who sang while fighting a fire on board their ship made the rounds.

Throwing the buckets on the fire near the explosives locker may have been doing about as much good as spitting in the ocean. But it was all we could do at the time. If the explosives went up, there would just be a big hole in the water where the Blessman, *and UDT 15, had been.*

The USS Gilmer, *an APD that was acting as the UDT command ship, came up to us as we lay there in the water. I had to climb up the ladder and get back on deck as the* Gilmer *approached so that I wouldn't be crushed between the two ships. Commander Kauffman was on board the* Gilmer *and he quickly had fire hoses, running off the* Gilmer*'s pumps, sent over to the* Blessman.

Now we had water power and could fight the fire with some chance of beating it. One of the Blessman*'s fire control crew, a hoseman, was standing over the aft hold playing the hose down into where the fire was burning. I told him we had to get the hose down into the hold and fight the fire where it was. He just looked at me and said, "Yes, sir. After you, sir."*

So I grabbed the hose and went through the hatch and down the ladder into the hold. Another UDT 15 officer, Bob McCullum, went down the ladder with me. We played the hose across the bulkhead between the fire and the explosives. Thirty tons of tetrytol and other high explosives wouldn't react well to a lot of heat, and the paint on the bulkhead was already blistering.

I didn't have much choice about going down into the hold and fighting the fire. If that much explosives went up, it wouldn't matter where you were aboard ship. Everything would be gone. What the bigger problem was involved the ship's ammunition locker.

The fire had already taken hold in the ammunition locker and the shells and other rounds were cooking off. The ammunition locker was right next to where our explosives were stored. Bullets and fragments were ricocheting off the steel walls of the hold as we fought the fire. The zing-zing of projectiles bouncing around was a bit disconcerting.

That kind of action I don't think took heroism. It was either do it or get blown up. Somebody had to do it. Besides, Bob went with me.

So we fought the fire and eventually won. Later on, the Navy thought a bit about my actions that day and awarded me the Bronze Star and a Navy Citation. For swimming in to the Iwo Jima beaches and drawing enemy fire, as the officer of the group, I received the Silver Star. Between the two, fighting the fire was the harder action.

It wasn't fighting the fire that was hard—that just had to be done. But I knew we had lost a lot of men in the initial bomb strike. We had moved the wounded and as many of the dead as we were able to the fantail deck at the stern of the ship. That was the only place that wasn't on fire at the time. Lying above that explosives locker were twenty-three of the Team's wounded as well as the members of the ship's company who had been hurt. Those men wouldn't have stood a chance if the explosives blew. And they couldn't move themselves to even try to get out of the way.

The shock of that blast had torn men's hands off, amputated legs and arms, and blinded others. They all would have been lost. But putting that fire out would at least give them a chance to live. Going in on the beach during a swim was hard, but at least that was just me and my swim buddy in harm's way.

I felt a considerable burden as I knew we had already lost a number of men from the Team; the number turned out to be eighteen later, as well as those from the ship's crew. If somebody didn't put that fire out, the number of dead would increase a lot.

We did get the fire out and saved the Blessman. She was later towed to Saipan for initial repairs. The blast from the bomb had been so great, it blew a hole in the side of the ship you could drive two large trucks through. The wounded had been removed to the Gilmer soon after we had the fires under control. Those of us who remained on board had to try to make the ship as seaworthy as possible. And there were other tasks that had to be addressed.

Our problem after the fire was in identifying the dead. It was only a day or two after the incident when I had to go into the blasted mess deck and try to identify what was left of my Teammates. That had to be done so that they could be officially declared killed in action. Otherwise, they would have to be declared officially missing in action, as per Navy regulations.

There have been easier jobs than going into that deck. Along with the Team's dead were the ship's crew. To identify them, several members of the ship's staff went in with me and what was left of the Team's staff. The problem was, we had already removed as many bodies as we could during the fire. Now we had to try to identify people by what was left, none of which was a whole body.

The group of us worked through the wreckage of the mess deck, the engine room, and other spaces that had taken damage. Throughout the areas there was just a mass of dead bodies. We looked for dog tags, or a piece of a body with a ring, tattoo, or other identifier.

In spite of our best efforts, there were some men we had to list as missing in action. There wasn't any question in our minds that they had been killed. We just weren't able to identify them.

In my platoon, I had to list two men as missing in action. Others in the Teams were listed as MIA as well, but these two were particularly my men. After we had returned to the States, I made sure to contact the families of those men. I told those people that their loved ones were missing in action but that I was convinced beyond a shadow of doubt that they had been killed aboard the Blessman that February evening. I felt it was my duty as their officer to make sure that my men's families did not suffer through years of false hope that their missing men would someday walk through the door.

UDT 15 returned to the United States and Fort Pierce after the bombing off Iwo Jima. Fully half of the Team had to be replaced. Besides the wounded and the outright dead, there were other losses to the Team.

When we returned to Fort Pierce, we were all subjected to a battery of psychological tests. Some of the men who had come back with me from the Pacific looked just as fine as anyone else around us. But the doctors later told me that those men could not continue operating. They were perfectly healthy physically, but were mentally scarred inside. My own swim buddy ended up in a mental hospital six months later.

So my Teammates received the help they needed, and UDT 15 was restored to full strength with replacements. We were going to be in on the invasion of Japan itself when the atomic bomb brought the war finally to an end.

We had our orders to get ready for the invasion of Kyushu, Japan, on 1 November 1945, my birthday. A few of the staff officers, myself included, knew the date we were training toward. The operation was very secret, but only the details. Everyone knew it was only a matter of time until we had to invade the main islands of Japan. That would have been a real suicide mission.

Those of us putting together the plans for UDT 18's involvement in the invasion had been told to expect up to 75 percent casualties. In spite of that, we were going ahead with the plans and training. The dropping of the bombs changed all that. As bad as the bombs were in the amount of destruction they caused, it was nothing in comparison to the loss of life an invasion of Japan would have cost. And that would be on both sides.

In spite of the tremendous cost of the war in terms of human suf-

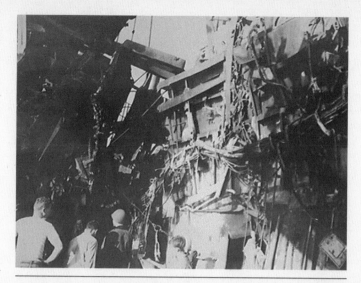

At 9:20 P.M., 18 February 1945, a five-hundred-pound bomb dropped from a Japanese plane went down the stack of the USS *Blessman* and exploded level with the mess deck. In the blast forty men were killed and thirty-four wounded. The explosion also set fire to the ship, coming close to detonating the tons of high explosives in her magazines.

From UDT 15, eighteen men were killed and twenty-three wounded. This is some of the carnage of the ship after the fires were put out. In this twisted steel, the crew of the ship and men of the UDT searched for the bodies of their comrades.

UDT-SEAL Museum

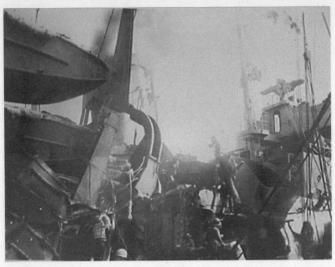

fering and loss, it was worth it. As expensive as the war was, even to me personally, if given the chance, I would volunteer again. Even with what happened, I would conduct myself as I had done before. When I look back on it, I think the price we paid as a nation was high, but the results were also high. And when I say "we," I mean the collective military might of the United States and the free world, not just the men of the UDTs.

As a fighting force, we were able to be a deterrent force to the black plague of Nazism, Fascism, and Japanese Imperialism. That's what we were fighting for, and we knew it.

The SEALs of today are carrying forward the traditions we established and paid for in blood. They are everything we ever were and more. They are far better today than we were, better equipped and better trained. We were in Model-T Fords and the Teams of today are in Corvettes. But in spite of all of their high-tech equipment and support, underneath is still the naked warrior of WWII who swam into the beaches wearing swim trunks, a knife at his hip, and a bag of explosives over his shoulder. Even in training today, the young men who want to become SEALs have to learn to be UDT men first.

When you're looking at a UDT or SEAL operator, you're looking at a man who is dedicated, is in excellent physical condition (or he's not going to last), and has a very high level of tolerance for personal discomfort. He will not quit. That is what they try to get you to do in training—quit.

If you are the kind of person who would quit, they want you out. There's no disgrace, because they don't want you to get into combat and then decide that's where you want to quit. When you've been dropped off and have to swim farther than you planned, are you going to give up? Or are you going to just keep going? That mental attitude is what may save your life or the life of the man next to you.

The invasion stories most people know about usually start as the boats hit the beach and the landing troops pile out into the face of enemy fire. What usually isn't told is the story that unfolds before that. The story of how someone had to go in and open the way through beach obstacles so that the landing craft could make it in to land their troops.

The NCDUs were the first ones sent in to open the way. At Omaha Beach in Normandy, the losses were very heavy among the NCDUs. Utah Beach had lighter casualties but there were still losses. The beaches at Normandy had a very slow gradient up from the low-water mark to the high-water mark. But the tides rose to a fairly high level. This meant the beaches were awash quickly, with the water level rising and covering the obstacles.

The obstacles on Normandy Beach had to be attacked while they were still out of the water. And in spite of herculean efforts on the part of the demolition crews, they couldn't destroy them all. Especially not in the face of the murderous enemy fire. And the NCDUs at Normandy were walking units. They wore standard uniforms, boots, and steel helmets. Since they weren't swimming, they didn't even have the cover of the water.

Those of us in the Pacific UDTs had the safety of the water. We loved it in the water, that was the safest place to be. An individual could duck and swim away if a spot was drawing fire.

The danger for the UDTs was in getting into and out of the water and in riding the boats to and from the beach. Once you were in the water, it helped make you safe. The poor guys at Normandy had to walk right up on the beach to try to outrun the rising tide.

The UDTs and SEAL Teams cannot be easily described. They have skills, courage, perseverance, tolerance for discomfort and pain. What they all are is dedicated. If they weren't, they would never have volunteered and completed the program. They seek out the challenge, they stand in line to get in. A lot of them don't make it, but they all want to try.

You have to like the challenge. Maybe it's the competition in the hardest arena there is. You have to believe in what you are doing and be willing to put yourself to the test.

On Iwo Jima, I had a radioman with me so that our boat could stay in touch with our APD further out. That radio was what we called a handie-talkie, an SCR 536, about a foot long and five inches square. If we could reach out with that radio half a mile on a clear day, we felt we had pretty good commo.

I spoke to a SEAL sometime back who was wearing a piece of equipment I didn't recognize. It was just a box that could be put in a large shirt pocket. When I asked him what it was, he told me it was his radio. When I asked him how far could it reach, "anywhere in the world" was his answer. That's just one small example of how much the technology has changed.

But it's the same man today who uses that equipment who would have been swimming off the Pacific beaches in World War II. The men themselves are individuals who have dedicated themselves to a mission, recognized its challenges, and accepted them. They are the guys in white hats, the good guys. And they are the very best we have.

Just like a good football player or other athlete, the men of the Teams accept that part of the game that includes the danger, the challenge. And there is no single type who can be pointed to and described as "a man who could be a SEAL or UDT." In my own unit, I had all types of men, all of them gung ho, but different.

Of my own six-man NCDU, who all became part of UDT 15, one was *a Golden Gloves boxing champion. Another, my own swimming partner, turned out to be a published poet. One became an engineer after the war. And one of the men of UDT 15 who lost his eyesight that terrible night off Iwo Jima, he beat his personal challenges and became a successful attorney-at-law.*

■ Chapter 14

PRISONERS OF WAR

On 9 July 1944, a very secret UDT mission took place that would turn out to be unique in the history of the teams. The Balao-class submarine USS *Burrfish* (SS 312) on only her third wartime patrol moved out from Pearl Harbor under the command of William B. Perkins Jr. on a special operation to secretly examine the Japanese-held islands of Peleliu and Yap in the Palau group of the far western Caroline Islands. To conduct the reconnaissance of the islands, the *Burrfish* was transporting a volunteer group of men from UDT 10.

The men consisted of two officers, a chief, and five enlisted men, all from UDT 10. The chief was Howard "Dynamite Joe" Roeder, who was already a veteran of UDT 2, and a number of the men had come into UDT 10 from the OSS Maritime Unit group. The reconnaissance operation was to be launched and received from the submarine, the men using rubber boats for transport.

The reconnaissance of Peleliu took place without major incident outside of an early mechanical failure on the submarine *Burrfish*. The men of the UDT-10 detachment were able to help in the repairs on the submarine working on the outside hull of the sub with a skill that surprised the crew of the *Burrfish*.

The next examination was of the island of Yap. The first rubber boat

The UDT swimmer in the center of the photo is wearing the 1940 model Lambertsen Underwater Respiratory Unit (LARU). The two swimmers on either side of the man with the LARU are both wearing early model dry suits for protection from cold water. In front of the swimmers is a stack of tetrytol explosive haversacks and individual blocks. The officer on the left is Vice Admiral Daniel Barbey, the commander of the U.S. Seventh Amphibious Force during WWII. On the right is Commander Francis Douglas Fane who brought the UDTs forward after WWII.

U.S. Navy

recon was conducted by Lieutenant Massey and a four-man swimmer team who examined the south end of the island. Chief Roeder and four men went on the last recon of the island during rough seas. The rubber boat operator was Chief Ball, who remained with the small craft while the UDT swimmers went into the island. The UDT men never returned.

With dawn approaching, Chief Ball had to return to the submarine with a single swimmer who had not been able to complete the swim in to shore. In spite of the great danger, the *Burrfish* patrolled just off the reefs of Yap hoping to see some signal of the lost UDT men in her periscope. With the weather deteriorating and the Japanese having possibly detected her, the submarine finally had to leave Yap waters.

The lost men from UDT 10 were Chief Howard Roeder, John MacMahon, and Robert Black. Documents later captured from the Japanese indicated that the men had been taken prisoner by the Japanese garrison on Yap after several days of search. In spite of what were probably serious interrogation techniques, the UDT men told only the cover story they had been given to tell in this eventuality.

Records indicated that the UDT men were shipped out to a Japanese prison camp in the Philippines when all additional records of them end. It is suspected that the men were part of a group of prisoners being transported in a military ship, against the Geneva Convention and other articles of war, that was probably struck and sunk by an Allied submarine.

All of the men of the UDT detachment, including the three men lost, received the Silver Star for their part in the operation. No more submarine-launched UDT operations were conducted for the balance of WWII. These three men are the only known POWs ever captured from the Teams.

Because of Japanese military policies, POWs were guarded by some of the worst dregs in the Japanese military. Besides wounded and disabled soldiers, who would have little love for the men of the forces that injured them, the Japanese also assigned sadists, drunks, and the simply inept as prison camp guards. This resulted in Allied POWs suffering some of the worst treatment imaginable. And the larger, fitter Americans were particular targets for some of the smaller-statured, insecure captors.

The Japanese treatment of prisoners caused the military men who had their comrades imprisoned to feel a deep and lasting hatred. There was a poor reckoning after the war in the war crimes trials of Japanese prison camp guards. It is indicative of how the Japanese treated prisoners that their own people were terrified to surrender, preferring death. Part of this attitude can be blamed on the Bushido code, which forbade surrender over death. But some of the less advanced Japanese troops may have thought they would simply receive the treatment their own people dealt out to the enemy.

Frank Meder Jr., Machinist's Mate, Second Class

We started training in Fort Pierce in September–October 1944 with about 700 to 800 fellows and finished with somewhere around 80. Up in Little Creek, Virginia, while waiting to be assigned to an amphibious ship, the announcement went out that the Navy was looking for volunteers for a suicide squad. This announcement was just one of the list of such things they read out every day. But I had been standing musters and basically doing make-work for a while and just wanted out of Little Creek. So I volunteered for UDT training.

The announcement was actually read off as volunteers for a suicide squad. None of us really believed that and it was probably just the announcer's way of showing his dislike of such units. For me, it was a way out of the area. If you had experienced Little Creek back in those days, even volunteering for a suicide squad wouldn't have seemed a strange way of getting out. Even after I arrived at Fort Pierce and was involved with the rugged training, I still thought that announcement had been a joke.

But the training was tough, though I didn't have a whole lot of trouble with it. Every day I saw more and more of the big guys dropping out and I would just say to myself, "I'm still here." Outside of maybe a stronger will, I don't think I had anything more than those bigger guys who dropped out. Probably much like me, the guys who volunteered for training originally just wanted out of something else. But I decided I wanted the program, so they quit along the way and I made it through. The hardest part of training for me was all of the running. The swimming, PT, and other things didn't bother me at all; I had been raised around the water.

As far as Fort Pierce went, I had been used to small towns, so the lack of facilities didn't bother me. The bugs that were all over the training areas, those bothered me a little bit. You can never get completely used to things like that. Even though I was from the New Jersey shore area and we had biting bugs up there, it was nothing compared to the swarms down in Fort Pierce.

After the final few of us graduated from the Fort Pierce training, we were sent out to Maui to continue with UDT training. At Fort Pierce, we had mostly gone through physical conditioning and demolition training. In Maui, the emphasis was on swimming. Besides swimming every day, we really got into the more sophisticated end of demolition training.

We learned how to blast ramps through lava rock so that amphibious vehicles could climb out of the water, and techniques for blasting coral heads so that incoming amphibs wouldn't dig just one track in and flip over. But the majority of the demolition training centered on lava work, blasting that kind of rock flow out of the way.

Though I had swum a lot as a kid off the Jersey shore, the waters off Maui were a lot nicer. The water was clearer and a whole lot warmer than the ocean off of Jersey ever got. Swimming around the coral was pretty and it held a lot of appeal to me. So did catching lobsters and other seafood. That part of the training I enjoyed a lot.

Back at Fort Pierce, we had been the first Team to leave the post with the designation of UDT. Other units had graduated before us, but they were put together into UDTs at Maui. But my Team, UDT 18, had left Florida with our designation and basic complement of officers and men.

Once we completed training at Maui, UDT 18 was sent to the Southwest Pacific, where we operated with the Seventh Australian Division in retaking Borneo from the Japanese. That turned out to be the last major amphibious operation of the war. At Borneo, we did something unique in the way of an operation that was copied years later in the Desert Storm.

Our operation was what we called a "hit-and-run." We would blast the beach one day, do a recon, and blast another beach somewhere else the next day. We did that action for four consecutive days. By this point in the war the Japanese knew that when the UDT swimmers had come into a beach and blown up the obstacles, an invasion of that site would take place very soon. By blasting different beaches, we were able to keep them off guard so that they never could figure out where we were going to hit. We also did it so they would move forces to reinforce the beaches we weren't planning to hit later.

The last day, we conducted the actual invasion reconnaissance and demolition swim. Then we led the assault troops in to the beach, which was also part of our job. Our deceptions had apparently worked well; the troops landed against relatively little opposition compared to what had been expected.

Though we had been pretty lucky on our operation, some other UDTs hadn't done so well. Even when the enemy didn't hit you, you had to worry about short rounds from friendly fire landing near you. One UDT had been bombed by accident when a flight of U.S. planes mistook them for enemy swimmers. But this was just something that happens in wartime.

For our operations off Borneo, the higher command had changed their tactics a little bit to account for us being in a target area. As we were going in to the beaches in our boats, we had the best fire support available. Naval gunfire came from everything from destroyer escorts to battleships, three-inch to sixteen-inch guns. And they pounded the beaches and the areas inland.

When we neared the beaches and began our real work, the heavy fire lifted. All we had to protect us then was the cover of the water and the LCS(L) (Landing Craft, Support) gunboats with their cannons and rockets which came in very close behind us and pounded the enemy positions. Those gunboats were right behind us and could see us, so they knew where we were and to shoot over us.

When we went in to do our preinvasion work, we were dropped off individually at 150-foot intervals. The swim-buddy concept that is so important now, we just didn't have yet. Our basic unit, what I think of when asked about the Team, was my platoon. That platoon was the unit of men that I was closest to. We worked together and supported each other. But for the operation itself, we operated as individuals with a common goal.

The men in the Teams, then or now, are dedicated men who want to be among the best. For forty years after the war I just didn't speak about what I did. The UDTs were very secret during the war and the habit of not talking just stuck. Now, with the expansion of the UDT-SEAL Museum, our association, and everything, we get together and remember about the good times we had.

Even though we worked very hard during an operation, we had fun during the other times. Going out on weekends when we could, we would go fishing demo-style. Half-pound blocks of TNT were much faster than using a hook and line. Using a PR (landing craft), we would chase whales and fish, catch lobster, and generally have a good time.

The work was tough, and the ops off of Borneo had some very hard aspects. Though we never really thought we had been given a job we couldn't do, there were some parts that were a bit harder than others.

Off of Borneo, I bailed out of the boat that had brought us in to the beach, and they tossed my charges into the water off the other side. Swimming up to my explosives, I would start towing them in to the beach. The packs floated, but there still were a bunch of them. Swimming in with one hundred pounds of explosives behind you is a chore. And with my explosives in tow, and the bullets flying past my head, that was the time I thought, "What am I doing here?"

Concentration on the job at hand keeps you from thinking about just what's going on around you. Swimming in, placing your charges, tying the lines up, swimming out, and getting picked up keeps you occupied. It's later that the thoughts of just where you had been and what you had done come up and you can get a little scared.

After operations, I had buddies of mine come up and tell me how they had seen enemy bullets flying all around me. I had just continued with my job and never even knew someone was shooting at me in particular. But the other guys told me how they had seen this one enemy sniper up in a tree shooting at me. I hadn't seen the guy and just didn't pay any attention to the little splashes around me.

Our job was what we were doing. Swimming in and blasting the beaches open was what we were trained for. There wasn't any fear because we just didn't have the time to think about it. Our thoughts were centered on getting in to the beach, doing our job, and getting out. That's what makes it work. If you have time to think about where you're going and what you're going to face, then you can get scared.

Doing the beach reconnaissance and demolition swim, that was what we did well and the water was our cover. Later, leading in the invasion boats, that was scary. In the boats, you could see all of what was going on around you. And you didn't have a lot to do. That was when you could think about things.

The troops we were working with were great. Mostly they were Australians and were veterans of serious campaigns. The troops we were with had a great deal of respect for us, and we had the same for them. These were the men who had held out against Rommel at To-bruk in North Africa. The Seventh Australian Division was called the "Rats of Tobruk." These were the men who had held out for thirty-three days under siege by the Germans. When they were finally brought out of the desert, they did all of the mopping up in the New Guinea operations and then were the troops at Borneo with us.

Those men thought we were the greatest. We blew open the beaches for them. We thought those guys were great troops and tough fighters. For us, we were just doing the job we had trained for.

Right before we left Borneo, we transferred over eight tons of tetrytol to the beaches for the use of the Australian army engineers. Moving that much explosive was work, but it wasn't something we weren't used to. We knew explosives, how to handle them, and what to expect. Some of the other people who were observing us may have gotten a bit nervous.

While on guard over the supplies, UDT men would take a smoke break. Lighting up cigarettes near a pile of explosive crates might look dangerous, but we knew exactly what we were doing and how to be careful. It didn't bother us and we really didn't care if it bothered them. We tossed around charges like some people just wouldn't believe.

We had been sent back to the States after the Borneo ops to train in cold-water operations. We would be among the first troops to go in against Japan itself. Before we reported for training in California, we were all given a six-day leave. But our leave was cut short and the Navy gathered us all up quickly.

We were rounded up in Los Angeles by the police, firemen, shore patrol, anyone they could send out to find us. We were taken back to Oceanside, California, then moved across the highway to Camp Pendleton, where we boarded a plane for Alameda. In Alameda, we boarded another plane that flew us all the way to Guam. That was my first plane ride and it was a long one. In Guam, the Navy had a ship waiting for us with all of our gear on board.

We had been scooped up in dress uniforms and didn't have a thing with us. We were picked up at the airfield in Guam and moved to our ship in dump trucks. There, we finally had a chance to change uniforms while we were under way to Okinawa. Once we arrived in Okinawa, we picked up UDT 21 and continued on to Japan. We joined Task Force 31 of the Third Fleet off of Honshu Island, Japan, and were ready to invade. That's when we learned that the war had ended.

There was a big relief that went through many of us when we heard about the Japanese surrender, and we were all thankful for it. Dropping the atomic bomb was one of the greatest things that could have been done. It saved thousands, if not millions, of lives. Many of those lives would have been members of UDTs, but it wasn't our lives, that were saved as much as hundreds of thousands of Marines and Army soldiers who would have fought to take Japan. Millions of men, on both sides, were probably saved by the dropping of the atomic bombs.

We were the first to go in to Japan from the fleet, us and UDT 21. The only thing in front of us as we went in to the beach was a minesweeper, and it didn't land. Our landing craft went right into the entrance of Tokyo Bay. Things were a little hectic at first during our reconnaissance and we were a little apprehensive about the situation. I don't think everyone quite believed the war was really over, and they sent us in to check things out.

Our main purpose in going in was to demilitarize all of the dock areas. While checking for mines and booby traps, we would also collect up all of the Japanese weapons and make sure any gun emplacements were rendered safe. We secured the area for the troops to come in.

The people of Japan were beaten, there wasn't any doubt of it when we saw the population. My first contact with a Japanese citizen was with a man who spoke English as well as I did. He was a Japanese officer who had gone to the University of Chicago before the war.

Our UDT had gone into Yokosuka Naval Base and that officer was in charge of a group of young men that we would probably refer to as sea cadets. We had walked into them while they were cooking something in a big pot; it looked like a bunch of roots to me, sweet potatoes or whatever. It certainly didn't look any good to me.

All of the personnel at the base had to be rounded up and I stood

The Japanese commander of a small fort overlooking Tokyo Bay hands his sword over to Commander Clayton of UDT 21 at the end of WWII. This was the first formal surrender of Japanese soil to a U.S. serviceman, an action that later drew the anger of General Douglas MacArthur.

Barry G. McCabe Collection

with the group of cadets and that officer while other UDT men moved through the area. The group of us were standing in the courtyard and I was sort of standing guard while the rest of the area was cleared. That officer and I just had a little general conversation while the buildings were being cleared and everyone else was brought out into the courtyard.

That first day didn't really prepare us for what we found later. As the UDTs moved up and down the shores, it seemed that every little fishing village we went into had its share of suicide submarines and suicide boats. Our mission now was to destroy all those munitions and war materials. We spent weeks just blowing up midget submarines. Among the stuff we found were caves full of torpedoes. There were even caves full of boxes of Belgian shotguns. Anything that the Japanese home guard could possibly have used against invaders, we found in those caves and villages. We found them, took them out to sea, and destroyed them.

The cost to an invading force would have been tremendous. From just what I saw, the cost to us would probably have reached 80 percent casualties. I saw maps of the beaches we would have been assigned to for Operation CORONET, the invasion of the southernmost island of Japan, Kyushu. The Japanese would not have given up one inch of the island without killing as many of us as they could have first.

Later in October, we boarded our APD for the trip home. We arrived in Southern California and our Team was decommissioned within a matter of days. Many of the guys left the Navy and went back home. Because I was a machinist's mate, my rate was frozen and I was returned to the fleet. Being sent from the Pacific to the Atlantic, I made seven trips across the ocean, ferrying troops back home. And that was in December and I wasn't prepared for the cold weather. I didn't even own a heavy Navy peacoat. Finally, I was discharged from the service in June 1946.

Personally, I never had a very high opinion of the Japanese or their military during the war. Most of this was due to their treatment of prisoners of war, which was cruel, to say the least. I had the opportunity to see both Germany and Japan after the war. To me, the Germans were a much humbler people than the Japanese. We really didn't see much of the Japanese fighting man, their combat troops. What we saw in Japan were the young kids and the older men who weren't fit for combat.

■ Chapter 15

THE LAST INVASION

The final major operation of the UDTs during World War II wasn't done against enemy resistance. Instead, it was the landings of the UDT men ahead of any other U.S. forces on the main islands of Japan. Though Japan had surrendered and the emperor had put out the call to his subjects to lay down arms and not resist, there was a question as to whether those orders would be obeyed.

So, as on so many occasions before, the UDTs went in first. Beach reconnaissance was done on the offshore waters, but a great deal of additional reconnaissance was done on dry land. For their last operation of the war, the UDTs would again be walking instead of swimming, as the NCDUs had done before them.

The men of the UDTs examined the beaches for mines and the docks and harbor facilities for booby traps. In addition, all of the Japanese naval craft that remained in Tokyo Harbor, along with any intact harbor defenses, were to be rendered safe. Some UDT operators pulled breechblocks from shipboard cannon and dropped them over the side. Others peered into dark, wet areas under docks and piers. But there were no incidents and the surrender plans went forward.

Later the men of the UDTs were given other assignments in Japan. And during these operations, the men learned just how expensive the final battles of World War II could have been.

Barry G. McCabe, Lieutenant (junior grade)

About a month prior to my receiving my commission as an officer in the United States Navy in 1944, a request went out for volunteers for an outfit known as combat demolition. They wouldn't tell us a lot about the organization, but they did tell us one of the requirements was that you had to be able to swim. Most of the fellows I was with at Columbia for my officers' training were going into amphibious operations, which meant ship-to-shore movements. That wasn't something I was particularly interested in, and since I could already swim, the demolition outfit sounded interesting.

A chief signed me up, took my information, and that was about it. When I came in to volunteer, the chief asked me how far I could swim. After I told him I figured about three miles, he said: "That's okay, we'll teach you how to swim."

That was the extent of my indoctrination into combat demolition.

In the month that followed, rumors were the order of the day. I was about the only person out of maybe 1,500 young officers at Columbia who volunteered for the new outfit. Scuttlebutt quickly had the outfit known as a suicide squad and my classmates referred to me as "Boom-boom."

The thing that was probably the most frightening centered around our leave after graduation. My classmates all received between a week to ten days of leave between the time they received their commission and the time they had to report for duty. I received a month's leave.

My friends all told me that the Navy gave me the long leave because I would never have the chance to go home again. Since I was all of nineteen years old at the time, all of the rumors tended to make me a bit apprehensive.

After my leave, I went down to Fort Pierce by train. It was early in the morning sometime in November and my first exposure to the training was interesting. As the train pulled in I heard all of these bombs going off and various explosions in the distance. When I reported for duty, I was told the unit was now known as underwater demolition. The term combat demolition wasn't heard again.

Getting involved with the training, I quickly learned how tough it was. But I was also becoming very enthusiastic about it. The hours were horrible and there was a lot of physical endurance training. But we also learned a lot about using explosives. It seemed to me that the primary emphasis was on demolitions and using explosives.

One thing that made the training quite unique was that I was right down in the mud with the enlisted men. Even though I hadn't spent any time at all in the regular Navy as a young officer, I knew this situation wasn't a normal one. Whether you had a commission or not, everyone did exactly the same training. You were hungry, you were bitten by bugs, you were dirty, wet, and tired, and so was everyone else along with you.

After about eight weeks of training at Fort Pierce, we all went on to Maui for further training. Once we arrived at Maui, we immediately began concentrating on swimming. We swam just about every day,

A UDT operator attached a Hagensen pack of high explosives to the center of a steel hedgehog obstacle.

U.S. Navy

and there was a five-miles-plus swim at least once a week. We would spend all day in the water sometimes. There was also a lot of additional rubber boat and explosives work.

During our training we had a number of individual tasks that we would focus on for concentrated periods of time. One of these tasks involved the rubber boat training. We would go out in the boats and paddle them over distance. We learned how to get some rhythm to our strokes and see how fast we could move while still going in a straight line. We had to flip the boats over in the water and then move them right side up. Many of the things we had to do in rubber boats training we never expected to do in the field, but we did them until we knew how to do just about anything with the small craft.

The idea was for us to feel totally comfortable with our equipment and abilities. There were hours of drill in things like swimming, rubber boats, and working with explosives. We would tie charges together on land, and in the water, and half in, half out of the water with waves crashing down on you. Then we would blow the things up. You got to the point where you could properly tie a charge into a primacord line in any situation. It became second nature to you.

The hours of swimming were supplemented with other exercise. We had hours of breathing practice. There was no real scuba gear available to us. When we went underwater, it was with the strength of your own breath. On land, we learned you could hold your breath longer than when swimming in the water. So we practiced the one to be better at the other.

We did some unusual training where we had to jump off a thirty-foot-high pier into the water while wearing full combat gear, sometimes even packs. That one we did a number of times. We had to do things that were unusual, things that you wouldn't normally run into during a day's work, not even in the UDTs. It was to help you learn to cope under almost any circumstance. This philosophy had been followed at Fort Pierce as well.

During our explosives training, we had learned how to tie a number of charges together with primacord so that they could all be detonated together. Individual primacord leads from the separate charges were tied into the main primacord line. To make sure we could tie the knots correctly, we had to tie them behind our backs, underwater, while holding our breaths. Once you can get through that exercise correctly, doing the correct knot becomes second nature.

After my graduation from training at Maui, I was sent out to join up with UDT 21. The Team was on its way back from the invasion at Okinawa and I met up with them on their trip in to the United States. We came back to the States at the end of July 1945.

The UDTs were created because there was a hole in the capabilities of the Amphibious Force to land on an enemy beach. This gap in abilities can be described in one word which is known to everyone who served in the Pacific in WWII: Tarawa.

Even though there was aerial reconnaissance that showed the reefs—intelligence dug out every piece of data that could be found on the area—the details were wrong. The recons hadn't worked and the landing craft were hung up on the offshore reefs. The Marines had had to wade in to Tarawa carrying all of their equipment; many of them drowned and others were picked off by the Japanese. And much of this was because the water over the reefs was too shallow.

An outfit was formed from the Seabees and Naval Combat Demolition Units to scout out the beaches, recon the waters, and blast the reefs. This new outfit was the Underwater Demolition Teams. And the Japanese learned from their errors as well.

The Japanese became clever in making obstacles of all kinds. Where there weren't enough reefs, they put up other blockages. Cribs

UDT trainees during UDTR basic instruction charge a rock outcropping with high explosives. The individual demolition charges are strung together with detonating cord "mains." The detonating cord will initiate all of the charges at once in a single huge explosion.

U.S. Navy

of logs were built in the water and filled with rocks. Concrete barriers with steel rails pointing outward were put up. And if there was space between the obstacles for landing craft to fit, the Japanese would string wires up attached to anti-boat mines. Striking the mines or the wires would cause the detonation of a large charge of explosives.

And in the UDTs, we learned how to destroy these and other kinds of obstacles. We filled the need for someone to go and see what the situation was, measure the waters, and chart the obstacles. After the information was delivered back to command, the UDTs could go back to the same area and blast the way free for the landing craft to arrive. When necessary, men from the same unit that went in on the recon swim would guide the first waves of landing craft in to the proper sites. But for myself and my Team, that mission was over.

In spite of not yet having been with UDT 21 on an invasion, I really didn't feel like I had missed anything so far. The training I had gone through was rigorous and complete. In spite of just having returned to the United States, I was looking forward to going overseas with the Team when they left again. The Team reported to Oceanside, California, for cold-water training to prepare for the invasion of Japan.

One of the big differences in the invasion of Japan compared to the rest of the Pacific campaign was that the waters would be very cold. They took us up to lakes in the mountains and put us in the water to see how long we could stand it. This kind of thing really took your mind off of the invasion itself. Then the atomic bombs were dropped and Japan surrendered. The war was over.

Here I was, a brand-new nineteen-year-old Navy ensign, and I had seasoned combat veterans under my command. As far as what the war had been like, I really hadn't experienced any of it yet. But some of my men certainly had. But I had a lot of learning myself to do yet and I probably didn't take into account that these men had a tremendous amount of experience among them. Some of the veterans in UDT 21 had landed with the NCDUs on Normandy Beach. And here I was, a nineteen-year-old officer telling them to stand at parade rest or whatever. I really didn't think of the consequences of that, but I learned.

When we heard that the bombs had been dropped, I thought that the war would be over and I would be going home soon. The war was over, but I wouldn't be seeing home anytime soon. Two UDTs were flown out to Guam, where they met ships loaded with all of their gear. And UDT 21 and UDT 18 were those two Teams.

We arrived in Tokyo Bay on August 28, 1945. The Japanese formal surrender was signed on 2 September on board the battleship Missouri. For about a month following that ceremony, we went up and down the coastline of Japan locating, gathering, and destroying suicide boats, midget submarines, and major weapons. But that first landing had been different.

When UDT 21 arrived at Japan, we were the first Americans to set foot on Japanese soil after the war. Before any troops arrived, paratroopers, anything. In a UDT of around one hundred men in five platoons, we would land in different places while checking out sites for the upcoming landing craft. One of the platoons had our commanding officer, Commander Clayton, on board when they arrived on a place called Futsusaki, a small peninsula at the mouth of Tokyo Bay.

Thought I wasn't with the platoon at the time, I have a copy of the picture of the Japanese commander at the small fort overlooking Tokyo Bay handing over his sword to Commander Clayton. That was the first formal surrender of Japanese soil to an American soldier.

Going in to Japan was an adventure and we were all a bit apprehensive. We only swam in once, during that first landing. That was to do a normal hydrographic reconnaissance and check for possible obstacles in the water. After that first time we would go in to shore in landing craft or our rubber boats depending on how we were conducting the mission.

We checked docks and beaches for mines and booby traps. And after the mission was over, we would return to our ship for the night. Even though the Japanese had said they gave up, the official surrender hadn't been signed yet. So there were mixed emotions about the war being over—maybe not all of the Japanese military had gotten the word everything was over.

There weren't any incidents for us at all. There was probably apprehension on both sides, given that the Japanese had lost and we were landing in their country. But nothing happened where we were. Later there were reports of isolated Japanese units elsewhere in the Pacific that continued fighting after the war was over. But they just hadn't gotten the word yet, or they didn't believe it.

Our role in UDT 21 in going in first was the same as it had been all through the war, to try to make the way in safe for the troops to land. When we got over there and started landing along the coast of the main island of Japan, we found dozens if not hundreds of caves on the shore. In these caves were hundreds of suicide boats. There were also midget submarines. Our job was to get rid of these weapons and it soon turned into a problem because there was just so many of them.

At first we tried burning the boats. Then because of the danger of hidden explosives, we would take them far out to sea and take axes to them. What went through my mind as well as others' was just how horrible any invasions would have been if we hadn't dropped the atom bombs.

With the vast volumes of materials and weapons we found, there was no question that resistance to an invasion of Japan would have been catastrophic. A lot of people on both sides would have been killed in that operation.

Japanese midget suicide submarines being removed from their caves along the shores of the main Japanese islands. This Kairyu "Sea Dragon" miniature submarine would have been launched from its rail trolley to attack Allied ships with its several thousand pound explosive warhead. Shown here are just two of the dozens of such suicide weapons destroyed by UDT 21 in their post-WWII operations.

Barry G. McCabe Collection

All of our troops would have been exposed to the hundreds of suicide boats and midget submarines we were uncovering. Losses among the Allied troops and ships would have been horrendous. The Japanese were terrific warriors. They could fight to the very end and then try to take you with them. And that was not just the soldiers. Every man, woman, and child on the main islands would have done the same thing to the best of their ability. They would have been defending their emperor and their religion.

The atomic bombs had been horrible in and of themselves. But the alternative would have been so very much worse. The alternative to the bombs would have been hundreds of thousands of casualties on both sides. In spite of everything, the atom bombs were the fastest and cleanest way to bring the war to an end.

Once the emperor had said the war was over, the change in the Japanese people toward us was amazing. They were polite and deferential. I walked among them after the war, meeting men who were younger than I was, in their mid teens really. These men had been trained to be the suicide boat pilots for all of those small craft we had destroyed.

Even those young men were polite to us. We were welcomed up and down the coastline. And this was only because the war was over, the emperor had said so. It was like the difference between night and day the way the people changed.

When we finally returned to the United States for the last time, I knew I was going to go to college and finish my education on the GI Bill. I stayed in the Navy a few months longer and received my promotion to lieutenant, junior grade. Then I just left the Navy and continued my life in the civilian world.

It was right after the war that the term frogman was coined, sometime between the end of 1945 and the beginning of 1946. We never used the term at all in the service; we always called ourselves demo men. It was some civilian writer, I think for the Honolulu Advertiser, who came up with the name when he was writing a story about us after we had finally been declassified. But the term stuck as a great name and we've used it for the men of the UDTs ever since.

In the years after the war I didn't even think much about what had happened. In recent years I met the people in the UDT-SEAL Museum where our history is being saved.

Now, I'm active in helping prepare young men for careers in the SEALs. Captain Andrew Bisset set up a program to help these young men who want to be SEALs prepare for the extensive training at BUD/S (Base Underwater Demolition/SEAL training) in Coronado. And we don't just prepare them for the physical part of the training but also the mental part. Becoming a SEAL is probably at least fifty-fifty, half mental and half physical.

As a WWII frogman, I can see that the young men going into the Teams today are a lot better prepared for what they will face than we ever were. But they have to be now, warfare having changed so much over the last fifty years.

The training we had and the training they have today is similar though, in one way: it's really tough. We had Hell Week and they still do today. That's one of the big breakers. And we both had technical training. But ours centered primarily on explosives. Theirs today is generations ahead of what we had.

As a WWII frogman, we only had a pair of swim fins, a face mask, a knife, a watch, and little else. All of a man's gear then would have fit in a small bag. Today they have vast amounts of equipment they have to learn to operate. A single man's gear in the SEAL Teams today can fill a small room, or at least a large closet.

To become a SEAL today, you have to have physical capability, upper body strength, the ability to swim great distances, and the ability to run great distances under any conditions—run, run, and then run some more. Run with boots on, run in sand, run uphill, run carrying things, run doing all of the above at the same time. That physical aspect is the one best known to the public.

But the other aspect, the harder one to build, is the attitude, the mental discipline. People coming in to training have to have the desire to become a SEAL more than anything else. Young men go into Navy recruiting offices saying that they want to become a SEAL, but they want to finish their education first. That's fine, the individual isn't ready quite yet to join the Teams. But it's a good reason and they can grow further as they learn.

Then there's the men who come in to join who say that they're qualified to become a Navy officer, but they want to be a SEAL so badly they're willing to go the enlisted route just to get in. The job is tough no matter what your rank once you get to BUD/S training, but there are more openings available for enlisted men than officers just because of the way the Teams are organized.

The failure rate for young men going into BUD/S from across the country straight from the recruiters and boot camp is about 70 percent. We help recruit for the SEAL Teams up in the northern East Coast. And we have SEAL candidates come up to us from all over the country. We help prepare them for BUD/S both physically, mentally, and psychologically. We tell them that when they get out there in training at BUD/S, it will be some of the most draining and discour-

aging work they will ever do in their lives. But they must have the attitude to get through.

We help these young men learn how to swim, run, and work out better. And we test them. The reason so many young men fail at BUD/S is not just that it's hard. Rather they were never prepared properly from their first day in the Navy. The recruiter has a quota to fill, and these young men come in saying that they want to be a SEAL and that's just fine with the recruiter. They're in the Navy whether they pass BUD/S or not. If the young man can pass the standard screening test, he gets in. But the level of the test, we feel, is too low. So we test our candidates at a higher level. And our young men have an 85 percent success rate in passing BUD/S.

That's better for the Teams, and for the Navy.

To have been in the Teams, then or now, is an accomplishment. Accomplishing the objective, no matter how hard, gives you a boost in your own eyes. You can look back on what you had to do and see that you got the job done.

■ Chapter 16

SCOUTS AND RAIDERS

The Scouts and Raiders continued their operations in both the Atlantic and Pacific theaters well after their initial operations in North Africa. The actions in the Mediterranean continued with additional personnel being trained at North African bases as well as at Fort Pierce. The Scouts and Raiders operated heavily in support of actions in the Italian campaign, especially during the several amphibious landings in Italy. The emphasis during the Italian operations was on scouting and reconnaissance duties.

A few S&R personnel were involved with hands-on intelligence-gathering operations off the beaches of France in preparation for D day. For the Normandy landings themselves, S&R personnel were available and were primarily involved with leading the initial landing craft waves in to shore. Operating from command ships, the S&R personnel were not able to use the most efficient means at their disposal to guide in the craft by infiltrating the beach areas the night before and setting up signaling stations. S&R personnel in the Mediterranean theater also operated as part of the Operation DRAGOON forces.

The three Scouts and Raiders officers lost during combat operations at Anzio in the Mediterranean Theater. On the left is Lieutenant (jg) Jerry Donnel, in the center is Lieutenant (jg) Carmen F. Pirro, and on the right is Lieutenant (jg) Kenneth E. Howe.

L. L. Culver Collection

Emphasis at the Scout and Raider School after the Normandy and Atlantic operations were completed was on training an officer corps in Scout and Raider skills. Once qualified, the officers would be able to act in a staff capacity for operations in the Pacific theater. Staff duty not being something that held a lot of appeal to many S&R School graduates, a number of the officers managed to get into the field and operate as often as they could.

Rear Admiral Dick Lyon, USN (Ret.)

During World War II I went from a Yale undergrad to a graduate of the Columbia University Midshipman's School, which made me an officer and a gentleman by order of Congress in all of ninety days—what was then called a "90-day wonder." I enlisted in the Navy while still at Yale on 9 October 1942. It was while I was at Columbia as a midshipman that a special recruiter came to the school shortly before our class's graduation.

The notice on the bulletin board read, "Looking for volunteers, must be strong swimmer." That kind of had my name on it, as I had spent more than a little time on the Yale championship swimming team, including a period as the team's captain.

That little bit of information in the notice was about all we were told about the new unit for some time. A meeting was held with the students who were interested. Those students who continued to have an interest after the meeting were given the opportunity to volunteer. I signed my name and soon after graduation followed my orders down to Fort Pierce, Florida.

Facilities at Fort Pierce were what might be called spartan. There was a tent, some wooden containers which at one point had contained rubber boats, and a cot that I was told would be my bunk. The bunk wasn't the most comfortable thing in the world. But the level of physical activity demanded by training would soon make it a very welcome sight.

Now I was a member of class eight at the Navy Scouts and Raiders School at the ATB in Fort Pierce, Florida. The choice of Florida for the training base, it was later explained to me, was because Florida's topography is the closest in the United States to the land and water we would find in the South Pacific.

The physical training at S&R School was tough. And it has some aspects in common with BUD/S training today. There was a lot of stressful physical exercise. Ensign Bell was running the school while I was there. Rank didn't seem to mean much among the students or the faculty. A young lieutenant (jg) named Phil Bucklew was there and he had been with the Scouts and Raiders since their very beginning.

Being right there on the water at the ATB, we did a lot of swimming. But that wasn't the toughest thing. Lying absolutely still in the sand and grass, not moving at all for extended periods of time, was a lot harder than any of the other physical activities. And the simple reason for this was the hundreds of thousands of sand fleas and other biting insects that swarmed all over the island training site.

For me, the swimming part was okay. But for others in the class it was a lot harder. We helped each other get through the different parts of training, though no one could help in beating the insects.

Part of the original training staff at S&R School had been from an organization called "Tunney's Fish." These men had been Specialist As (Athletic) and they were in the Navy to help develop and run the physical training program for the entire service. They took a particular interest in the Scouts and Raiders training program, so we received some of the most advanced physical training and conditioning in the Navy at the time.

There was another unit training at Fort Pierce right alongside of us that we knew quite well, though we didn't work with them directly. The Naval Combat Demolition Units had come down much earlier from Camp Peary, Virginia, and became the forerunners of the Underwater Demolition Teams for the Pacific theater. These guys were in the camp right next to us and there was kind of a constant friendly rivalry between the two units. Things never got out of hand, but there were varying degrees of mischief performed between the units. Even then, it seemed a fellowship of special warfare was developing between different units who all went into harm's way.

The Scouts and Raiders trained in the same place where Naval Special Warfare had spent its infancy. SpecWar, as it is known today, was really born with the NCDUs at Camp Peary early in 1943. Though the UDTs operated in the Pacific, the Scouts and Raiders and NCDUs had performed critical roles in the actions conducted in the Pacific theater.

My class was a bit unusual in that it was made up entirely of officers. Previous S&R classes had been a mix of officers and enlisted men, but our class was mostly very junior officers; we had some fifty ensigns. Our few very senior guys were at the lofty rank of lieutenant (jgs). The class was all commissioned officers apparently because the graduates were expected to work as independent operators in the China theater. Later, I was assigned to the Seventh Fleet in the China area, acting as the scout intelligence officer for the fleet commander.

The mission of the Scouts and Raiders met the name very closely. We were training to scout an area and perform raids on targets at or near the beaches. As officers, we directed and led these operations, though not a lot of active operations took place during the war. The only real exception to this was in the China theater, where a number of the S&R officers did conduct field operations. Mostly, especially for me, we ended up doing staff work in the scouting field.

It was after the war, when I had extended for a year, that I was able to do some active scouting actions in China. That was a year I performed intelligence-gathering work and scouting, sending back my reports to the commander of the Seventh Fleet.

The early missions of the Scouts and Raiders were not known to us. They were a secret unit and their history wasn't one of the subjects taught during training. They had been actively involved in the war since Operation TORCH in November 1942. But none of us were given a lot of information as to where the previous classes had been involved. We didn't even know where we would be going.

About half of my class ended up along with me at the Administrative Command, Amphibious Forces, Pacific Fleet in Pearl Harbor, known as ADCOMPHIBPAC. From that command, we were assigned to do our jobs further out in the fleets.

My last assignment, and the one I extended for, was as part of the staff of the commander of the Seventh Fleet in his Intelligence Section. At the time the war ended I was in the Philippines and my job was to conduct reconnaissance and scouting ops in the area of the islands. The target we had been looking at particularly was the island of Mindanao, with an eye to conducting an amphibious assault at Davao.

The war ended and the operation never took place. I eventually found myself in Shanghai with Com Seventh Fleet, after taking troops up and landing them in Japan. We conducted the recon on the beaches off of Wakayama, Japan, where no obstacles were found.

The elements of the Thirty-third Infantry Division I had been traveling with landed safely and conducted their occupation duties soon afterward.

The reconnaissance conducted on the beach was done in much the same manner as those done by the UDTs. I swam in to check out the beach and the offshore waters since I was not only the scout officer, I was all of the scout troops as well.

Scouts and Raiders disappeared at the end of World War II. They had been a specialized unit that existed only during the war years. Any of the S&R men who remained in the Navy and later became part of Navy Special Warfare did so through the UDTs.

The mission of the UDT through World War II and Korea, and to a lesser degree in Vietnam, was making sure that a beach or landing site was cleared for an amphibious assault.

After World War II, I eventually transitioned into the UDT. I had left the Navy after WWII and returned to civilian life to finish my education. When the Korean War broke out, I went back into the Navy and went through UDTR with class two West Coast in 1951. Personally, I didn't have a lot of trouble going through UDTR. I was still a pretty young guy and my S&R training wasn't that far behind me. It was the presence in the water—the water training that was such a big part of Scout and Raider training—that helped me in UDTR. In the UDTs, swimming and water work was the primary mission, so they received a great deal of emphasis in training. That aspect of training hasn't changed to this day.

So to continue my career in Navy Special Warfare, I had joined with the UDTs on the West Coast, and soon was part of the recommissioning crew for UDT 5. The need for additional West Coast UDT operators to operate in the Korean War supplied the push to bring back UDT 5. It was very soon after commissioning that the Team had deployments on their way to Korea and were performing UDT operations there.

Our skipper in UDT 5 was Lou States, who had been on the original crew of UDT 11 during WWII, eventually becoming commanding officer of that same UDT in time for a number of their invasions. He came back during the Korean War as a reservist and helped in the commissioning of UDT 5. When he assigned me as the intelligence officer for the new UDT, Commander States made his feelings very clear.

"Now, Lieutenant Lyon," the CO told me, "I want to make something very clear. You don't have to be intelligent to be an intelligence officer."

He was looking right at me during that statement, and I wondered if he was trying to give me a message there. But it was a great Team. Many of our crew and officers were experienced WWII UDT men. We had fourteen officers and one hundred enlisted men in our original crew muster for UDT 5. With all of our WWII vets and the experiences they brought with them, I feel it was the best UDT Team the Navy ever had.

At the beginning of the 1950s in Korea, the UDTs were again involved in combat operations, theoretically only to the high-water mark. That was not where many of the missions ended. When UDT 5 was in Korea, I was assigned by my skipper to go into Wonsan Harbor in later 1951/early 1952 on an operation. There were reports that a very small enemy mine had been detected along the beaches in Wonsan Harbor. Wonsan Harbor is a huge harbor; the mouth of it is nearly ten miles across and there are nine beautiful little islands inside of its protected waters. We controlled the islands, waterways, and harbor, but Wonsan is well north of the thirty-eighth parallel, in what is now North Korea.

The mission I was given was to spot the suspected mines from a helicopter. The bird took off and landed from a Navy LST; I flew in that and spotted the mines, making note of their location. Then I would later return with a MINERON 3 explosives ordnance disposal officer and a two-man rubber boat. Going over the side of the boat, I would swim down with a pair of twenty-four-inch bolt cutters and shear through the mines' mooring cables. The mines would float to the surface, where they would be secured. We would then tow them to a nearby island and render them safe.

Through that procedure, we recovered some unusual new mines that were loaded aboard the APD Diachenko. They were returned to the States for study and are now on display in a Navy museum at Indian Head, Maryland. The new mine I had been specifically sent to recover we rendered safe and were able to get into the mine's casing to examine it. We found the still-dry packing slips within the mine casing, all written in Russian.

The Mark II SPU (Swimmer Propulsion Unit) as adopted by the UDTs in 1962. This was an improved model over the Mark I SPU, which was first used in the late 1950s. The SPU allowed a swimmer pair to operate over longer distances underwater and take more equipment or explosives along with them during an operation.

U.S. Navy

The Korean War started with the invasion of the North Koreans into South Korea on June 25, 1950. The war was fought up and down the peninsular country, with the Allied forces led initially by General Douglas MacArthur. The basic conflict of the war was never finally resolved. We still face one another in North and South Korea across the demilitarized zone on the thirty-eighth parallel. Weapons are aimed at each other and have been so from 1954 to this day.

The war in Korea was never declared and was the first major armed conflict between the Communist ideologies and the rest of the free world. It is often referred to by people today as the "forgotten war," even though over 50,000 Americans lost their lives in it. For myself, I left Korea in 1952 and watched Pusan fading over the horizon. I said good-bye and I will never go back to Korea. It remains a tragic situation, the constant state of tensions between North and South Korea. Though geographically it certainly appears that Korea should be one nation, politics and ideology prevent that from ever happening.

The most recent descendant of the WWII Teams is today's SEAL Teams. A SEAL is a member of the United States Navy Special Warfare Forces. The name is an acronym made up from the words SEa, Air, and Land. In view of the fact that the seal is a kind of a water animal, the name worked very well, since the SEALs spend a great deal of their time in the water. The mission or work of the Navy SEALs covers all facets of Navy Special Warfare, and there is real meaning to their name since they gain access to their area of involvement from the sea, the air, or on land—for instance by submarine, parachute, or by landing on a beach and moving overland.

UDTs were the Underwater Demolition Teams. Their mission was to conduct beach reconnaissance. Prior to a landing on a beach for an amphibious assault, the UDTs made certain that the beach area and offshore waters could be safely moved across by our armed forces in landing craft. And the UDTs would clear the beach of any obstacles, either natural or man-made, that blocked the safe approach of landing craft.

The NCDU were the Naval Combat Demolition Units and they were the first of the beach clearing units for amphibious invasions. The units were formed from volunteers primarily from the Navy Construction Battalions or Seabees. Assembled first in 1943 in Camp Peary, Virginia, the NCDUs subsequently moved their training site to Fort Pierce, Florida. They later became the Underwater Demolition Teams. Their mission was essentially the same as that of the UDTs.

Scouts and Raiders were to do scouting and intelligence gathering for commands needing the information for the planning of amphibious operations. The raiding portion of the name comes from their ability to quickly strike at objects and installations from the sea and then leave the area. The intelligence-gathering aspect of the S&R mission became important for landing troops on beaches. The Scouts and Raiders did not survive World War II as a unit and their mission became part of that of the UDT.

A Scouts and Raiders beach recon would involve going to examine the beach approaches and the beach itself up to the high-water mark on the shore. Scouts and Raiders worked surreptitiously from submarines, rubber boats, or other small craft to examine a beach area or raid against a target near the water. The missions were done in the dark of night and undercover. The great majority of the UDTs' missions involving reconnaissance work was done in broad daylight.

Though the Scouts and Raiders spent a lot of time swimming in the water during training, actual combat operations done as swimmers was much rarer. S&R people spent the majority of their time on land conducting scouting operations. Scouting would be done to gather intelligence on an area without making contact with the enemy. Raiding took the form of small, fast destructive actions conducted against the smaller enemy installations. The men of the Scouts and Raiders could work in platoon-sized units all the way down to operator pairs, depending on the mission requirements.

The UDT had a much more restrictive and defined mission statement during World War II and the island hopping campaign in the Pacific. Their primary mission was the recon of beaches prior to amphibious assaults. The critically important primary mission of the NCDUs, which they carried out in Europe, was the clearance of beach obstacles.

Even though the UDTs always concentrate on the effort of the Team as a whole, individuals can stand out. Doug Fane is one of these individuals: he was the first man to put together a written history of the Teams, their operations, and their creation in his book The Naked Warrior. As an individual, Doug Fane is one of those people whose mold was broken after he was made.

An integral part of Navy Special Warfare from the early years and into Korea, Doug Fane was one of the forward thinkers who moved to expand the UDTs' doctrine, their missions, and their capabilities. He helped ensure the continuation of the UDTs despite the cutbacks after World War II and their significant participation in any of the Navy's involvements up to and into the Korean War.

The original mission of the Underwater Demolition Teams limited them to operate to the high-water mark during World War II and for some time afterward. In Korea, this changed and we went up on dry land for operations, some of them well away from the water. Demolition raids were done, tunnels and rail lines were blasted, and prisoners were taken for interrogation. Over time all of that kind of work became part of the UDTs' capabilities.

The mission that was going to broaden Navy Special Warfare, the creation of the SEAL Teams or someone like them, was something that a number of us could clearly see was coming. When the SEAL Teams were commissioned in the early 1960s, I, like many others, was curious about the name. The SEa, Air, Land acronym made a lot of sense, and led to further training for me.

To become qualified into the SEALs as a Navy captain, I went to Lakehurst, New Jersey, in 1965. There, I received my wings and became jump-qualified. The term *pretty cool* took on a whole new meaning for me while jumping over Lakehurst from 5,000 feet in the wintertime. Comfortable *also wasn't one of the terms I would use to* describe that particular course of training.

■ Chapter 17

SACO AND AMPHIBIOUS GROUP ROGER

The Sino-American Cooperative Association (SACO) was part of a 1943 agreement between China and the United States on mutual military cooperation. The target of the cooperation would be the Japanese forces that had been in China since the early 1930s. The United States would provide material and trained personnel to act as instructors and advisers in their part of the agreement. The Chinese would supply facilities, support, and troops.

With U.S. assistance, the Chinese raised a guerrilla force capable of operating against the Japanese. U.S. personnel, considered far too valuable to risk by the Chinese government, were not allowed to even accompany their troops into the field on operations. Allowing the

U.S. advisers to fight was completely out of the question. It was not until October 1944 that this order was rescinded by Chiang Kai-shek himself.

Additional trained U.S. personnel were wanted for the SACO project on a priority basis to increase the number of Chinese guerrillas available for the final push against the Japanese empire. Under the code name Amphibious Group Roger, a training program to prepare U.S. volunteers to work with the Chinese guerrillas was established. Supplying men for Amphibious Group Roger was one of the last missions of the Scout and Raider School before it was closed at the end of the war.

Rudy Boesch, Command Master Chief Boatswain's Mate, USN (Ret.)

It was in April 1945 that I arrived in Navy boot camp. The war against Germany ended while I was in boot, but there was still heavy fighting against the Japanese in the Pacific. After we graduated from Boot Camp, they lined us all up and asked if anyone wanted to volunteer for a special outfit. When I put my hand up, I looked around figuring to see a hundred more hands raised. But mine was the only one up. I was told to step out of the formation and very soon I was on my way to Fort Pierce, Florida.

When I arrived in Fort Pierce I reported in to Scouts and Raiders School. At that time I had no idea who they were or what they did, but I eventually found out. The mission we were being trained for was to go to China to organize Chinese guerrillas for actions against the Japanese. In addition, the Chinese would be in on the first waves for the invasion of Japan.

It was a special mission, training guerrillas, and the Scouts and Raiders was one of the first of the Navy's Special Warfare units. While I was at Fort Pierce, the Underwater Demolition Teams were training at the same base, doing most of their active demolition training on the next island north of us. We were separated from the UDT trainees by only the width of a street between rows of tents. There wasn't any real interaction between the two units, besides the normal level of competition between two special outfits. There wasn't any animosity between us and the UDTs, at least none that I ever knew of.

As we got deeper into training, we started to learn how to speak Chinese. At this time I was all of seventeen years old, so all of this was a great adventure to me. The adventure continued as we went out to Lake Okeechobee and conducted inland water training.

It was while we were out in the swamps around Okeechobee that our instructors told us all to come in, that they had some announcements to make. They told us that we were going to stop what we were doing and go back to Fort Pierce. The atomic bombs had been dropped and the war with Japan was over.

Back at Fort Pierce we had all been living in tents. The base was being closed and they told us to start tearing down the tents and burning them. Even with the about five hundred students in my class, it still took us about five days to tear down the entire base except for the original civilian buildings.

Once the Amphibious Base at Fort Pierce was eliminated, we were put aboard troop trains and sent west to California. From California, about three hundred of us were put on board a ship heading for China. It looked like I was going to see China anyway, along with a bunch of my classmates. There was the three hundred of us going west, and we passed about three million U.S. troops coming east and going home.

When I left Fort Pierce and headed for China, I was back in the regular Navy. Going aboard a ship in China, I spent eighteen months basically guarding Navy assets. Finally returning to the States, I was put on board a destroyer, where I stayed two years. Now I had a chance to put in for some shore duty and I requested Germany, so the Navy put me in London, England.

It was while I was in London that I saw some literature on the UDTs, a write-up in All Hands magazine, and how they were looking for some volunteers. So I applied and was accepted. In 1951, I started UDTR (Underwater Demolition Team Replacement) training with class six on the East Coast at Little Creek. A winter class in southern Virginia.

There were no permanent instructors for the UDT training then. Volunteers and other men would be assigned from the Teams to run the training program. Most of what we did at Little Creek was physical. If the instructor couldn't find anything else for you to do, there was always PT or running. Demolitions training was given, but it wasn't as sophisticated as it became for later classes. What they wanted to know was if you wanted the program badly enough to go through all of the work involved. So the physical end was made the hardest.

Our Hell Week was memorable; it was cold and it was loud. Since we were a winter class, the weather was cold and the wind could come in from the Atlantic like a knife. The instructors didn't have the same restrictions as they do in training today. We didn't use ear protection, and as long as it didn't kill you or mess you up permanently, it was okay. So for training, they exposed us to blasts from twenty-pound demolition charges.

The blasts from those explosions are probably the reason my ears are still ringing today. Those twenty-pound packs would pick you right up off the ground and slam you back down. A bit rougher than the quarter-pound charges they use today. But class six finally finished training, and all of about twenty-five guys finished. From there it was on to the East Coast UDTs.

When Roy Boehm picked his men for the first SEAL Team, I was one of the people he chose. When the SEAL Team was first being put together, Roy wanted everyone in the Team to already be jump-qualified, or at least as many as possible. Not everyone in UDT 21 had gone to Jump School, so his pickings were limited. At that time I was one of the very few, if not the only, chief who was jump-qualified in UDT 21. When the names were called out at the muster on January 8, 1962, to go over to SEAL Team Two, I was the only chief petty officer listed. So I became the chief master at arms for SEAL Team Two, a position I held from 1962 to 1988.

Within a short time we had two more chiefs, a corpsman, Doc

Stone, and a storekeeper chief, Hoot Andrews, in the Team. I had been notified prior to that muster that I would be in the new SEAL Team. I had been on a Med (Mediterranean) deployment when I received orders to report back to Little Creek. When I returned to UDT 21, I was told that I would be reporting to the new SEAL Team. My only answer to that was, "What's a SEAL Team?"

But when the Team started, it was a very small, tight unit. Not everyone on the muster list had arrived; there were only about thirty-six men on board at the very start. But we stayed physically active from day one.

When we didn't do PT or running, we played soccer and other games that would build up and keep up our leg strength. At the start there wasn't a lot for the men to do; we were still lining up the schools and the specialized training. Once the training programs had been set up, everybody was going somewhere. When we started going to the Army schools and the Air Force and Marine schools, it seemed like you were going to a different school every week. And I went through my share of the training just like everyone else in the Team.

As the chief master at arms for the Team, I was responsible for keeping a handle on my bunch of hardworking, hard-playing new SEALs. But there really weren't any problems. Most of the men I had known for years in the UDT and I could handle them without any trouble. When it was necessary, I took care of all of the discipline myself and never had to bother the front office (CO) with it. It made it easier on the person that had to be disciplined and it made it easier on me that the officers didn't have to be officially involved.

One aspect of my job at SEAL Team Two was running the daily PT. I enjoyed doing PT myself, and when I was put in charge of the Team's PT, I really enjoyed it. There was a certain amount of fun in the fact that I always knew when I was going to stop doing a certain exercise or run. But the men who were following along never knew. We had a good physical outfit that was in top shape all of the time.

Everyone always made PT, no one got out of it without a good reason. And they all completed the runs, or at least as much as I wanted *them to. Sometimes, you could go a bit crazy running and jogging too much. Some games were played too, where guys would try and duck out of a run by hiding from the very end of the line. But those tricks worked only once. And they kept everyone trying which made things fun.*

■ Chapter 18

THE COST

World War II officially ended with the formal surrender of Japan on 2 September 1945. U.S. casualties included over 400,000 dead and almost 700,000 wounded. Of the approximately 3,500 men of the World War II UDTs and NCDUs, 148 individuals were wounded and 83 lost their lives.

By the war's end, thirty-four UDTs were under commission, with several of the Teams still in training, preparing for Operations CORONET and OLYMPIC, the invasions of the main Japanese islands that never had to be carried out. The almost thirty commissioned and staffed UDTs were gathered in Southern California in the fall of 1945 and decommissioned. Five postwar UDTs were assembled from the remainders of the UDT personnel who didn't go back to the fleet or left the service. Reorganizations kept the new postwar UDTs from being officially commissioned until more than six months after the end of the war.

On 21 May 1946, UDT 1 was commissioned, the first of the post-WWII UDTs. The UDTs were divided between the Atlantic and Pacific Fleets and would be stationed at Coronado, California, and Little Creek, Virginia. Even-numbered Teams would be on the East Coast and odd-numbered Teams on the West. In June 1946, UDTs 2 and 4 arrived at Little Creek after having been transferred to the Atlantic Fleet.

Commander Francis Douglas "Doug" Fane, USN (Ret.)

My father was English and drowned in the North Sea just before I was born; my mother was from a well-known family from Aberdeen on the eastern shore of Scotland. Between my two parents, the sea had an effect on my life from the very beginning.

I had become involved in the Underwater Demolition Teams during World War II and was the last wartime commanding officer of UDT 13 prior to it going over to Japan for occupation duties. When UDT 13 was decommissioned on 3 November 1945, I remained with the post-war UDTs, later becoming the commanding officer of UDT 2 stationed in Little Creek, Virginia.

After World War II the UDT had to expand its range of operations if it was to be effective in the modern Navy. One of the first things that had to be done was to take the men of the UDTs underwater. During WWII, the UDTs had worked in a very limited way with some underwater breathing apparatus, but never operationally. Instead, the length of time swimmers could work underwater was limited by how long they could hold their breaths.

During the war, the UDTs could swim in to a beach on the surface of the water because they were being covered by the heavy fire of Navy ships pouring in on the enemy. Without that cover, the swimmers could have been easy targets for light weapons, mortars, and small cannon.

The way to approach an enemy beach, if you are not to be seen, is by coming in underwater. So I had the men under my command learn to swim long distances underwater using oxygen breathing apparatus. That let the men reach the beach unseen, which would keep them from being killed.

Later on, we used the aqualung as invented by Cousteau and Gagnan in France. The aqualung used compressed air and was an open-circuit system; you breathed the air once and exhaled it out into the water. Using air made the system safe and easier to use, with a much greater range of depth, but the bubbles from the air could give away your position.

So to keep from giving away where the swimmers were underwater, we used the closed-circuit oxygen rebreathers. That system reuses the same gas, scrubbing out carbon dioxide and replacing the used oxygen. It is a dangerous system, limited in depth, but leaves no bubbles to track a swimmer. The system we first used was an Italian rig, the Pirelli. With that system, we could swim up to a beach completely undetected, then crawl out and recon the beach itself.

The first real underwater combat swimmers had been the Italians in World War II and even limited attempts in World War I. I had gotten permission from the Chief of Naval Op-

During a diving equipment demonstration in the early 1950s, this UDT underwater swimmer is wearing the Pirelli Model LS-901 rebreather. Due to the single breathing hose causing a possible buildup on carbon dioxide during use, this system was sometimes called the "Black Death" by the operators who used it.

National Archives

erations to go over to Europe and learn what the British had done during the war, what the French were doing after the war, and to learn everything I could from the Italians. The Italians had conducted successful underwater operations against British ships at Gibraltar and elsewhere. They had sunk British warships, and they had a lot to teach us.

Meeting with the people from all of the different countries face-to-face allowed me to gather the information I wanted firsthand. After over six weeks of travel and study I returned to the U.S., accompanied by one of the Italian swimmers who was willing to work with our people in the UDTs. Bringing all of this information back to the United States, we incorporated parts of it into the mission capabilities of the UDTs.

Captain Draper L. Kauffman (right), considered to be the Father of the UDTs, and a swimmer from UDT 21 stand on the bow of an LCPR in the 1950s. The swimmer is wearing a Draeger Lt. Lund II breathing rig with the two green-painted oxygen bottles across his stomach.

U.S. Navy

A very good friend of mine was Commander Draper Kauffman, who was both a tremendous man personally and I felt a great swimmer, having spent his time in the water with the UDTs he helped start during World War II. Kauffman was up in the Pentagon at that time and he quickly grasped the importance of what I had learned and what it would mean to the Teams. He helped make sure that my information got to the right people in the Navy and on the Joint Chiefs of Staff. The UDTs received the go-ahead to continue developing their new underwater capabilities.

For our closed-circuit underwater breathing equipment we used the Lambertsen Amphibious Respirator Unit (LARU), which had been developed in 1940 by Dr. Christian J. Lambertsen. The LARU could give a good swimmer one hour underwater without releasing a trail of bubbles. The system had been used by the OSS Maritime Unit during World War II during their very limited operations.

After we had established that underwater operations could be conducted with the equipment we had, we extended the types of operations we could perform. We worked from submarines, locking in and out of the torpedo tubes, though that didn't work very well. And we operated a "Sleeping Beauty" one-man submersible from the deck of a submerged submarine. To prove to those on higher command that we could do the operations as we said we had, we also filmed them underwater. That too was a first for the Navy. These were some of our experiments in 1948.

Now I felt the main thing the UDTs could do was swim long dis-
tances underwater. With our new training program, the men could
conduct operations covering several miles underwater without sur-
facing. We learned many of our initial techniques and methods of op-
erating underwater from the British and the Italian swimmers of World
War II. It was to those pioneers I felt we owed a debt of gratitude.

Captain Norman H. Olsen, USN (Ret.)

The importance of what the UDTs did during World War II has been
borne out by history. For the landings at Tarawa in the Pacific the plan-
ners didn't have what proved to be good intelligence on the beach and
the waters offshore. When the Marines came in, their boats grounded
on reefs offshore and hundreds of men drowned during the assault.

That incident at Tarawa brought home the necessity of reconning
the beaches ahead of time and finding out which would be the best
for landings. But that was only one factor.

The other factor was that it was well known that we—the Allies—
would have to go in to Northern Europe, where the beaches would be
heavily defended. There didn't really exist a unit that could go into a
beach area like that and open it up for invasion craft. Both of those
factors were real missions and the men of the NCDUs and the UDTs
performed them.

If there hadn't been any such thing as the UDTs, or NCDUs, World
War II would have probably turned out the same. Some organization
would have to have been given their mission. The results of not doing
the beach reconnaissance and obstacle demolition would have been
a much greater rate of casualties and losses among any invading
force. Parts of the Pacific-island-hopping campaign would have really
had a problem in just getting on the beach. And in parts of the Nor-
mandy invasion, particularly on Omaha Beach, the NCDUs took very
heavy hits. Those beaches would have been even harder, if not im-
possible, to secure if someone had not made it possible for the in-
coming waves of landing craft to reach the shore.

Like so many other things, the UDTs basically went away in the postwar cutbacks. The Teams barely survived that time, and if it had not been for farseeing individuals such as Doug Fane, the UDTs may have disappeared entirely. The Teams had been decimated and he found additional missions and capabilities for them. Then the Korean War came around and suddenly we were in the thick of it again.

People in the military were scrambling to fight a ground war again. Units had to make do with what they had, the UDTs among them. But in Korea too, the UDTs conducted their missions well, including additional ones they hadn't been really trained for. Afterward, it was much the same thing as had occurred after WWII, with cutbacks and restrictions reducing the size of units and the funds available for them.

In the 1960s, the cycle repeated itself. We geared up for Vietnam and the new SEAL Teams showed themselves to be immensely capable and flexible in their operations. But afterward, the small units again suffered reductions, the SEALs and UDTs among them.

Today, Special Operations is a household name. They are at the leading edge of a lot of things that are going on in the world. Back in the earlier days they always seemed to be an afterthought by command. "By the way, we have a lousy job. Let's give it to these guys."

■ Chapter 19

OUTBREAK OF THE KOREAN WAR

In an act that startled much of the world, the Communist forces of North Korea surged across the thirty-eighth parallel that divided their country from their democratic brothers to the south. At 0400 hours on 25 June 1950, the North Korean People's Army (NKPA) crossed the thirty-eighth parallel in force. The government of South Korea staggered and almost fell. U.S. President Harry Truman told his Far East commander, General Douglas MacArthur, to support the South Koreans with ammunition and equipment.

As the South Koreans continued to fall back, support was soon ordered in the form of U.S. air and naval forces. A small detachment from UDT 3 was taking part in maneuvers in Japan when the Korean War broke out. These frogmen were soon ordered on emergency behind-the-lines demolition operations to try to slow the NKPA offensive.

The UDT men were now going up on dry land to attack targets that could be approached by the sea. This was the first land combat operations the UDTs performed, but they would be far from the last. The flexibility and adaptability of the UDTs was about to be tried to its utmost.

Lieutenant George Atcheson, USN (Ret.)

While I was an ensign on board a destroyer on the East Coast, I came across an article in a magazine put out by the Bureau of Personnel. As I remember, the article was titled something like "Warriors in Trunks" and was about the Underwater Demolition Teams of World War II. According to the article, the Teams were still active in the Navy, and that sounded like my kind of place to be.

They were accepting applications to the UDTs and I put mine in. My chit was accepted and I was ordered out to Coronado, California, to begin my training. There were no formal training classes then on the West Coast, this being around the spring of 1948, around April. As people arrived, they were assigned to a Team and underwent kind of an intensive on-the-job training.

We went out to San Clemente Island and conducted rubber boat exercises. And we did a lot of swimming, practicing with the dry suits that were to protect us from the cold. There were also a great deal of exercises, long-distance swims, running on the beach, and so on.

In July 1947, UDT operators train for demolition missions off the shores of Little Creek, Virginia. In the center of the IBS are stacks of demolition charges and spools of detonating cord for stringing the charges together.

U.S. Navy

When I arrived in Coronado, I reported in to UDT 3. That was always my parent Team of the two, UDT 1 and 3, which were the only two Teams in Coronado at that time. UDT 3 was commanded by Lieutenant Commander Wolmanick, and the CO of UDT 1 was Lieutenant Al Seares, who had been a Fort Pierce/Maui–trained UDT man in World War II.

In spite of there not being a specific class and such, I feel we had pretty good training. And I don't feel I missed much by not going through a formalized course or program. That kind of thing always seems to pick up a lot of Mickey Mouse "make work" parts that should be avoided whenever possible.

Both enlisted men and officers entered the Teams in this manner on the West Coast at that time. I was the only new officer to begin with, but another arrived while I was still being introduced to all of the skills needed for the job. Enlisted men of various ratings came in from time to time as well. As men left the Teams, were discharged from the Navy, transferred, or whatever, new men came in to keep up the unit's strength.

In the spring of 1950, I had taken a ten-man detachment from UDT 3 to Japan. We were going to do some beach reconnaissance in support of some amphibious training the Marine Corps was going to give to various units of the Eighth Army. So my detachment and I were in Japan when the North Koreans crossed the thirty-eighth parallel on 25 June 1950 and invaded South Korea.

The thirty-eighth parallel was a political device that had been cooked up between the Americans and the Soviets at the end of World War II. The Soviets had a faction in northern Korea who were Communist. The so-called South Koreans were more democratically oriented, and that made them our kind of guys. All that part of Asia, including Korea, Manchuria, and a good chunk of China, had been occupied by the Japanese for some time. Korea had been practically a colony of the Japanese since almost the beginning of the twentieth century. With the dropping of the atomic bombs and the fall of the Japanese Imperialist Empire, there was a question of how we could even deal with the surrender of all these people.

There were millions of armed people in these parts of Asia. And their arms had to be taken away, they had to be fed, and their economies restarted. So to separate the problem into smaller parts, the politicians decided to divide Korea along the thirty-eighth parallel of latitude. The Soviets would take care of the surrender of the northern part of the country and the Communists there. And we would handle the surrender of the Japanese in the southern portion. That resulted in North and South Korea.

It was at 0400 hours in the morning on 25 June 1950 that the North Koreans made what turned out to be their big mistake. They crossed the thirty-eighth parallel in large force and very quickly took Seoul, the capital of South Korea and the historic capital of Korea itself. Then they proceeded to take almost the whole of the Korean peninsula in a very fast series of movements.

The whole world, including the Soviets, probably hadn't expected any such action on the part of the North Korean government, certainly not at the time that they launched the invasion. The Soviet delegation had walked out of the UN in a huff over some quibble they had with us. When the North Korean invasion was brought before the UN Security Council, the Soviets weren't there to veto the vote to support the government of South Korea. That wasn't a mistake they were ever going to make again.

We certainly hadn't expected the invasion. In fact, the then secretary of defense had recently made a speech stating that we didn't really care what happened to Korea. Within a week the north had crossed the parallel and had taken the south away from us. So that was pretty much a complete surprise.

There was some shock that went through the U.S. armed services in Japan, but the overall reaction was not that big a deal at the very start. It sounded like it would be a very tough thing to fight the North Korean army. American forces, such as they were, and South Korean units had collapsed very quickly in the face of the heavy North Korean advance. The People's Army swarmed down from the north until they were finally held up by a line of resistance around Pusan, known as the Pusan Perimeter.

The Pusan Perimeter surrounded a small corner of Korea with Pusan in the middle. The North Koreans pushed up against the perimeter, pressing the remaining U.S. and ROK (Republic of Korea) forces very hard. But with their backs to the sea, the last operating military units had nowhere to go and held their ground.

No one was ready for the sudden outbreak of the war. My men and I had been quartered with the Army's Fifty-second Heavy Tank Battalion in Japan, which had actually been a parade unit and little more than a company-strength unit of light tanks. What the Fifty-second had done during their occupation of Japan was wax and polish their tanks, paint the grease fitting red, keep the markings bright, and see to it that all of the men wore yellow scarves. They turned out for parades and other functions; they were supposed to look good. And these were the men who were suddenly thrust into combat in Korea.

When the news of the Korean invasion arrived where we were stationed in Japan, I may have been excited; I just don't remember. We were quartered with a U.S. Army unit down near the beach, where we had been working in Japan. As the officer in charge of the detachment, I went down to a phone and called the Mount McKinley, which was the command ship of Rear Admiral James M. Doyle, commander of amphibious Group One.

When I asked the commanders on board the McKinley what they wanted me to do, all I got back was some hemming and hawing. Finally I was told to come down to the ship. Going back to our barracks, my detachment gathered up our gear, said good-bye to the soldiers, and all of us piled into a weapons carrier truck that was assigned to us. Going in to Yokosuka from where we were at Camp McGill, we boarded the McKinley. We operated out of there off and on until Team One came out and we could actually join back up with them.

We stayed on board until ordered to Sasebo, Japan, to board an APD there. We were flown from Yokosuka to Sasebo, where we boarded the APD Diachenko.

Very quickly, my unit was put into action against the enemy forces. Command had the idea that if my men and I could do some demolition raids behind the lines in North Korean territory, we might be able to distract some of the North Korean attention on the Pusan Perimeter. The hope was to force the North Koreans to remove some of their troops from the front to police their rear areas, which were vulnerable from the sea.

We were the only demolition men there, so the job fell to us. Our knowledge of demolitions was very good, but our experience on dry land operations was very limited. High command seemed to not have a great deal of experience in choosing targets either. The first target chosen for us was terrible; if we had gone in on it, we never would have survived. The first choice of target would have been like going in to San Diego and trying to blow up the Naval District Headquarters.

The second target was much more realistic for a small group of demolition men like us. There were a small pair of bridges that we were to destroy, a railroad bridge and a highway bridge, near Yosu, which was south of the Pusan Perimeter and now behind enemy lines.

We rode in the Diachenko for the trip to Yosu. Arriving late at night we boarded our LCPRs for the trip in to shore. Two of us were going to paddle in a rubber boat from where the LCPR had released us. Once we had checked out the target, Warren Foley, who had gone in with me, would signal the rest of the men to come in with the explosives to load the target.

The little intelligence photography we had of the area was old, dating from World War II. When we arrived on shore near the bridges, we found there was a thirty-foot embankment that had to be climbed in order for us to get up to the bridges. So we circled around and made the best of our situation.

The North Koreans discovered us and our distraction never worked, as they were able to run us out of there before we loaded the bridges. I threw a couple of grenades that I had brought with me at the ten or so North Koreans who had come out of a tunnel and spotted us. That was about the size of the fight. Heading back to the beach, one of my own men shot my hat off as I approached at the run, mistaking me for the enemy in the dark. But that was our only casualty of the operation. We got off the beach all right, returned to the ship, and went back to Japan.

Very soon after that first mission, UDT 1 arrived in Japan along with a platoon of Marines from the First Marine Division Reconnaissance Company to act as backup. I joined up with them and we went on to do some fairly respectable operations that worked out considerably better than that first one.

Looking back on the situation back then, the demolition of an enemy target was kind of a watershed moment for me. Up until that time everything had been training. Any other time we had blown something up, it had been rocks at San Clemente or something like that. To actually have blown up something that had belonged to the bad guys was a new step in the right direction.

The three demolition raids we conducted kind of run together in my memory, they were so much alike. Even though they were several hundred miles apart, the target sites were similar. They resembled each other in that there was a short stretch of railroad close to the beach, and it ran between two tunnels. The beach would be an open area where the train came out of one tunnel and just went into another.

Usually, we would try to blow up the tracks between the tunnels. A few times we tried to blow down some of the tunnel entrances, but that never amounted to much. You have to prepare a tunnel for demolition a great deal, drilling holes and placing a lot of charges. It's more like mining or construction blasting than military demolitions. We just didn't have the time on target to do that kind of work.

We were out of the water entirely during those three demolition raids. There was a small contingent of a couple of officers and enlisted men who first swam in to look around the bench. We had an infrared sniper scope that would let us look around the beach area in the dark a little bit from the rubber boat, but it didn't work too well. But there was never anyone on the beaches acting as guards or anything during our operations, so we were lucky that way.

On one later operation, we weren't so lucky. With the Koreans, I went back to one of the places that we had gone to earlier with the UDT. On the second trip, there were some North Koreans on the beach and things got hot fast. Several of my Koreans were lost, my interpreter was shot, and it was just a very bad evening.

But that operation during which we finally lost a man wasn't for some time to come. After those first three successful demolition operations in a row, we had been getting kind of cocky about our abilities. On the third op, a group of us had been on the beach talking as if there weren't any problems at all. Being that we were operating at night, behind enemy lines, with very limited immediate support, the lack of problems could have changed very quickly if we had been discovered by the North Koreans.

Marine Major Ed Dupris from the Marine reconnaissance company was in charge of the operation. He became fed up with our nonchalant attitude about where we were, what we were doing, and our talking amongst ourselves. In his best parade-ground voice, that Marine Major called out, "Quiet!" We all quieted down quickly after that.

But those operations were our first real "frogman" ops, in which we got to blow something up that belonged to somebody else. There were veterans of WWII operations in our Team, but a number of us, myself included, were brand-new at this sort of thing. Conducting combat operations behind enemy lines, and getting away with it and not taking any casualties, was kind of exhilarating. So sometimes our enthusiasm got the better of us.

What the command wanted to do was take advantage of our demolition experience and knowledge. A lot of the railway system in Korea had been built by the Japanese during their long control of the country. A great many of the Japanese-built rail lines ran along the eastern coast of the country. To avoid major tunneling through the mountain systems close to the coast, the rail lines were laid out near the shoreline. That made them accessible from the water and that was why the UDTs were chosen to attack them.

We could come ashore in rubber boats and carry our explosives up to the targets. This wasn't much more than an extension of our normal water demolition ops, so the logistics for this kind of operation were already met by the Teams and our APD transports.

Specific targets assigned to us included the rail lines themselves, bridges, and the tunnels. There was somebody in command who thought you could blow up railroad tunnels as easily as any other demolition target. But you can't really demolish a tunnel quickly without a lot of preparation. Setting off even a very large charge of explosives in a properly engineered tunnel isn't much different than firing a big cannon or rifle. The power of the explosives just goes down the tunnel and out the ends.

We could blow up the tracks, but the enemy could fix those fairly quickly. So our operations weren't as long-lasting in their effects as our command planners might have liked. But we did give the enemy something to think about with what was happening in their "secured" areas.

Korea was much like World War II might have been if we had gone in and fought the Japanese in China. It would have been a land war with no real infrastructure as we knew it in Europe. There were small villages spaced out with no good roads between them. It was a pretty primitive countryside. And because of the farming practices of the Koreans, it was tough to get along in the field. If you just cut yourself slightly, it could become infected quickly just from the dust in the air. It just wasn't like anything else. But I had no real experience in land warfare anywhere else in the world.

A frogman was a demolition swimmer initially. He could swim almost anywhere and take care of obstacles in the shallows. Or he would take note of what the obstacles were, measure the beach gradient, and come back to his ship and make a report. That information would be told to the high command and it would tell them what they would be getting into if they tried to land in a particular spot. Like the frog that he's named after, the frogman is an amphibian; he can also get along on land.

Even though we were UDTs and not really intended for land combat, we did not feel at all out of place or uncomfortable during our land operations. During the first little operation we did with only the ten guys from my detachment, we felt a lot more confident going in than we did after we arrived on-site. Our lack of experience kept me from preparing for the operation as well as we could have.

When we first went in, we hadn't prepared to swim in with weapons. Doing that just hadn't occurred to me. We had a fairly long swim in, about five hundred yards, and the tide was ebbing, so the swim must have taken us over half an hour. And we weren't wearing trunks; you don't go ashore in a bathing suit behind enemy lines. You go in wearing clothes you can live in if you have to. So we were wearing fatigues with long pants and shoes, sneakers anyway. I began to realize right away that I would like to have had a lot more training for this kind of operation than I had as I was going in to shore.

In the way of weapons, I was carrying a pistol and some hand grenades. Foley had some grenades along with him as well. We had additional weapons, a Thompson submachine gun, along with us in the rubber boat. That was our primary piece of firepower and it had been my idea to take it along. It wasn't all that good of an idea; we would have been better off taking M-1 carbines along for both of us. Originally, I thought we could swim in with a Thompson, but that didn't work out too well. Neither Foley nor I could swim very far dragging along a ten-pound steel anchor, and that didn't include any ammunition for the weapon, which weighed in at about two pounds apiece for thirty rounds.

So we left the submachine gun behind. It was bad enough swimming with just a pistol and several hand grenades. Weapons are just a dead weight without flotation. But when we ran into an enemy patrol, it was good to have with us what we did. But I wasn't really glad about the situation until we were back on our rubber boat and heading to the ship. Still, I was glad I had something. Later even my limited small-arms experience would come in handy on another assignment.

The Joint Advisory Commission Korea, or JACK, was the cover name for CIA activities in Korea. All the actions of this organization were highly classified at the time and many were done with the cooperation of the U.S. military. But even then, it was fairly common knowledge that JACK was an organization created by the CIA for their paramilitary actions.

Initially, my involvement with JACK was to assist in creating an Escape and Evasion organization in Korea to help downed aviators. No one wanted to be caught by the North Koreans; their reputation for treating prisoners was not a good one. A lot of things that later came out about the Koreans' treatment of prisoners enraged the American public.

The idea was that the aviators would be told where so-called safe areas were and that they should make for those if they had to bail out of their aircraft. Teams of Koreans trained by JACK would be in those safe areas to try to locate the downed aviators before the North Koreans did. Once the teams had the aviators in hand, they could take them down to a beach where a boat could pick them up or get them someplace where a helicopter could come in and snatch them out.

So I was picked to go and work with the JACK organization as a UDT officer. The initial idea was that as a trained UDT man, I was supposed to know how to land rubber boats and how to maneuver them through the surf. So I was brought in to teach the Koreans those

Navy SEALs

skills. The trouble was, we didn't have any rubber boats available to us. We were up in the mountains of Japan, at a place called Camp Drake north of Tokyo, with a hundred or so Koreans and a bunch of various Army, Air Force, and Navy officers, to train these guys.

So I ended up teaching the Korans how to throw hand grenades and shoot various weapons. We didn't have any real curriculum, classes were kind of invented as we went along. The idea was for us to turn the Koreans into kind of a guerrilla force by this time. We were still involved with setting up the E&E units, but there would be other missions for these same Koreans to run.

Later I went to Korea and was attached to a JACK unit over there. They put me to work training a thirty-man group of Korean guys. We ended up doing essentially what the UDT had done when the Koreans first crossed the thirty-eighth parallel.

For our operations, we would land, after maybe a couple of swimmers had gone in to shore first and made sure that no one really serious was on the beach. Predesignated guys would be sent out to establish a perimeter around the landing site. The rest of us would act as the powder train and pack the explosives up to the target, the little bridge, railroad tracks, or whatever. Once the explosives were set, everyone would withdraw. The fuse pullers would have stayed behind, and when the first boats were back in the water, the fuse igniters would be pulled.

We usually ran a fifteen- or thirty-minute delay on the charges. Once the fuses were burning, the fuse pullers would get on out of there. With the pullers recovered, we would all paddle back out to the ship. This was all done at night and we could usually hear the charges go off. The next day, if it was appropriate, the APD would pull in to the target area and everyone would try to see what we had done.

One time, we blew a little railroad bridge. The next day, as we went in to see the target area, a small train came along and went off the bridge. The Koreans usually put an engine on the back of the train so that they could pull it back into tunnels if the trains came under fire. They managed to pull back part of the train but the front engine stayed on the broken bridge. That was kind of pleasant to see, that our work had made some troubles for the North Koreans right there.

The end of the Korean War was unique in that it never really ended. Instead, it seemed to just kind of fade away. The politicians and military people started negotiations at Panmunjom, northwest of Seoul. Things started to calm down a little bit. The front was well north of the thirty-eighth parallel and it wasn't a line anymore, more of a conventional-war frontal situation. It was referred to as the bomb line among the American and UN forces. You just didn't go north of the bomb line.

We had stopped bombing the North Koreans pretty much and the amphibious operations had ended. The UDT operations were no longer being conducted. My Korean guys still had work to do, but the ops were intelligence operations rather than demolition raids. And on the ops, none of the Americans, myself included, were allowed to go on shore. The Koreans could go because it was their country. But the active combat just kind of petered out.

Finally, there was a cease-fire that was formally agreed to. It wasn't really even an armistice. And there were some very big loose ends left hanging in the last agreements. They were some large islands in South Korea where there were the UN prisoner-of-war camps.

The camps held thousands of North Korean and Chinese Communist prisoners. A lot of those men didn't want to go back to North Korea or Communist China. Instead, they wanted to stay in South Korea or go on to Nationalist China in Taiwan. There were a lot of really hard-nosed Communist guys among the prisoners and the situation became a very touchy one for the UN forces.

The war just never really was resolved. It's still going on in a very small way. The North Korean operations with their spy submarines that ran aground are just one example of the aggressions that are still felt on both sides of the border.

It seemed to me that maybe some of what we did in Korea helped lead in to the creation of the SEALs. I was never in any strategic thinking sessions after or during Korea. But it was obvious from the start of Korea that the UDTs had been trained for World War II. It was also obvious that World War II was over, that there wouldn't be any more major amphibious operations with beach obstacles, reefs, and things like that.

What we had shown the strategic planners on command staff was that the UDTs had a lot of potential. The demolition skills, the swimming, the gung-ho spirit, and all of that made for a flexible unit. But to make them really useful, they had to broaden the UDTs' capability. They had to be made into a commando unit that was heavily armed, motivated, and very mobile. The SEALs would do parachute jumps and boats, which were first performed by the fifties era UDTs. And the SEALs do the HALO-style parachute jumps, which take steady nerves. From what I have heard, the SEALs have been very effective whenever they have been used, if they were used properly.

It's that last caveat that's important. The armed services have the tendency to use people and units improperly. That puts them in situations that they aren't trained for. I don't know why, but that was the kind of thing that first got the UDTs up on dry land during the Korean War. And sometimes these things work out for the best.

Looking back on the Korean War, I kind of consider it as my war. In spite of my having gone into the Navy in 1943, I spent all my time in training and never saw action. As an aviation cadet, I had just gotten my commission as an air navigator when the war ended. Staying in the regular Navy, I guess I felt the same as a lot of other guys, that we had somehow missed something by not taking an active part in World War II.

So I had felt that, which was a subjective thing. Objectively, I think we had no choice but to get involved in Korea. It would have been a terrible mistake to simply let the Communists take over the entire peninsula, and make the same mess of it that they have made of their own country now. It also would have been strategically bad if we had let South Korea fall. Our whole Far Eastern situation would have been much different if we hadn't gone in there and done what we had to do.

At the start of my operating in Korea, I didn't hold much affection for the people there that I later came to have. I was prepared to like them a lot, as I was born in Beijing, China, and lived there till I was about sixteen years old, my father having been in the diplomatic service. I have very warm memories of the Chinese people. The Koreans have been described as the Irish of the Orient; they are a very stubborn and proud people. That makes it hard to teach them things sometimes. They feel they know how to do it better than you do very quickly, and sometimes they do.

The Koreans that I knew, that I worked with and trained, and got to know well, I have a great deal of affection for. These men were brave and stoic, you couldn't tire them or wear them out. They were just great soldiers. It's a different culture, so it would be hard to say just how tough they really were. But they could stand a lot and just keep going.

The North Koreans as an enemy I didn't really know. They had a good reputation for toughness and held a hard discipline. The troops were also motivated and they believed all of that propaganda that they were told. Or at least they had to pretend to believe it or they would have been killed. It is such a different culture from ours that it's very hard to really compare the differences. But the fact that they were good, tough soldiers isn't argued very much at all.

Being in the Teams was great fun. It was the best duty I ever had while I was in the Navy. I would have liked to have stayed in the Teams for my entire career, but I was a regular officer and had to move out of the UDTs to continue my career advancement. Later this was changed and you could stay in the Teams as an officer and continue your advancement. This was called a career path and there just didn't used to be one in the UDTs.

Now being in the UDTs and the SEALs has become respectable in the regular Navy, or at least it's a lot more accepted than it used to be. Today, being in Special Warfare is almost respectable while back in the old days it was almost a backwater. You were never going to make great rank if you remained in the UDTs back then.

In the Teams you had the comradeship every day. They were good company, those Teammates I served with. There wasn't a lot of spit and polish in the UDTs like in other outfits. And the easygoing camaraderie existed between the officers and the enlisted men, which it didn't anywhere else in the Navy, at least certainly not like it did in the Teams. It wasn't like the respect wasn't there. We weren't buddy/buddy and they didn't call me George. But they thought of me as George and they knew I could do the same job they did. It wasn't like a ship where the officers are very separate from the men by both rank and tradition.

When I think of the Teams, that's what I remember. The congeniality and the fact that it was just fun. We were very proud of doing what we did. You knew you were part of something special when you were in the UDTs. I certainly felt pride in what we did and what we accomplished, and I'm pretty certain everyone else with me felt the same way.

It was great to be in the kind of outfit where you knew you were special. And no one else really knew what you did and they couldn't do your job even if they did know what it was. When you were asked, "Where are you stationed?" and you answered, "I'm with UDT 3," well, then they just looked at you differently. It means a lot, and I think the same thing must be true today, if not even more so.

Gung ho is a Chinese word meaning "togetherness." In general, it means working in harmony. Marine Colonels Edson and Carlson had a lot of experience working with the Chinese and they picked up the term for the First Marine Raider Battalion during World War II. It became their slogan and spread throughout the Marine Corps. Now it has become part of the general vocabulary as meaning a hardcharger, going straight ahead, and working as a team to get the job done.

The SEALs have an enormously high reputation today and they uphold everything we held dear back during the Korean War. They really are Gung ho, with a capital G.

Chapter 20

ROTATIONS

As soon as the West Coast UDTs were organized as part of the Korean War effort, the Teams set up a rotation among themselves. In an effort to keep the limited manpower of the UDTs from becoming too exhausted, the deployment time was set at six months. This did not include travel time across the Pacific to the UDTs' staging area in Japan. That long trip could easily add several months to a six-month deployment time.

The UDTs deployed to Korea also operated as part of the Pacific Fleet. Operational platoons would take part in fleet landing exercises and other actions as they were directed. UDTs also conducted their normal reconnaissance and hydrographic survey operations in Korean waters. There was also a new mission they conducted that had them facing an old enemy: water-based mines.

Eugene Poole, Seaman Second Class

In late 1951, I joined the Navy Reserves, where I didn't stay very long. By early 1952, I was put on active duty in the Navy in time for the Korean War. During my civilian work, I had been a lifeguard for Santa Monica. Several of the people who worked for our organization had been UDT operators during WWII. It was they who first introduced me to the Underwater Demolition Teams and caused me to search them out when I was activated.

Doug Fane became my hero, as he was the man who got me into the UDT. When I first went in to the training compound back in 1952, it was really just a group of Quonset huts on the beach in Coronado.

Commander Fane was just sitting in his office in one of the huts when I and my friend walked in wearing civilian clothes. There was some first-class petty officer sitting in the front office who asked us what we wanted. When we told him we wanted to see Commander Fane, we were brusquely told that he was busy. We made some pretty unprintable comments to the petty officer and eventually got in to see Fane.

We explained our situation to him, that we didn't want to be where we were on a destroyer. His name had been given to us as the man to talk to about getting into the UDT program. We had references for him and had a few names of individuals we could mention to him. After we told him the rest of our background, he went to see what strings he could pull to get us off our ship and into the UDT.

Within about two months we were off of that destroyer just as it was getting ready to leave for Korea. Then we were officially at the lowest possible rung in the UDTs; we were trainees.

We officially arrived in Coronado in the summer of 1952, barely in time to be part of class six. My friend and I were both from the same reserve unit and it turned out we were the first reservists ever to go into training. The UDTR (UDT Replacement) course was about 16 weeks long back then, with Hell Week being the seventh week of training. The two of us started training during the fifth week, so we had to push kind of hard to catch up. The fact that we arrived in pretty good shape was what helped us catch up with the rest of the class.

The most memorable thing about training was just getting through it. Everyone has heard about the rigors of training; it was tough and it was strenuous. But overall I enjoyed it.

After graduation, we went in to UDT 1. Our first overseas deployment came soon after our arrival, when the Team left for Korea. The Team was stationed at Camp McGill, Japan, just outside of Tateyama and across Tokyo Bay from Yokosuka. We deployed from Camp McGill as units to Korea. The Team operated in different parts of Korea, up and down the western side, primarily in the Yellow Sea area. We reconned beaches, did some demolition of coral heads, and cleaned obstructions out of harbors. After that, we went back to our base in Japan.

From Japan we were again sent out, but this time to a safe area around Okinawa and the Ryukyu Islands. The work off of Okinawa was similar to what we did in Korea, maybe cleaning out a harbor for the Navy or reconning what had been sunk off some beaches. Then we would go back to Japan. We might be flown out somewhere for an operation of several days, then back again to Japan. Trips were taken on destroyers for shorter operations, just a few days or so. Then again back to our main base.

Most of our work in the Yellow Sea up in Korea centered around a number of beaches and little harbors. The intent seemed to be to examine and chart those areas to see if they were suitable for landings. At my level in the Team, I don't know any of the overall or strategic value of what we were doing. For me, it was simply a "go here and do your job" sort of thing. We were happy just to get back on board or back to wherever we were staying that night after we were done. The waters there were pretty cold.

All of the demolition operations I went on were water-oriented. We didn't do any land operations. There was one platoon that did a demo op that involved blowing up a bridge and that required them to go up on land away from the water. For my Teammates and myself, though, all of our demolition work was on islands that as far as I know were right around the thirty-eighth parallel, maybe a little bit above it. Those islands were supposed to have been in friendly hands. At any rate, we didn't have any incidents.

There was one harbor where some mines were found that we had to deal with. For the operation, the UDT that I was with didn't have to clear the mines or blow them up. Instead, we had to go in and mark the location of each one.

These were large water mines that were floating just beneath the surface. These weren't something that I would have volunteered to swim up on. But we didn't have to do this in order to complete our mission. Instead, we would observe them from the surface and drop a marker buoy nearby. Then we made note of the location of the mine on a chart. It may be that EOD (Explosive Ordnance Disposal) came back later and cleared them out—I wasn't involved in that later operation.

I had some concerns while looking over the side of the boat at a few hundred pounds of high explosive, armed and ready to blow if we struck one of the horns. The thoughts centered on "What am I doing here?" and "Why aren't I up there in the air with that Corsair?" Those mines are nasty things. But you don't think of the danger much, you just go ahead and do your job.

While working off of Okinawa earlier during that deployment, it was hard not to think sometimes about what had happened there not ten years earlier. When you operate in the UDTs, you're part of a Team. You do not do anything on your own: your Teammates are working right alongside you, even if it's just your swim buddy. So while my Team was functioning in its normal capacity right then, there were thoughts about the Teammates who had preceded us

UDT operators bring their IBS ashore after a mine clearance operation off Wonsan Harbor, Korea. Locations of the mines and other obstacles would be noted down on the plastic slates the men have hanging from their necks. This operation took place on 26 October 1950 during the first year of the Korean war.

National Archives

and worked these waters during World War II. They had led the way originally.

The specific Team areas, where they had operated, were unknown to me at that time. Nothing that I was aware of had been written about their operations off Okinawa. Since then, I've seen reports and accounts that have told me a lot more about what happened offshore during that last great island invasion of World War II. As far as I knew, I hadn't been swimming off of any of the same beaches that had been the targets back in April 1945, but then again, I might have been.

You would look at the island now and then and think of what it must have been like back then. Thousands of men died on Okinawa, and many were killed just getting to the island. And there were the occasional reminders of what had happened that made things stand out starkly to you.

For example, we had to do a recon on a harbor off of Okinawa and I found a sunken landing craft down in about thirty-five feet of water. The craft was lying on the bottom, upside down, and had been there since World War II. I wondered just what had happened to that craft, how had she gotten to the bottom? Why was she upside down? And what had happened to the men who had been aboard her?

It was one of our boats and she could have hit a mine or been struck by a bomb or shell. There was no way to really know. But finding things like that made you wonder about the situation back then and what went on to cause that situation to develop. There isn't any thought of danger to yourself generally. The UDTs had a job to do and you just did it. That was what we had signed up for.

Chapter 21

RECONS

The success of the WWII amphibious operations conducted in the Pacific were very familiar to General Douglas MacArthur. He used this experience to his great advantage in the audacious landings at Inchon, which turned the tide of the Korean War and nearly resulted in the defeat of the NKPA. As the North Korean forces were driven back well past the thirty-eighth parallel and almost to their northern border with China, the war took an ominous turn when the Red Chinese People's Army "volunteers" joined with the North Koreans. Now U.S. and UN forces were faced with one of the largest land armies in the world.

The reinforced NKPA drove the U.S. and UN forces back south past the thirty-eighth parallel. To maintain his options, MacArthur had earlier ordered further preparations for possible amphibious operations, both to put forces on the beaches or evacuate cutoff or threatened units. The demolition skills of the UDTs were also put to use in destroying facilities that were being abandoned in the face of the Chinese and NKPA forces.

Rod Griggs, Electrician's Mate, Second Class

Originally, I had volunteered for the service because I was a young fellow and I wanted to get into the war over in Korea. One of my desires at that time was to do my duty for my country. My choice of service was the Navy, and one day a call was issued for volunteers for UDT training. I had been raised on a lake, was an excellent swimmer, so I figured that I could do some good in the UDTs.

Personally, I don't believe in Communism, I never did, and I thought the conflict in Korea was a just war. They called it a police action, but it was a war no matter what name they gave it. And I wanted to be more involved. The ship I had been stationed on had been conducting a lot of antisubmarine exercises. I figured there wasn't much chance we'd chase down any North Korean subs—I don't think they even had any then—so the Teams looked like a way to get into the action.

The Korean War was the first real armed conflict between the Communists and the free world. We had to keep the Communists from moving forward, and the Korean War did that. The later cold war, the Berlin Wall, and other incidents, they weren't active combat. The Korean War was.

In August 1952, I was accepted for UDTR training with class six on the West Coast. Training was a long seventeen weeks that took just about everything you could give. The biggest single week of training was Hell Week, but everything that was demanded of you prior to then made you numb through that ordeal. The first six weeks of training was a lot of physical work. They condition you, get you in shape, and then put you through Hell Week to see if you also have the mental toughness to do the job.

It was after Hell Week that you started to receive the more technical training. Then we had to learn flashing light code, demolitions, gradients, and beach conditions. That last was really the kind of information we would be going after on a hydrographic reconnaissance. And we also received a little bit of training on booby traps, disarming mines, and other explosive studies.

It was the numbness I felt that helped me get through Hell Week. You would get maybe two hours of sleep during the night and then they would get you up for a march through the muck. You're so tired and worn-out that you run solely on stamina. That's what they want to see you show before they spend time teaching you the nuts and bolts of being a UDT man.

After graduation, I was assigned to UDT 1. It was just shortly after we had completed graduation that UDT 1 deployed to operate in

Korea. That was about February 1953. We went aboard ship in February and took about thirty days to cross the Pacific to Japan. Our base in Japan was Camp McGill near Tateyama on the eastern side of the mouth to Tokyo Bay, a short trip from Yokosuka where the ship pulled in.

The thirty-day trip across the Pacific was memorable. The ship was an AGC, an amphibious force flagship, basically a converted WWII liberty ship. In the middle of one of those Pacific storms, the ship cracked up both sides of the hull. We had been sleeping in the mess hall when the crew came in, woke us up, and tossed all of us out. Then they stripped off all of the insulation from the walls and welded up the cracks. That was roughly in the middle of the Pacific. I knew the crew could handle the situation; the ship wasn't really breaking in half, just kind of cracking in the middle.

Even when we were in Japan, we hadn't been told where our operations would be. That kind of decision, where the command wanted us, was made well above the Team level. We were a Team of about one hundred people divided into four action platoons and a headquarters. For missions, some platoons would be sent to one place while other platoons would go someplace else. We all went to Korea together as a Team, but this was after we had been in Japan for a few months. We had gone to Hokkaido to recon some beaches there. And we had gone to Okinawa to clear some beaches for practice Marine landings.

After those operations, we returned to Sasebo, Japan, and waited for an APD, a high-speed transport, to pick us up and take us over to Korea. When we arrived in Korea, we received our orders where to send the platoons. All of our equipment, rubber boats, LCPRs, and whatever, were aboard the APDs. So we worked from those ships while off Korea. The major Korean operations that I was involved in consisted of beach surveys, the normal UDT op.

We had different ways of surveying beaches, using swimmers in the water or measuring from boats. On the swimmer beaches, the operations went much like the standard UDT op from World War II. We would work from our WWII-vintage plywood LCPRs, putting a number of swimmers in the water. For some beaches, it would be a line of fifty swimmers spaced out at roughly the three-and-a-half-fathom (twenty-one-foot) depth line. The swimmers would raise their arms to help everyone line up for the swim in to the beach.

Going in to the beach, we would have our plastic slates, drop our lead lines at regular intervals, and write down the depth on our slate. Then the line would move in to the next interval and repeat the measuring. What we would do was measure the gradient of the seafloor as it sloped up to the beach. That told the planners what kind of ships could land on that beach.

Ships—the LST, for example—required a depth of 14 to 15 feet under the stern, as I remember, while the bow needed only four feet of water under it. Since an LST was something like 328 feet long, calculating where it could nose in to the beach, drop her bow ramp, and unload while still being able to get off the beach later was easy.

There were two things about swimming in the water off of Korea. First off, the water was never very clean; mud, silt, and whatever suspended in it kept you from being able to see very far at all underwater. Second, the ocean around Korea had something like a 30-foot tide. So we would always conduct our surveys at low tide. The rest of the recon could be done by observing the beach high-tide line.

And the water around Korea was cold. If the temperature was below sixty degrees, we had to wear exposure suits to protect us. Around Korea, we wore the suits all of the time. The exposure suits were Italian Pirelli rubber dry suits, basically a waterproof rubber suit you wore over a set of long underwear. The suits kept you warm by trapping a layer of air in the long underwear between the suit and your skin. As long as you didn't cut the suit or let any water into it, it worked pretty well.

So the Navy was taking care of us with the equipment we were getting. We had used aqualungs in our operations off of Okinawa, but none of them were used on the Korean ops that I was on. We would just make the swim in and hold our breaths for any time that we had to spend underwater.

I was not involved in any land operations while off Korea. In fact, we were told to stay away from the people who were conducting such things. On some beaches, we would set out a perimeter to maintain the security of our site. On one operation, I was assigned to go ashore prior to the landing and watch one end of the beach. Another man from my UDT was watching the other end of the beach. We were both armed, but there wasn't any enemy contact or other incident.

The lack of incidents was a good thing for us; we weren't supposed to make contact with the enemy. We were an intelligence-gathering outfit, our information was valuable, and we had to get back with it. Then the cartographers could draw up an accurate and complete chart of the beach. If even one man was missing, then information he had gathered about a coral head or other obstruction might be missed, as well. In that case, a ship coming in to a beach and running aground wouldn't be able to do its job. So we had to do ours to prevent that.

Two UDT combat swimmers wearing the early model dry suits. It was because of suits like these that the UDTs were first able to operate in arctic and antarctic waters. These suits and improved versions aided underwater operations off the coast of Korea during the Korean War. The suits trapped a layer of air, usually formed by a set of long underwear, to insulate the swimmer from the cold water. The black device below the neck is a flapper valve to allow excess air to escape.

U.S. Navy

The only time I even heard of any UDT men making contact with the enemy and actually getting into combat was early in 1951. The men were from UDT 1 and they had been getting back from a survey when supposedly friendly Koreans on the shore opened fire on them. Two of the UDT men were killed, an enlisted man and an officer, and five more were wounded. Some of the wounded men were later returned to our Team. The UDT men hadn't been armed and weren't able to return fire. The machine guns aboard their LCVP just didn't have the range to cover them.

We—that is, the men just doing the job—never really knew where we were. The job was just to survey the assigned beaches. We could have been above or below the thirty-eighth parallel, with North Koreans on the shore around us. We kept watch on shore but remained sneaky and always avoided contact. That was just part of how we did our job.

There were other actions the UDTs did in Korea, such as cutting the North Korean fishnets, going on shore for demolition raids, and blowing up the dock facilities at Hungnam prior to the time when the North Koreans and the Chinese military forced all of the UN forces back down the Korean peninsula.

In Korea, the UDTs would alternate being on station. UDT 1 might be over there and were relieved by UDT 3, then UDT 5 would relieve UDT 3. The tours were six months long on paper, but you had to add two months of travel time—thirty days to get there and thirty days to return—to the overall deployment. So a UDT was away from Coronado for eight months at a time during the Korean War.

My one tour over in Korea came just before the signing of the cease-fire on 27 July 1953. We were just packing up to return to the United States when they announced over the ship's PA system that the armistice had been signed. So we were the last UDT to do a combat tour during the Korean War. I have the Korean Medal with two stars on it, indicating I was in three different combat zones during the war. So we traveled a lot up and down the coast of Korea during our deployment.

Soon after UDT 1 returned to Coronado, I volunteered for a trip to Alaska. The USS Burton was a Navy icebreaker heading up to Alaska and they always carried six underwater demolition men on board. In case the ship penetrated into the ice fields and was frozen in, we had the capability to go into the water and blast the ice from underneath. That would create a leed of open water that the ship could move through. Building up some forward speed, the icebreaker could then keep going forward, busting through the ice with her heavy reinforced bow.

Another duty we had during that trip was to try to do demolitions under the ice in order to clear channels for boat landings. That was an experiment that didn't work too well. We could do the demoli-

Navy SEALs

tions, but you couldn't run a normal boat through the heavy slush that resulted.

This was seriously cold water, twenty-eight degrees at the intake of the engine room. Cold enough that some of the salt water would freeze up and become ice, joining up with the snowmelt and other buildup floating on the surface. The operations were very interesting, in spite of the fact that I broke my eardrum on one dive.

For protection from the extreme cold, we wore padded aviator's underwear under our Pirelli suits. Then we put wool suits over that. Vaseline protected the exposed skin of our faces and tight gloves protected our hands. What happened to me was that the Vaseline sealed my ear to the hood of the rubber suit. When you go down with an aqualung on, you try to clear the ear and equalize the pressure on either side of the eardrum. If you can't equalize the pressure by swallowing or blowing into your mask, you try bobbing in the water to open the passages up in your ear. If your ears don't equalize, the pain can get pretty bad.

A UDT swimmer moves to the edge of an ice pack in frigid Arctic waters. Though his fellow sailors do not appear particularly uncomfortable on the landing craft nearby, without his protective suit, the UDT swimmer would be killed by the cold waters in minutes.

U.S. Navy

I had been bobbing and suddenly my ear was clear and the pain had gone away. I thought the ear had cleared, but what had really happened was I had created a vacuum between my ear and the suit and had popped the eardrum outward and ruptured it. So I had a bad ear and couldn't dive anymore on that trip.

Other than the problem I had on that one dive, going under the ice was a very interesting experience. It's very beautiful underneath the ice, with light filtering down through the snow and overhead cover. The water is very clear and there are very few things floating around or moving through it. There are air pockets under the ice, some of them so large that you can go up into them and breathe out of the water.

The trip was very interesting at the beginning, but after you've seen ice for a week or two, the next two months aren't very interesting. So things became boring after a while and stayed that way. Our path was up the inland passageway, through Canadian waters, and we went from Juneau, Alaska, over to Kodiak.

An interesting incident occurred while we were at Kodiak. The mail was being delivered in large rubber containers for air pickup. One of the bags was dropped in about seventy-feet of water and the ship wanted someone to go down and get it. I and another diver went down to pick it up. There was no problem finding the bag, it was just lying on the bottom right off the pier where it had fallen. But while we were down, a real big fish came along and scared the hell out of me for a moment. But we rescued the mailbag and received a standing ovation from the ship's crew when we surfaced.

My discharge was coming up relatively soon after the Alaska tour. UDT 1 was deploying again, and since my time in the service was almost up, I stayed behind in Coronado. Finally, in November 1954, I left the UDT and the Navy and returned to civilian life.

Life in the UDTs had been good in general. We had quite a few more privileges than the rest of the people in the Navy. We were an elite group and that came with some perks. We had early chow passes, although we had to exercise every day to earn them. There was less "spit and polish" discipline in the Teams, and the rank consciousness that was so prevalent in the regular Navy you didn't see in the UDTs. Aboard ship, it was "yes sir, no sir." When you were swimming with an officer, you were learning to trust each other with your lives. That makes the command situation quite a bit different, and a lot more relaxed.

■ Chapter 22

HEAT AND COLD: MINES AND THE KOREAN WINTER

The environment of the Korean War ranged from hot and dusty in the summer to blistering cold in the winter. Cold-weather fronts would sweep down from Mongolia and Russia in the winter, bringing with them shattering cold. And it was in this environment that the UDTs operated on land, without the necessary supply line for cold-weather clothing. Few UDT operators who spent the winter months in Korea have a fond memory of the place.

And in the constantly cold waters off Korea were floating mines. These dangerous packages could hold hundreds of pounds of high explosive, enough to blast a hole in the hull of a capital Navy ship. Actions were conducted by the UDTs to search out and mark or destroy these mines—procedures that occasionally led to very close calls as the men met the floating bombs.

The safe handling, disarming, or simple disposal of the floating mines required additional technical training. This gave the UDTs another skill to add to their list, one that proved invaluable as their operations and missions increased in technical complexity.

Louis J. DeLara, Senior Chief Boatswain's Mate, USN (Ret.)

At the beginning of the Korean War, I was a civilian in Pittsburgh, Pennsylvania. I had been in the Navy during World War II, and unknowingly to me, on my discharge from that service, I had signed a reserve clause on my papers. Nothing ever showed up in my mail and I didn't have any drills or anything like that to go to. Still, I was a member of the inactive reserves of the U.S. Navy. The start of the Korean War very quickly changed all that. I was one of the first guys reactivated for service.

The situation was thoroughly miserable and I didn't want to have any part of this thing that was going on over in Northeast Asia. But the Navy took a number of ships as well as men out of mothballs. I was assigned to one of these old rustbuckets as it came out of storage and immediately went to sea.

That ship cruised into the bay of San Diego. All I wanted to do was get back out of the Navy and go home. One day I happened to notice this LCPR in the water with big shark's teeth painted on it and a bunch of suntanned guys running around on the deck.

When I asked one of the other guys aboard ship who those people were, he said, "They're frogmen."

"Where are they stationed?" I asked.

"Over there." He pointed across the bay at the Amphib Base in Coronado, then looked at me and said, "That's a volunteer organization. Are you thinking about joining?"

I thought yeah, it was a way to get off of that ship. So I submitted my request, and it was approved. The ship was getting under way and they called over to the Amphib Base and told them about this man they had on board who would be shortly reporting for training. The ship was leaving about a month early, but they were willing to send me over to the base before we left. The folks over at the Amphib Base agreed and now I was off the ship.

The situation was one that made me at least semihappy. Then I reported in for training. A gentleman by the name of Hughes, who is still a very good friend of mine, did so too. "Lou," he told me, "we're

Two SCUBA-equipped UDT swimmers are entering the water from the bow ramp of the LCPR. This small craft was one of the famous "Higgins" boat designs of WWII.

going to get into this training and get a jump on the rest of the class. We're going to get up early and get into some exercise."

This guy was out of his mind as far as I was concerned. I was off of that ship and that was the big thing for me. The upcoming training wasn't something I was worried about. But five o'clock the next morning, here he was rattling me up and out of my rack. Then we were running around that base, and that was the start of it.

Then I got into training. And the more I was involved, the more I felt like I was putting money in the bank. Now I had an investment in what I was doing. Then I became semidedicated to it and I found I had put too much time and effort into what I was doing. By that time you couldn't get me out of the program. So that was how I became a frogman.

My class, class six, was a winter class. We graduated in 1952 and immediately were sent over to Korea with UDT 1. The men I was with and the work I was doing drew me in. And the more I was involved with it, the more I became committed to the service. Before I realized it, I had become a dedicated career Navy man.

Originally, training was just a way to get off that ship. But it grew quickly into something that had a life of its own. Guys like Hughes and others like him that I met while in training helped me get through the hard parts. And the extra pay you received as a member of the UDT didn't hurt either.

During an interview with the trainees they had early on, they passed around this questionnaire to find out why we wanted this training. When I looked at the questions, I just said that I wanted the extra money. One of my friends told me not to put that down. He suggested that I write how this was the best way I could serve my country and the Navy. How I was dedicated and my becoming a frogman would be to the best interests of the service. I agreed and put all of that down, but I really did want the extra money initially.

After graduation, I was assigned to UDT 1. There were three Teams on the West Coast then. The Navy had just commissioned UDT 5 to join with UDT 1 and UDT 3 at Coronado. At that time the Teams were made up of about 120 men total, officers and enlisted. Whether we ever were up to capacity, I don't know. But we did average between 75 and 80 enlisted men and maybe 10 to 12 officers. These were broken down into four operating platoons and one Headquarters Platoon.

The whole Team went on combat operations off to Korea. The operating mandate for the Teams calls for us to do reconnaissance and clear obstacles for an amphibious landing. We also tried to acquire intelligence about the trackability of a beach and where its entrances and exits were. That was so that once the landing forces had gotten to the beach, they would know if the surface could hold tracked or wheeled vehicles and how they would get off that thing. And that was our basic mission.

In Korea, as time went on, we found ourselves going inland on missions. That wasn't where we were supposed to be, according to our basic mandate, but it wasn't like we were in violation of the Geneva Convention or anything. But we were getting more and more involved inland. Now we were putting out perimeters to protect our site and blowing up railroads and bridges. That became our more usual mission.

All in all, that kind of inland work, the operational type of things we were doing, proved abilities and helped raise the SEALs years later.

The operations we did took us up and down both coasts of Korea a number of times. For an inland demolition operation, we would go in on an APD at night to within range of our target. We would launch from the APD into our rubber boats for the paddle in to the beach. There would be two boats usually, each with a crew of six, so there would be about twelve people, not quite a full operational platoon, on the op.

Getting in to the beach, we would put a few people out to sneak in and make sure that we could come up and get in there with the boats. Then we would land and set up a perimeter, putting some people out in a circle so that we wouldn't be surprised by someone walking up on us. Then we would make our way up the beach. We had maps and whatever with us to guide us in to the target and we carried our explosives with us.

Once we got to the target, we set our explosives, which were on a timer. Then we armed the timer, retracted from the target, pulled in the perimeter, and beat feet out of there.

Even though we were out of the water, we had no real problems in conducting our missions. We had been doing some land operations training in the years before and during the Korean War. So we certainly felt confident in conducting the ops that we did. And we didn't go that far inland. Most of our operations were directed at targets on or near the water.

Back in World War II, the Naval Combat Demolition Units and the UDTs were assigned primarily to demolish beach obstacles. And beach obstacles usually meant right in the water. It was the Army's demolition people who took care of those targets up on the dry beach itself. The high-water mark was the normal limit of UDT operations.

As the war went on, the UDTs found it to their advantage to conduct some limited land operations. Training was done in handling small arms, setting up command posts and perimeters, and being able to move about on land. Then we could attack targets on the beach as well.

In Korea, we were able to put that training to some use, and we learned more. Few of my memories of Korea are fond ones. Mostly I was there during the winter months, and that is a cold country. Also, we were a poor outfit at that time. I was running around the hills of Korea, a long way from the water, with an old pair of boots on, the soles half-gone and one of my toes sticking out. A wrapping of tape kept the worst of the snow and mud out.

You could line up a platoon of UDT sailors at that time and no two people would be dressed the same way. There would be a Marine hat on one, Army boots on another, and an Air Force flight jacket would be a considerable fashion item. This was where our clothing came from—the other services. We would do training runs to different bases and see what they were willing to trade. This usually was to everyone's advantage. We would offer all of the fish and lobster they wanted if they gave us what we wanted. What really made things bad was that it was just so miserably cold in the winter.

Sometimes we would get a break and go back to Yokosuka in Japan. That was the forward location that the UDTs were based out of. There were barracks at an old Army base in Kamakura where the UDTs, Seabees, and whatever other Navy units were in at that time were housed. Those were some pretty fun times at the base because the camaraderie was great and so were the guys I worked with. But the operations were always cold.

UDT 5 had another mission later in the war that got them pretty cold and wet. Basically, what happened was that the North Koreans had strung fishnets out to sea. This was feeding the enemy forces and keeping the fish from getting to the South Koreans. So UDT 5 was given the assignment of destroying the nets and whatever at sea. That cut down on what the North Koreans were getting as well as giving the South Koreans a much better catch.

One of the things we encountered all over the place in Korea were

These UDT operators clamber across the rocks on the shore of Korea during Operation FISHNET in mid-September 1952. Their mission was to destroy or capture North Korean fishing nets to help cut off a source of supply to the enemy.

National Archives

mines, especially in the water. It was the UDTs' experience with mines in Korea that led to a modification of the Teams' manning levels to include qualified EOD people. That school taught men the art of rendering an explosive device harmless or getting rid of it. Qualified members of the Teams, and even the SEAL Teams today, would be sent on to EOD School to learn how to safely handle and dispose of mines.

The safest way to get rid of a mine is to blow it up. Just let the mine function, preferably not by striking a ship. For the landings at Inchon, the approaches were mined. The UDTs were sent in there to locate and clear the mines. The water was pretty murky, so just wandering around was not the way to look for a mine. Instead, a helicopter would fly overhead and an observer in it could see a shadow in the water cast by the mine. We would leave our boat and swim over to the mine with a Hagensen Pack.

To destroy the mine, we would put the shoulder strap of the pack over one of its horns. Then you would take the line from the pack and put it around the mine, securing it to another horn. Cinching the line down tight to keep the pack close to the mine, you would then pull the fuse device, step back, and just watch it blow.

After doing that for a while, a number of us, including myself, were sent to EOD School. There I found out that the horn of the mine I was pressing against to secure my Hagensen Pack was soft lead and only required a few pounds to bend or crush it and detonate the mine. That horn had a glass ampule of electrolyte in it. Below the horn were battery plates wired to the mine's detonator and ready to go. Breaking the glass let the electrolyte flow down to the battery plates, create a current, and boom!

Fortunately, no one in the Teams was ever hurt messing with an antiship mine. One time aboard our APD troop transport an announcement came over the PA system calling out a warning about a mine in the water and sending us all to the opposite side of the ship. So naturally, we all ran to the other side of the ship to see the mine.

This one single mine slid along the side of our ship, bouncing several times against the hull and finally slipping past the stern. On the fantail were some men with automatic weapons. When the ship was clear of the mine, they opened fire on it. Not more than half a dozen or so rounds had been fired when the mine blew up. That was about the luckiest day for our UDT and that APD.

In today's schools, the Korean War is taught as having been heavily involved with an air war. There were more than a few ground-pounders involved trying to capture and hold the real estate the planes flew over. One famous piece of dirt was a good-sized bulge of land known as Pork Chop Hill. Both the North Koreans and the UN forces wanted that hill for a strategic advantage over the surrounding area. Each side had determined that the other wasn't going to get it. That hill was fought over for months, with a tremendous loss of life. That hill kind of exemplified the ground combat in Korea.

A lot of the UDT work had to do with the water, but not all of it was offensive in nature. With the heavy involvement of aircraft in the war, there were also a number of air losses. The Korean War was probably

Prior to going out on a mine clearance operation, these UDT operators receive a premission briefing. The cold waters off Korea require the dry suits for underwater operations. The black "ear" on the side of some of the dry suit hoods is a one-way rubber flapper valve to allow excess air to escape as the men enter the water.

National Archives

the last great war of dogfighting in the air. Now missiles are used; then, it was mostly plane to plane with cannons and guns.

And we did a lot of pilot recovery. You would stand by on board ship if you saw a plane in trouble over the water. If a plane popped its canopy, you could see the pilot eject. Then we would all make the best effort we could to get to the pilot before the North Koreans did. We had a pretty good success rate in conducting that mission. Taking a fast boat, we could get in to the pilot quickly and pull him out before a larger, slower craft pulled up.

The involvement of the Teams in the war included risky missions, beach reconnaissance, mine clearance, and things of this nature. The Marines and the UDT worked together a lot on operations. The Marine Corps is a dedicated unit of fighting men, professional and extremely capable at their job. We thought highly of them and I like to think they thought a lot of us.

There was an element of danger in everything we did in Korea, maybe a bit higher than what the average soldier or sailor faced. But we had a pretty decent record on our operations. There were UDT operators wounded, and I believe we even had several killed. But for the most part, we conducted our operations with minimum casualties.

The Korean War concluded with a cease-fire and not really an end to the conflict. Though there was still a lot of cleanup work to do off of Korea, the Teams went back to Coronado, and for the most part we were in the States for good. Somewhere along the line during the war, the Navy had changed UDTs 1, 3, and 5, to UDTs 11, 12, and 13.

When I returned from my third tour in Korea, I was assigned to Underwater Demolition Unit One, which was the overall command unit for the UDTs. Commander Doug Fane was the man in charge of UDU 1 at that time. Fane was the equivalent of today's admiral of SpecWar; he was in charge of all of the Teams on the West Coast. There was a group of about ten or twelve of us at UDT 1 that Fane had working on various secret projects and the development of new equipment.

Manufacturers and other companies would send new gear down the line to our unit for testing and possible use by the Teams. It could be a new diving device or swimmer propelling device of some kind. Testing those items is what justified our workday.

An officer by the name of Bill Hamilton, a lieutenant at that time, was always hanging around our unit. I didn't know him as a frogman or as having come through training. He wore flight wings, so I knew he was an aviator. Looking to one of the guys who had been there longer than me, I asked him just who this guy was. "He's our air officer," I was told.

But UDT wasn't conducting air operations at that time. We would jump out of helicopters without parachutes, from 75 to 80 feet in the air. But that was about the extent of our air operations. If you wanted to get back into the helicopter, it would have to drag a Jacob's ladder behind it, down into the water. You caught the ladder and crawled back aboard the bird that way. This was long before the parachuting requirement entered the Teams.

What I came to find out about the "air ops" officer later was that he was with the CIA. In his efforts to expand the operations of the UDTs, Commander Fane had a lot of dealings with the CIA. To the best of my knowledge, Hamilton was one of the men working with Doug Fane on those projects.

Commander Fane was a lieutenant commander when I first met him. He'd had some problems on the East Coast earlier involving a demolition operation and was sent over to Coronado. He was a heroic, brave man who always led from the front. A good example of his attitude was shown when we were locking in and out of submarines.

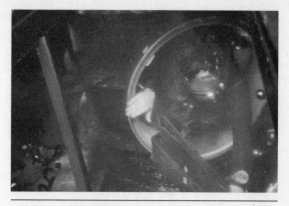

During underwater training, a SEAL exits the hatch of a very crowded submarine escape chamber.

U.S. Navy

Subs didn't have a real good system for locking swimmers in and out en masse while the boat was underwater. We could use the submarine escape hatch, which was about the size of a trash barrel, to move a few guys at a time. We would squeeze, literally, four guys into this small steel barrel, to get out of the sub while it was under way.

This was a pretty inefficient way of moving divers in and out of a submarine, so Doug Fane thought it might be a good idea to go out through the torpedo tubes. The procedure would be to crawl into the torpedo tube through the loading hatch inside the submarine. Then you'd flood the tube and open the outer doors. The water could be leaked in reasonably slowly, the pressure would be equalized, and the swimmer would go up the torpedo tube and out into the open water. This sounds easy until you realize that the tube is only twenty-one inches in diameter. A swimmer and his breathing rig would be very crowded inside of that tube. But it did work.

Getting back into the submarine was a little different. First, you had to work your way into that greasy tube, and then crawl down in the absolute dark to the loading hatch. Banging on the side of the tube would tell the people inside the torpedo room that you were ready. They would close the outer doors, blow the water out of the tube, and open the interior hatch.

The problem was, there was no way of controlling the air pressure that was used to eliminate the water and clear the torpedo tube. What they did was hit the button that normally fired a torpedo. The firing button dumped the boat's high-pressure air lines into that tube in a hurry. That air pressure was enough to send a snug-fitting 3,800-pound Mark-14 torpedo up and out of that greasy tube like a cork from a bottle.

During the first torpedo-tube-lock exercise, when we opened the tube holding Doug Fane, we found him bleeding from the eyes, ears, and mouth. It was obvious to all of us that the sudden air pressure had really done a job on him. Standing there in the torpedo room, a little shaky on his feet but standing on his own, Commander Fane said, "I don't think this is going to work too well."

I and quite a number of other Frogmen really learned to appreciate the man. He was a tremendous leader and a real example of what it meant to have guts. There was another occasion when we were out on a diving operation on a wreck and I spotted a big, beautiful lobster—it must have been about ten pounds. When I came up to the boat, I told Fane about the great lobster I had seen on the bottom. "Well, why the hell don't you get it?" was all he said.

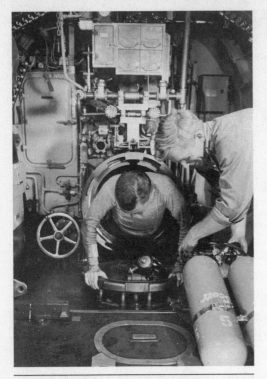

Inside the cramped stern torpedo compartment of a submarine, a UDT swimmer backs into the open torpedo tube. He will don the mask of his Scott Hydro-Pac after getting into the tube and then drag the tanks in behind him. Then the operator's swim buddy will enter the tube face first, pushing his air tanks in front of him.

U.S. Navy

"Because right next to it is a real big moray eel," was my answer.

"Goddammit," was all he growled as he went over the side. Fane went down to where that lobster was, pushed the eel aside, and came back up with a really nice dinner. "That's the way you do it," he said to me when he was back on the boat. Doug Fane was a real good man to have leading us in the Teams.

By the latter part of 1961, there were some rumors making the rounds of the Coronado Teams about this new formation, a SEAL Team or something of that nature. We didn't know what it was about. Little by little, it became a reality.

What was done was the UDTs were drawn on to supply the personnel for this new SEAL Team. A lot of people were under the impression that the SEALs were a completely new outfit. What they were was UDT sailors under a new name and mission. Once that was done, the SEALs did go on to a lot more technical training. They were given weapons training, taught languages, they were even taken up into the mountains and taught how to ski.

The SEALs had a new operational mandate that justified their going inland for intelligence gathering and other missions. Whether it was capturing an enemy chief or rescuing hostages, all of this was under the new mandate of the SEAL Teams. The UDT mandate remained the same.

The SEAL Teams continued drawing manpower from the UDTs. When a man graduated from training, he didn't go into the SEAL Team, he went into the UDTs to get some experience first. Eventually, the UDTs were completely absorbed by the SEAL Teams. The last component of the UDTs to go was the Swimmer Delivery Vehicle units. These were consolidated and became the SDV Teams, one on each coast.

As an EOD-qualified individual, I spent time in both the SEAL Teams and the UDTs during the Vietnam War. If there was an accident or a piece of ordnance didn't operate correctly, I was one of the people who was sent in to check things out and investigate what happened. Vietnam wasn't a place that really impressed me at all. The *guys in the Team did some beautiful work there, and a lot of the operations weren't fun. It was a lot of very hard work and occasionally very tricky to pull off.*

The Teams had some ordnance in Vietnam that they tried to modify in the field on occasions. Normally, you never touch that kind of thing, and you certainly don't modify it. Ordnance is approved of by the Bureau of Ordnance and is controlled. The way they send it to you is the way you are supposed to use it.

But the SEAL Teams had some leeway in those rules. They could alter weapons and ordnance if they felt it would give them some advantage in completing a mission. There were times when some SEALs felt that a piece of ordnance would work better with their design. And sometimes people got hurt.

There was a backpack-carried rocket system made for the SEALs that had three rounds of 3.5-inch bazooka rockets. The fuze system ended up being at fault. The system turned out to be very unstable because in a safe position, where it wasn't supposed to fire, it fired on three occasions. Several of the people hurt in these incidents were friends of mine. The weapons and materials issued to the SEALs were sometimes experimental. And the guys using them earned their extra pay.

■ Chapter 23

THE LIGHTER SIDE

Only the West Coast UDTs participated in the Korean War. Even though the West Coast had to commission an additional UDT, UDT 5, to meet their commitment to actions in Korea, they continued to decline offers of assistance from the East Coast Teams at Little Creek.

Support personnel were assigned to the UDTs to assist in the completion of their mission. Although these men were usually not qualified as UDT operators, having never gone through UDT training, they had technical skills that the Team needed, skills the UDT operators lacked. These people were the only nonvolunteers in an entirely volunteer outfit.

But the appeal of the UDT lifestyle would draw some of these individuals into trying their luck at UDTR or Underwater Demolition Team Replacement training. When they completed training and joined a Team, they often conducted Team operations in addition to their original technical job. Even though they may not have gone on a single combat tour during their time in the Teams, some of these operators made an impression on the UDTs that would endure long after their own Navy careers came to an end.

Jack Tomlinson, Draftsman Second Class

Prior to enlisting in the Navy, I had been a flooring designer at Armstrong Industries. When I found out that I was in line to be drafted into the Army, I decided to enlist in the Navy. Because of my civilian designer background, the Navy sent me to drafting school. The school was in California and after graduation I was scheduled to go to a Seabee unit at Little Creek, Virginia. Instead, I was issued a set of orders sending me to a unit called UDT 2, also in Little Creek, and was assigned work as a cartographer.

At that time I had no idea what a UDT was or what job they did in the Navy. A cartographer I understood—I would be drawing naval charts and maps. When I first started to work with what I learned were the Underwater Demolition Teams, I did the drafting work from information the swimmers obtained by measuring and observing the offshore waters. Part of my job was to go out with the unit on exercises, so I was able to watch the men go through their paces.

My first thought after watching the UDT in action was that these men had to be crazy to do the kind of work that they did. Rolling out of high-speed boats, swimming off "enemy" beaches and dropping lines into the water, and then being snatched back up by the high-speed boats.

My second thought after watching these actions was that there was no way a skinny little guy like me could ever do it with them. The UDTs were an all-volunteer outfit. I was assigned to UDT 2 not as a swimmer, but specifically as a draftsman and cartographer. After I had been in the unit for a while, I spoke to the commander and found out that there was no way I was going to get a transfer from the UDTs to another unit. So I decided to try out for the next training class.

My class was class eight in 1952 and it took place right there at Little Creek. The training was something I never want to go through again. It was very strenuous, difficult work. Looking back on it now, I realize that much of what they had us doing was intended to test and stretch our mental capacity. This testing reached a climax during Hell Week, kind of the highlight of the training. Once an individual passed through Hell Week, he was pretty much on his way to the Teams. The real hard weeding-out of the volunteers was completed during that week.

What got me through Hell Week personally was probably nothing more than my determination to accomplish it. A young fellow by the name of Wendell Witherow buddies up with me early on, and through most of the course, we poked each other to keep going when one of us flagged a bit.

I graduated with my class and returned to UDT 2. Now I was one of the Team. Probably my most vivid memory of being in the Teams was actually making it through training. Some of the forced marches we had done, I really don't know how I completed. There was pain and discomfort at a level I hadn't experienced before. In spite of the throwing up, the arms and legs aching, the desire to just collapse and give it all up, your buddy would prod you a bit and you would just keep going. And the instructors just kept asking for more, and more, and more.

Individuals who enter the UDT or SEAL Teams seem to me to have to be nonconformists. They're not the image the public holds of giant men with huge muscles. Instead, the average UDT operator got through training because he was a regular guy who had a strong mental capacity. It was an individual's will that got him through training much more than his physique.

Once you had gotten through the training, you became a member of a UDT. Each man in the UDTs had his own specialty, and each man worked as part of a Team, using his skills for the good of the whole. Everything in the Teams is done under the buddy system. The training exercises and swimming exercises were all done as a Team and each man worked with his buddy on the same job. Throughout training and during operations, there was no thought to the individual, only the Team. The stand-alone individual wouldn't have survived in the Teams, much less through training.

So many things were going on in a tactical operation that one man couldn't hope to accomplish the mission. And the water is a dangerous environment. Each man in the Teams had to know he could count on his Teammate to help him if he got into trouble. Just as he would help if needed. You covered each other, always.

We didn't train to operate against any specific enemy. In the UDTs then, our mission stopped at the dune line on the beach. We didn't go inland yet; that was to come later. Our training mostly was to clear paths and to destroy ships. A team of combat swimmers could attack a ship at anchor with explosives, and that was one of the operations we practiced for.

On a mission, we weren't even really armed. Our gear consisted of a knife, a packet of shark repellent, and a plastic slate. This was enough for the operation at that time. The lack of equipment didn't bother us since there was no real need for more. We didn't go on shore, so we didn't need guns or other weapons. Communications were conducted from the boats, so there weren't radios with us in the water. We just did water work and that was enough.

Later I was able to leave something with the Teams that was a bit more permanent than the charts and maps I had been making.

There was an advertisement in a Norfolk paper about a contest for all of the personnel of the Atlantic Fleet. My partner in the chart shop brought it to my attention and suggested I enter. The competition was to design a symbol for the Underwater Demolition Teams. Before then, there had been a number of different signs and kinds of mascots used. During World War II, a stylized octopus with its multiple arms waving explosives had been used a few times. But nobody had come up with something that everyone liked.

Having been a designer and not an artist in my civilian work, drawing wasn't really what I did. But a lot of the guys in the Teams had me do different drawings, cartoons, and whatnot, so my sketching skills had become fairly good. I submitted about four different designs to the contest, which isn't a very large number in most design work. You just don't do you best work right at the beginning. Instead, you kind of warm up to the subject, change things, develop others, and sometimes just turn your back on it for a while.

The early sketches had been all right, but they just didn't really grab me. So I put everything away for a bit. When I picked it back up again, I started making sketches. The first idea that came to mind was based on our name. To the public, we weren't the Underwater Demolition Teams, we were the frogmen, a name that had been coined just after WWII. So my new character sketches centered around a frog.

So I had this little frog down on paper. To make him look a bit more Navy, I gave him a white enlisted man's hat. We had a reputation for being tough in the Teams, so I gave him some heavy muscles and a serious expression. A stock of dynamite in the frog's hand came from my memories of training. The instructors had thrown these little packets of explosives at us during Hell Week.

The lighting of the explosive came from the fact that during training, we had a bosun's mate by the name of Mark O. Lewis. When we went south for further training, all of the trainees had been put up in the bow of this APD for the trip down to the Caribbean. The rough Atlantic waters bounced us all over the place during the trip. Instructor Lewis used to stand in the door of our compartment smoking a great big smelly cigar, doing his best to make us all sick. It was that memory of Instructor Lewis with his cigar and his throwing explosives at us that gave my design his cigar and stick of dynamite.

That design, Freddie the Frog, became the official insignia of the

U.S. Navy's Underwater Demolition Teams. Being its creator was quite an honor, and it would have been an even greater one if I had known about it. No one notified me of anything and the design wasn't accepted as an official symbol until some years had gone by and I'd left the service.

One day when I came down to visit the UDT-SEAL Museum in the early nineties, I found out that my drawing had been adopted. The then curator of the museum, Chief Jim Watson, showed me all of the different ways my design had been used.

Freddy the Frog, the official Navy symbol for the Underwater Demolition Teams. In his mouth is a burning cigar and in his right hand, a stick of dynamite with a lit fuse.

U.S. Navy

As a cartographer in the UDT Team, I was really part of the Intelligence Section. When the Team went out on a predemolition run, the men were dropped off in pairs, spaced out at intervals from the boat. They would swim in, making depth soundings and recording their information down on plastic slates. This was also when they made any notes of obstacles.

When the swimmers were returned to the ship, the intelligence officer interrogated each man on details of their swims. Then they would deposit their plastic slates with me. I would transfer that information onto charts that were used by the Amphibious Forces to plan their landings. The same charts could be used by our own UDT to plan a demolition swim if we were going to go back in and blast away obstacles.

Chapter 24

COLD WATERS, COLD STARES, COLD RIDES

Besides swimming the cold waters off of Korea, the UDTs conducted operations in the late 1940s and through the 1950s well north of the Arctic Circle. To support distant military facilities across the northern cap of the North American continent, the men of the UDTs opened landing sites on beaches that were covered with thick ice through most of the year. Cold-water diving technology was still in its infancy during these operations and the men of the UDTs suffered through extremes of cold that taxed even their well-known endurance.

Cold wasn't the only threat the men of the UDTs faced. In the warmer waters of the tropics, cold wasn't a problem, but some of the denizens of those waters could pose a definite hazard. Encounters with some members of the ocean's population could be difficult only if you weren't aware of them. Others made you very aware that you were the interloper in their territory.

Even with new diving equipment that allowed a swimmer to remain underwater for hours, the length of a UDT combat swimmer mission was still dependent on the muscle power of the individual. UDT operators were superbly fit, but miles of swimming could tax the most powerful of men. Add to the swimmer's load the weapons, explosives, or equipment needed to complete a mission, and the distance he could cover decreased greatly. Mechanical means for extending a combat swimmer's range and carrying ability were developed throughout the 1950s and into the 1960s. But a new drawback was found in using these aids.

Commander Donald Balzarini, USN (Ret.)

Like so many other people, I probably first heard about the Underwater Demolition Teams by seeing the Richard Widmark movie The Frogmen. *Then there was a* Life *magazine cover and article called "The King of the Frogmen," with Tiz Moresson in the title role, as I remember. That really looked like something I wanted to do. Having done a lot of swimming and other water sports, I figured I'd give it a try.*

While I was at Navy OCS (Officer Candidate School), they were asking for people to volunteer for UDT training. Passing the screening tests, I asked for the West Coast and received orders for Coronado. Class 17 started in July 1956 and I was a part of it. The sunny Southern California weather doesn't have a lot of effect on the cold-water currents off Coronado. It didn't matter that it was summer; we did our share of shivering.

Particular stories can be told about any number of individual classes, but we all had pretty much the same experiences. We were all cold, wet, and miserable. The instructors beat us with hard work and PT, had us running and rolling around in the sand. Generally, it was an ordeal. For myself, I didn't particularly like to run and I didn't start out in training as one of the best runners. Swimming I didn't enjoy particularly either, but it was a lot easier for me than the running. Paul McNally was our class proctor and he would just go out and run forever. We would be trying to follow him and he was just running and running and running.

Probably the worst run I can remember at UDTR was during Hell Week. Our instructor for that "evolution" was Al Huey, and he was acting as the "good guy" instructor in contrast to the "bad guy" instructors. Just another mind game they played on you in training.

Instructor Huey was going to take us on an easy run, just a half mile over the sand dunes, down to the Del Coronado hotel and back. At least rumor had it that we would be having an easy run. As it turned out, he took us and ran us past the Hotel Del Coronado, down to the North Island fence. Then we went past the Del again and con-

tinued halfway to Imperial Beach. It was the most miserable run I had ever been on in my life. What we had been "told" was going to be one mile turned out to be twelve.

So Hell Week lived up to its name for us. You could "fight back" in your own way. We decided on the last night to make our own changes to the route the instructors had laid out for us for an "Around the World" rubber boat trip. We were to start near the Del, go across the land to the bay, paddle around the Amphibious Base and down to Imperial Beach, then cross back over to the ocean and paddle our IBS (Inflatable Boat, Small) north to the Hotel Del. We thought that route was ridiculous and decided to cut it a little short.

When we went around the Amphibious Base, and didn't think we could be seen, we cut into the base and headed overland. Stopping at the BOQ (Bachelor Officers' Quarters) and the enlisted barracks, we grabbed up a couple of six-packs, sandwiches, and things and figured we were going to fool the instructors and have an easy night of it. You get a little ding-y by the end of Hell Week.

Back into the ocean we went and we paddled on toward Imperial Beach. We had gone about a hundred yards when we could see the instructors on the beach. And they were just motioning us in. We went in to shore and there were the other boat crews standing at attention. The instructors, it seemed, were capturing each crew and having them do additional "fun" things on the beach.

We had a slight problem, though. Before taking our boat back into the water, we had taken one guy, Billy Davis, and sent him on another mission. He was going to go and find a friend of his nearby who had a truck. They were going to drive down to Imperial Beach, meet up with us, and drive us back to the base. That way we wouldn't have to paddle back. So when we were captured, Billy was off looking for this truck.

The instructors took us back to the Hotel Del and held a big beach party, and we were the entertainment. We would paddle out through the surf, up to the North Island fence, back in to shore, check in, run down to the Del Coronado, and check in to where the party was going on. Then we would do the whole thing again. This was the evolution we did all night.

So Billy Davis wasn't with us. He was still looking for us in Imperial Beach and had no idea that we were up doing our little circuits. It came to be around 4:00 or 4:30 in the morning and we were allowed to go back to our barracks and get cleaned up and some sleep. About 5:30, we were awakened in time for our morning PT and whatever down on the grinder. It was Saturday morning, the last day of Hell Week. As the leader of our boat crew, I had to turn in a muster report. Billy was in our boat crew, but he still hadn't shown up. I couldn't turn in a false report and I certainly didn't want to report him missing and get him in trouble.

So I went up to Instructor McNally, our class proctor, and told him I had a problem. He asked me what the problem was and I told him that Billy Davis was missing. And about that time Davis came running onto the grinder. He had been looking for us all over and finally just conked out to sleep at about 4:30. The sun woke him up and he came and found us. And we got away clean with our misfired little plan.

About noon that day we were secured from Hell Week. We all went to our quarters, showered, and just absolutely crashed. Some non-UDT guys woke me up around 4 P.M. Getting some of the other guys together, we actually went out and partied after completing Hell Week and being up all week. Finally, I got back to the BOQ about 11 P.M., fell into bed, and woke up sometime Sunday afternoon.

It didn't seem to me that the enlisted men going through training were treated any differently than the officers. The instructors took people that they weren't really sure should be in the Teams and seemed to give them some additional attention. But the rest of us mostly shared the abuse evenly. The officers, of course, had some different evolutions during training that we had to plan and lead. But the general treatment was about the same for us all.

In later classes that I observed in the late 1960s, there seemed to be a lot more verbal abuse from the instructors than we had to face a decade earlier. There was a lot more swearing at the trainees and such. Demeaning more than anything else. That's gone away again; it seemed to have just been around for a few years, perhaps with just a few instructors, and that was their technique. All trainees were scumbags; that was something we learned the first day at training, if not before.

Until the day you got into the Teams, we were all given a goodly helping of misery. Then came the day you graduated and you were welcomed into the Teams as a comrade. We didn't have a big graduation ceremony such as they have nowadays. We had a small outdoor graduation in front of the base theater. There were about twenty-five of us who had made it and there was just a feeling of elation at our accomplishment. We were part of the Team now. It was a wonderful feeling that can't really be described.

To get through UDTR—or what is called BUD/S today—you have to have a certain level of physical ability. That's tested during the screening programs and you have to have it just to get through the quarterdeck. But we've had world-class athletes who didn't make it through. Mentally, it's nice to be able to turn off the pain. But what you really have to have to get through training is that desire to make it to the Teams. That's the heart. You see some scrawny little wiry runt make it through to graduation while some big hulking guy didn't make it to Hell Week.

Physically, I was just kind of typical, five-foot-eleven, 180 pounds. My size was just kind of ordinary. Some of the other guys we had were well-built, muscular quitters. It was the desire—you had to want it. And it was sure worth it when you made it through.

Everything we had done to get to the Teams was worth it. And what seemed to be the best thing about it was that they paid us to do our jobs once we got into the Teams. Some of us would have done what we did for nothing. We lived on the beach in Coronado; you could go and jump out of airplanes, blow stuff up, and they paid us. That was pretty good.

The friends you made in the Teams, your comrades, your pals, these were great people to be with. That carries on to the present day. The men in the SEALs today are real professionals, but they also know how to really enjoy themselves when they can. They fight hard and they can party hard.

A Teammate is someone you can count on for your whole life. These are people you will be able to depend on no matter what the situation is. No matter how difficult the situation or task is, you will not be alone. Your Teammate will be there to help you. And if he isn't enough, more will come. A Teammate will not disappear, he will not bail out on you, he is there, unconditionally.

It's not that you can always recognize a SEAL or a frog in a crowd of people. Truthfully, you can recognize the phonies before you spot the real ones. The guys who are not SEALs or frogs but claim to have been, they stand out more. The big thing that trips up the phonies is the simple truth that once you have gone through training, you will never forget your class number. And that number is not classified. Training isn't what's classified in the Teams; some missions and capabilities are. If a guy claims to have gone through training and he can't remember his class number, he's a phony. If he says his training was classified and secret, he's a phony. Everyone who has ever gone through it is very proud of their class, as well they should be.

Once I graduated from UDTR and got into UDT 11, we did a lot of training ops along the coast of California. We did recons and amphibious landings, learning our craft and polishing our skills. The first real deployment I went on was the Arctic DEW line support operations. The Distant Early Warning System was set up along the far northern edge of North America and it was designed to spot a Soviet attack coming in on the United States over the North Pole. The radar and other sites that made up this line had to be manned and those people needed to be resupplied on occasion.

A detachment from UDT 11 flew from San Diego up to Kodiak, Alaska. From there, we flew on to Point Barrow, the northernmost point of Alaska. From Point Barrow, we used bush pilots to fly us in to different sites all across the North American continent. We would do beach reconnaissance, ice demolitions, and other actions to try to

UDT 12 operators paddle their IBS in frigid Arctic waters as they return from an underwater charting mission. The ice floes floating about them demonstrate the extreme cold of the water. Even in their insulated dry suits, the UDT swimmers suffered from the cold every time they entered the water.

U.S. Navy

see if these sites could be supplied by ship. We spent about six weeks up north of the Arctic Circle, traveling from Point Barrow to the Boothia Peninsula and back.

There had been cold water in Coronado, but wet suits weren't available in the Teams back then. You could go and buy your own, which many of us did. In the Arctic waters, we would wear our wet suits under the issue dry suits we had. The dry suits work by keeping a layer of underwear dry that's between your skin and the suit. But dry suits almost always leaked and that got the long underwear wet and you got really cold really fast. The wet suits kept you warmer longer.

Where you really felt the cold was on your hands, because we didn't wear gloves. And your face also got very cold. And this was cold from frigid water. It wasn't very much fun diving under the ice or working in Arctic waters. It was just unbearably cold. But it was beautiful once you went under the ice. The water was this great color, and it was very interesting. But it wasn't something you would do if you didn't have to.

Under the ice, the surface was a light white gray. The water was a very deep blue looking down. Looking around you, the water had a greenish tint, but didn't have any real color to it. The overhead cover of snow is what controlled the amount of light that penetrated the water. It could get dark but not really black.

We had a contest one day with a big tub of half ice and half water. The challenge was to see how long you could stay in the water before you climbed out. I lasted maybe thirty seconds. But the guy after me lasted forty-five seconds. Then the time just kept growing. The final time was something like twenty-five minutes that someone stayed in this ice bath. Again, that was from mental discipline, because the doctors said you couldn't stay in that thirty-two-degree water for that long. But some guys did.

The experience of working the DEW line was enjoyable. Seeing caribou, walrus, small whales, and polar bears, as well as the Eskimo culture was worth the work. But the work was hard and we earned every sight we saw. But we never had any close encounters.

There was one occasion with some Eskimos that was noteworthy. A couple of the guys were on the ice in their wet suits when some Eskimos approached. They must have looked like a couple of seals—the animal kind—and the Eskimos started taking shots at them. It was their arm waving and jumping around that caused the Eskimos to finally stop shooting.

There was another time when a bush plane crashed. The UDT men on board had been wearing their wet suits and were able to get the pilot out. They were all lucky to be alive after that incident.

There was another wildlife encounter I had out in the Pacific that took place in a lot warmer water. It was a night operation and Ron Smith was swimming off to my right. As Ron tells it later, he looked over his right shoulder and just saw this huge mouth in the darkness. Whatever it was, it struck him in the shoulder. He didn't know what it was and swam in to shore pretty quickly. We always teased him

Standing amid floating ice floes, a UDT swimmer comes close to resembling an aquatic seal long before the Navy SEALs were commissioned.

U.S. Navy

later, saying that he hit the beach and kept swimming across the sand until he hit the rocks.

When we checked Ron out later, we could see where he had been bitten on the shoulder. The puncture wounds looked like what a sea lion would leave if it nipped you. As near as we could figure out later, Ron may have gotten between a mother sea lion and her pup. He wasn't hurt real bad, so the situation seemed funny later.

There was another time when we were operating off of Wake Island in the Pacific that didn't seem so funny afterward. The first couple of days out we were doing reconnaissance and prepping a channel where we were going to blast through the coral. There were a few sharks around but nothing seemed bad. We set our shot off and the next day went back to the site. Now there were sharks all over the place. We went out through the surf and they literally chased us back to the shore.

We waited another day to let things settle down. The sharks had probably been feeding on fish and whatever our shot had killed. So we went out again to do a recon and see how our demolitions had gone. We paddled in IBS out there and Dick Swenson and I hit the water. We separated a little bit and just skin-dived down the thirty or forty feet or so to the channel we had shot. There were quite a few sharks still around.

I swam back up to the surface and looked down at a shark that appeared to be looking at me. That shark just kind of leveled off and started coming up to where I was. Now I knew how a fly felt on top of the water as a trout came up to eat it; the only trouble was that I was the fly and that shark was a really big trout.

He was about six feet away when I kicked at him with my fins and he swerved away. Then that shark just started circling me. He was about eight feet long and I was spinning around as fast as he was circling to keep my eye on him. The IBS was about fifty-feet away and I was working my way toward it as I spun in the water. The guys in the boat had no idea what was going on.

When I got to the boat, I wanted to get in, but I also didn't want to take my eyes off the shark. Finally, I just about swam straight up out of the water and into the IBS. Swenson was something like a hundred yards away and he too had no idea what was going on. So we paddled over and jerked him into the boat. Then I explained that there was a shark going around who looked very interested in us. So we went back in to shore.

The next day there were still sharks, but fewer of them. There was a cloudy layer in the water where we had blasted the coral. You had to swim down through the cloud layer to get below it and see just what the blast had done. It was a little disconcerting to watch the sharks moving in and out of this cloudy layer when you had to go back through it and not be able to see anything for a moment.

There was only one known incident in which a guy from the Teams was killed by a shark. That was in April 1963, when Lieutenant John Gibson of UDT 21 was attacked and killed by a shark in Megans Bay on Saint Thomas. The shark was later caught and they found parts of Lieutenant Gibson inside its body that proved they had gotten the killer.

But for all of the operations the UDTs and SEALs have conducted in the water, there have been very few attacks of any kind from the critter there. Some guys have been bitten by morays while catching lobster, and more than a few guys have had encounters with sea urchins and jellyfish. There have been guys who have disappeared, though.

When I first came into the Teams, one of the first things I was involved in was a memorial for a lost teammate. This guy had been diving off of Panama and just disappeared. It could possibly have been a predator or shark attack, but the sea is a dangerous place even without the things that live in it.

The "cruel sea" was an expression we've heard more than once. But the UDT mission is inherently dangerous. We've had more people killed since 1950 in noncombat than combat. Training accidents, equipment testing, or just operations have taken Team lives. It is just a dangerous environment.

Little mistakes when diving, working with explosives, or operating can kill you or your Teammate quickly. But when you're in the Teams, you don't think of the dangers. These things can happen, but you train constantly to see that they don't. When you worry about what can happen too much, it's time to get out.

But there were some interesting times working with new equipment. In the late 1950s, we were developing what were called SPUs or Swimmer Propulsion Units. These were battery-powered electric motors in a waterproof casing connected to a small propeller. The SPU could tow a swimmer a longer distance than he could swim, keep him better rested, and allow him to take more equipment/explosives with him.

The first SPUs in the Team were jury-rigged items the guys had made themselves. The first official SPU came to us in the late fifties. Chief Gagliardi and I went up to the Aerojet General Company in Southern California and picked up our first unit. The device was maybe three and a half or four feet long and a foot or so in diameter.

It was January when we went to pick up the unit. The company had a tank of water outside we could test the SPU in. And that water was cold. Right away we noticed a problem with the SPU, and it has been the same problem they have been struggling with ever since. The vehicles are cold to operate. When you are swimming, you're doing enough work that you'll keep yourself warm, especially in a good suit. When you're just hanging on to an SPU and riding around, you can get very cold, and very, very bored.

Later SPUs became bigger and you could sit inside of them. They were miniature submarines that were flooded rather than being dry inside. The driver would have something to do, but those of us just riding along would get bored and cold. Today they're developing warmer suits, even heated ones. But until they come up with a completely dry submersible to be used by the Teams, people are going to get cold and bored.

The history of the Teams hasn't been well documented over the years. Those of us who were doing the job wanted to be operating and not filling out paperwork. A lot of the history, the personal stories, have been lost. Now we are fortunate to have the UDT-SEAL Museum in Fort Pierce, Florida. The people there are really trying to gather the history through documents, recordings, photographs, and artifacts. The experiences of the people even from World War II can be saved now and kept for future generations.

The UDT-SEAL Museum is built on the training land that was used by the first UDTs and their forerunners, the Naval Combat Demolition

A UDT underwater swimmer using the Mark II SPU. His swim buddy would ride along behind him on an operation, being towed above and behind the man operating the SPU.

U.S. Navy

Units, during World War II. Initially, the training done at Fort Pierce was for the invasion of Europe. Then the Teams were created at Maui and Hawaii and their manpower came from the Fort Pierce training site. Now there is a home for the Teams' history on the site where they really had their beginnings.

■ Chapter 25

BEACH JUMPERS

In warfare, deception has always been as valuable a weapon as a firearm, vehicle, or ship. A specialized naval deception unit was founded during World War II based on an idea of a man who was well versed in the art of illusions. That man was the actor Douglas Fairbanks Jr., then a Navy lieutenant, and the unit he proposed would become the Navy Beach Jumpers.

The Beach Jumpers were an elite unit that used modern sound effects, electronics, and other tricks to make a group of small craft appear to be a much larger task force. These Beach Jumper units were first used as part of Operation HUSKY, the invasion of Sicily, in July 1943. The German forces were convinced that they had detected and repulsed an Allied landing force. Instead, a Beach Jumper unit had fooled them into directing some of their limited assets to an area that wasn't threatened with a landing.

The Beach Jumpers are among the most unconventional units that ever were active in combat. Though not used for the Normandy invasions, the Beach Jumpers proved their worth in other actions during World War II. After the war, they were retained in the Navy. Eventually, the Beach Jumpers were assigned to the same organizational command as another Navy unconventional warfare unit, the UDTs and later the SEAL Teams.

Commander Peter C. Dirkx, USN (Ret.)

I spent practically my entire naval career in the Navy Special Warfare community, from my first entering UDTR class fifteen, a winter class on the West Coast in 1955, to my retirement in 1981. When I first left boot camp in the Navy, I was assigned to Beach Jumper Unit 1 in Coronado. We were berthed in an adjacent building to the UDT barracks there. Every payday, we tended to give our paychecks to the UDT men in a crap game. Since our money was going to them anyway, the men finally convinced several of us to join the Teams. So another man and I in the unit started training together, based on our friendship with the UDTs guys.

A Beach Jumper Unit at that time consisted of four aviation rescue and reconnaissance boats along with their crews. Our mission was mainly one of cover and deception. Later it evolved into something more sophisticated, but at that time it was basically about simulating ships that were not ships by making the small boats sound and seem to be much bigger. That system could deceive the enemy into thinking a unit was either landing where there really wasn't anyone, or a much larger force than there really was steaming by offshore.

When we first volunteered for UDT training, we didn't have a clue about what we were getting into. Part of what kept us going was the friends we had in the next barracks. They promised that if we failed training, we would quickly be boarding one of those long, gray ghosts (Navy fleet ships) in the harbor and never see land again. That helped us continue through training when things really got bad.

And things did get pretty bad during training. We didn't have many of the "habitability items" that made working in the water at least a little more comfortable. Wet suits were pretty much unknown and the water could be really hard to get into. The training hasn't changed in its overall goal today, but the Navy has gotten a lot bet-

ter at running the students through. And the habitability factor has changed.

Does it make you a stronger or better person because you didn't have hot showers, hot meals, a wet suit? That's a question I just don't have the answer to. Comfort level isn't something that comes up a lot in BUD/S, and it didn't in the days of UDTR either. It's all relative to the time anyway.

Some things didn't change noticeably; our Hell Week then was pretty much the same as Hell Week now. There were five and a half days of misery, pain, and pure hell. Swimming, nuisance exercises, paddling the rubber boats, and only an hour or so of sleep each night. The constant movement, constant going, and staying awake all of the time, that was matched only by the constant harassment from the instructors.

It was the teamwork, the fellows in my boat crew, that helped get me through that long week. We hung in there and said we were getting through to each other. And that meant a lot when you were dead tired and just wanted to fall off of the tube (the side of the boat) into the water and just sleep forever. In fact, we did have people fall asleep while paddling the rubber boat and slip into the water. We'd have to grab them and pull them back. That's what got all of us through, our Teammates.

The thought of quitting is always in your mind during training, but I never seriously considered it. There was the thought that all of the misery and cold could be stopped in a moment, but then the thought would go away as you worked with your boat crew through the next evolution.

Cold is something everyone has experienced at one time or another. But then there's COLD. Being cold is dropping off the side of the rubber boat off San Clemente Island In December, when the water is 49 degrees and you don't have a wet suit. That's cold. You are so cold when you come out of the water that you don't have any feeling at all; you're numb all over. We did that to see if we could sustain that kind of cold. And we did those freezing cast and recoveries off San Clemente more than once.

Then comes the time when you hear the phrase "Secure from Hell

Week!" Those words cause the greatest feeling of relief in the world. It is probably the best thing you have ever heard in your life. Secure from Hell Week. You just want to lie down and sleep for a week, get warm, take a hot shower, eat. And there's also a sense of accomplishment. You know you've crossed the roughest period of the training.

After many weeks of training, a lot of them spent on San Clemente Island, what stands out in my mind is some of the really great instructors we had. When we went out to that island, we had to erect the tents, the instructors' tents first of course, at eleven o'clock at night. Then we could put our own tents up. And all of this work was done in what felt like gale-force winds. Every morning we would get up and do our PT and then hand-to-hand combat, followed by the day's training. In the evening it was fall out for semaphore and flashing-light drill. Then came the night exercise.

We didn't have showers. So you would come back off an exercise, peel off your wet clothes, and climb into that sleeping bag with all of the sand that came with you, and try to get warm. Walking out of the tent one evening, when we were being rousted out for some more signaling drill, I asked, "What are they trying to prove?"

An instructor, Chief McNally, looked at me and said, "Son, we aren't trying to prove anything. We want you to try and prove something to yourself."

These words stuck with me for the balance of my training and the rest of my military career. That was the single most significant thing I remember from my training.

We had about one hundred people start the class; we graduated thirty. It was a very proud and gratifying moment for me, and that sense of relief again, when we finally graduated. And there was a sense of excitement as well. Now we were looking forward to going into a Team. And I knew the Team I was being assigned to, UDT 11, was leaving for Japan in January. So my next biggest interest was to get my name on that list of men going to Japan.

So class 15 graduated training on December 15. I went over to UDT 11 and we left Coronado for Japan the first week of January 1956. I stayed over there with the Team until May 1957. For our mission we worked off of APDs (Assault Personnel Transports) on advanced force operations all over the South Pacific. The APDs included the Weiss, Bass, and Diachenko, and I rode on all of them at one time or another. We covered the same ground that WWII UDTs had gone to—Iwo Jima, Okinawa, and all of the other islands in the South Pacific. The operations we did were part of the amphibious exercises for the fleet. And we did demolition training.

There was an amphibious exercise off of Iwo Jima one night when we disembarked the ship into our PRs at 3 A.M. We took our PR (Landing Craft, Personnel, Reconnaissance) in and conducted our hydrographic reconnaissance and beach feasibility study from the boat. This was generally the same mission the UDTs had always done and was our part of the advanced force operations. It was around four o'clock in the morning when we were out on the water and a pitch-black night.

Iwo Jima has a black volcanic ash beach with a steep gradient. There were twenty of us from the UDT aboard that PR going in to the beach that night, and all we could hear was the surf crashing on shore. The next thing that happened, the boat had been lifted up on a wave, and we were surfing in to the beach. We hit the beach and the next wave hit our boat. Twenty people were scrambling out of that boat as the waves and surf came in on it. Within a half hour there was nothing left of that thirty-six-foot plywood boat except the engine block. We lost six boats on that particular operation, working in the middle of the night. And that was without any enemy fire or anything coming at us from the island. Just the power of the sea and the steepness of the shore.

In Japan, things went a lot easier for us. We initially stayed at Camp McGill, but it was closed while we were over there. So they moved us to the Yokosuka Naval Base. Each time we deployed on an exercise, it was on an APD, as used by the WWII and Korean UDTs. We spent thirty days one time doing a hydrographic survey of what was Siam then on the same APD. With twenty-some people on that ship, it was a pretty notable exercise. There wasn't any water available for showers or really washing up, so anytime it rained, we stood on the fantail and scrubbed up in nature's shower. When we got into

Bangkok after thirty days, the fleet commodore ordered the APD alongside another ship to take on water. He thought we all looked a little scrungy.

I have to give the WWII UDTs who spent months on those same APDs a lot of credit. I never thought much about them, but to spend thirty days on the same class of ship, they had to have been pretty hardy souls. We only had a detachment of some twenty UDTs on board, but there was also an equal number of Marines on the same ship. With roughly forty men on board besides the crew, we stayed on our side of the ship and the Marines stayed on theirs, both groups trying to stay out of the crew's way.

We returned to Coronado and it wasn't long before I was on another deployment. In 1957, I was one of the UDT 11 crew who went on a DEW line deployment to the Arctic Circle. Our job on the DEW (Distant Early Warning) line was to do a reconnaissance on the beaches that the Army was going to use to bring in supplies to remote sites. We would conduct a hydrographic reconnaissance off the beaches and make up charts for the Army. Large ships were bringing in the supplies and the Army forces were using small lighters to move the materials to shore. It was a little-known fact then that the Army had more small boats than the Navy. But they still needed to know the offshore waters.

Our base of operations was located at Point Barrow, Alaska, but we were taking aircraft inland to a number of the sites. The planes were DC-3, twin-engine prop jobs, and the only way we could get back off the small strips at the sites was with JATO (Jet Assisted Take Off) assists. These were rocket bottles strapped to the outside of the planes, fired to build up speed fast.

The runways we were landing on were so short that we had to touch down on exactly the right spot to safely land. If we overshot the spot, the pilot would often fire off the JATO rockets to get us back up in the air for another try. There were other times when we had to fly low across the strip to chase the herds of caribou away to clear the way for our landing.

On one site in particular, we went in with a Cessna-170 light plane.

We loaded our rubber boats, Fathometers, and other gear into the plane. Then the three of us who were going stuffed ourselves into the small cabin. The plane was piloted by a twenty-year-old kid whose father was with the FAA up in Fairbanks. This youngster was an experienced bush pilot who flew into these sites all of the time.

My memories of that trip were pretty good ones. My son was born while I was in Alaska, and I received notification while up there. And going in to the sites was fun. The people would be so glad to see us they would really put out a spread. They were cooking caribou steaks and beef, baking pies, just being wonderful hosts while we were there. So it was a very enjoyable experience.

We had been exposed to very cold water while in training, but this was the Arctic. Landing in the water unprotected would kill you quickly. Every time we flew in to one of these remote sites, we were wearing our Pirelli dry suits. These were the two-piece models worn over long underwear for cold-water protection. We wore those in the aircraft in case it crashed. Those were our survival suits. We wore the Pirellis in the water, and they would let us operate and withstand the temperature for a short period of time at least.

Most of our reconnaissance in the Arctic was done from rubber boats working with a Fathometer. We had to get in the water only when it was absolutely necessary. We didn't do any demolitions on that particular trip. Though we were prepared to, it just wasn't necessary.

Just a few years later there was a new excitement in the UDTs. The SEAL Teams were coming along and a lot of men were interested in just what was going on. Still in UDT 11 at the time, I was selected to be one of the "plankowners," one of the original crew members of SEAL Team One on the West Coast. But I had orders already cut to go to Key West and be an instructor at the Underwater Swimmers School. The assignment was one I couldn't afford to turn down because my wife was pregnant with our fourth child. She had already delivered three other children while I was deployed somewhere, and she made it very clear to me that I was going to be around when this one entered the world.

So even though I very much wanted to join this new organization, I had to decline, and went to Key West instead. Later, in 1968, I was back in Coronado and was able to join with SEAL Team One while they were active in Vietnam.

■ Chapter 26

MATERIALS, THE TOOLS OF WAR

The side that can bring the most production to a war is usually the one that wins. In an all-out war of attrition, it's the side that runs out of men and materials last that wins. This was well proven during World War II when a German antitank unit officer was heard to comment how he had run out of shells before the Allied side had run out of tanks.

The UDTs of WWII pride themselves on the fact that they operated in the field with almost nothing in the way of equipment. At that time a full issue of gear for a WWII frogman going in on an op without explosives would fit in the average child's book bag.

After WWII, the UDTs were not as well funded as they would have liked, suffering as they did the same dislike by conventional Navy units as any other service's unconventional forces. The UDTs got by on relatively little and made do with what they had or could get their hands on. In the mid-1950s, this changed a bit among the more farseeing members of the Navy's command structure as the UDTs began to rise in prominence.

New materials and supplies came in to the UDTs along with new missions. It took supply personnel who were not only familiar with how a UDT operated in the field but were qualified to operate themselves to know ahead of time what materials would be needed for an operation or even the day-to-day running of a Team in the field. With the advent of the new SEAL Teams, the need for good supply personnel was even more important, given the wide variety of unusual and exotic weapons and equipment the Teams used. But these supply personnel also had to be familiar with the bureaucracy and red tape of a very large Navy in a peacetime situation.

James H. "Hoot" Andrews, Chief Storekeeper, USN (Ret.)

When I volunteered to go into underwater demolition training, I joined up with other volunteers from all over the fleet. This group is gathered together and that composes a class. In this mob of strangers, I didn't know anyone. The only way I found to get someone's attention—to talk to them or whatever—was to call out "Hey, Hoot!" That would cause them to turn around to see who was calling them Hoot. The spin-off of that was by being nicknamed Hoot.

It was 1951 when I joined up with class seven on the East Coast at Little Creek. We started training in May and finally graduated in August. I was only twenty-four years old at the time, and I would never go through it again. The instructors we had were volunteers from the UDTs there at Little Creek. There wasn't a trained cadre of instructors like they have today in Coronado. Each Team, UDT 2 and 4 then, would just supply a number of experienced UDT men to act as our instructors. These individuals would vary from day to day, so we never knew just who might be running what evolution.

The Amphibious Base at Little Creek back then was hardly as built up as it is today. There were long stretches of mudflats, stagnant water, and the instructors made sure we were put through every inch of it. I always tried to make sure I was up in the front of the group when we plowed through the muck. After 160-some guys during the early days of the class had run through the same patch of mud, it would be so churned up that the guys at the back of the pack ran the risk of sinking totally out of sight.

And there was a lot more to occupy your training time at Little Creek than just mud. Going across the obstacle course would give you a new experience of the word pain. Or crawling through the mud-flats on your elbows and knees, with just your chin, nose, and eyes barely above the surface of the slime.

The Seabees had been one of the first sources of manpower for the Teams back in World II. And they seemed to still be mad about our taking their men when they built our obstacle course at Little Creek. They seemed to have taken every Seabee who was sadistic and had him design part of the obstacle course. It was terrible! It was awful! And we had to go through it every day during training.

The instructors even added a bit of competition to the obstacle course. They would see who could go over it the fastest, timing the whole thing. I never was one of the faster people. I was just about in the middle of the pack. But I did finish; a lot of others never did.

Class seven started with 169 men and we graduated 34. When I graduated with that proud few, I was assigned to UDT 2, later redesignated UDT 21. UDT 4 was also later redesignated as UDT 22. During the early 1950s, we still worked with the same limited equipment the Teams had used in World War II. The salvage yards were hit often to help us keep our boats and other equipment up and running. As far as individual gear went, they were issuing a pair of coral shoes, a web belt, K-Bar knife, face mask, and a pair of fins. During training, we had to qualify to earn those fins by swimming a mile under a certain time.

But those fins we had were a synthetic rubber WWII type that wouldn't bend and they just didn't last very long. But that's what we had to live with.

In 1954, I was sent to the Bureau of Ships to help formulate and implement an allowance list for one Underwater Demolition Team. Prior to my leaving on that assignment, I went around to all of the department heads in the Team. They were told to give me a complete list of everything they needed to operate, from screwdrivers to toothpicks or whatever.

Taking those lists, I collated them to eliminate the duplication factor. And that was the basic set of information I used to put together the allowance list. Each department, or code, as they would say at the bureau, had an allotment of equipment to begin operations. And then a listing of consumable materials to continue operating. These codes had to explain why something was needed and how much it would cost to purchase and maintain.

There were more than a few problems with some of the materials I ordered. The 5 or 10 gross (720 or 1,440) of condoms I ordered from the Naval Supply Center in Norfolk caused me to get a phone call. Some woman in the requisitioning department at the supply center wanted to know what we were going to do with 10 gross of condoms. I had to explain to her that these materials were necessary to waterproof firing assemblies used to detonate explosives in the water. She accepted my explanation and said that I should include on all my future requisitions for this item the words For Government Use Only.

Another item on the allowance list caused a little more stir in some offices. We had to go to the various bureaus that were concerned with all of the different items on the lists. For each bureau, we had to give a presentation justifying why we needed the things on the list. At the Bureau of Medicine, they wanted to know why I had listed 460 two-ounce bottles of brandy. The doctor who asked the question said he was wondering what we were going to do—outdrink the enemy?

We had a very good reason for the request. For our mission, we were responsible for the entire hemisphere that included the North Atlantic and the Northern European area. If we were tasked with a mission up in the Arctic, then we would have a platoon, twenty-five men, in the water in the morning and possibly again that afternoon. When the men came in from such a swim, the corpsman would issue each of them a two-ounce bottle of brandy. That could easily amount to fifty such bottles a day, and if there was a night operation, the total was seventy-five bottles a day.

We had to operate on the premise that we needed to supply ourselves independently for 90 days, until an auxiliary train came up and bought us a resupply. Adding all of the numbers together and using the equations the Bureau of Supply had come up with, that gave us 460 bottles for a platoon. And that answer satisfied the medical officer.

Later, in the fifties, I went over to the Nuclear Navy and became qualified to work as a chief of the watch on the new nuclear submarines. Before going aboard the George Washington, one of the first of the operational Polaris missile boats, I had gone through the initial outfitting, loading, location system, and records on board. It had been a very trying time and everything was starting to go very smoothly. Since I had been in underwater demolition before, I still carried that job code as part of my record. Even though I was a storekeeper chief, I still had that UDT code.

When Roy Boehm took the assignment of setting up the SEAL Team, he was having a very hard time getting anyone to respond to his needs for equipment. He had just written out a list on a pad and was trying to get some cooperation in filling it. That was when he got in touch with ComSubLant (Commander, Submarines, Atlantic) and went up the line to track me down.

When the George Washington pulled in to Holy Loch, Scotland, on what was my third patrol with her, there was a set of orders for me to report to SEAL Team Two. I didn't even know what that was. I had just received my qualifications as chief of the watch on the George Washington and the captain called me up to his stateroom.

He wanted to know if I had put in for a transfer to this new duty on my orders. My answer was simply no, and that I didn't even know what a SEAL Team was. So he said he was going to do everything he could to squash the orders. That started a flurry of messages and paperwork crossing the Atlantic from Washington, D.C., to Holy Loch. When the final message came in with year, date, and time group stamped on it, it said, "Negative, transfer." So I went back to Little Creek.

When I had gotten back to Roy, whom I had known well in my UDT 21 days, I learned what was going on. I have absolutely no regrets about my transfer. All of the guys I had been in Underwater Demolition with before were part of the new Team. Roy had brought them over, picking and choosing his men carefully. Some of the guys had been out on operations when they received the word that they would be reporting to SEAL Team upon their return. They were still plankowners, they just had to complete their operational commitment before they could ship over.

Plankowner is a uniquely Navy term. The term dates back to the days of the sailing Navy and wooden ships. It refers to a member of the original crew for a newly commissioned ship or shore activity. Each plankowner is qualified as such when he is assigned to the new unit by order. The name comes from the Navy tradition according to which each sailor owned one foot of the deck planking of the ship. In this way, the crew and the new command were brought that much closer.

So at SEAL Team Two, I was back making up new allowance lists. My first attempt was to try to get us more money, but that didn't go over too well. The SEALs were a new concept and the traditional Navy didn't like the idea very much to begin with. What the Navy at large wanted was seagoing men and ships to carry them. They wanted conventional warfare, and our type of unconventional warfare wasn't seen as the kind of thing that would enhance anyone's career at the Pentagon or elsewhere. But President Kennedy had been the one to start the idea going forward. He wanted the military to have these new capabilities and that meant we were going to have them.

To set up an allowance list, you first take the mission statement that is issued by the higher authority in the Navy and usually comes out of the CNO's office. That statement is matched up with the personnel complement, the number of people you are told it will take to carry out this mission. That's the basic piece of hard paperwork you have to have before anything else comes up. Equipment, clothing, weapons, everything is dependent on your mission statement and personnel.

At the beginning, the SEALs didn't really have anything. The Team was doing the beg, borrow, and steal routine from everywhere, including the UDT right across the street. Gear would be checked out from UDT, used for an operation, and then returned. There was no real paperwork kept to help them out or to be used as a guide.

ComPhibLant (Commander, Amphibious Force, Atlantic) was our command, and the supply types didn't know what we were or what we were doing. The folks over in command just considered us a bunch of misfits. In 1962, everything was top secret, even the name "SEAL," so we couldn't explain anything in very much detail. From the time I got to the SEAL Team, I went through the same procedures I had gone through before. They worked and we could at least eventually get what we needed.

Part of what I was doing really was repeat work. Besides using the mission statement and personnel lists, I picked up a copy of the UDT allowance list to use as a base. And that was the same list I had written years earlier. There were elements in the two units' mission statements that overlapped—Sub Ops, Air Ops, diving equipment, recharging compressors, things like that were the same whether it was for the SEALs or the UDT.

The armory with our weapons in it, that was a very different story from what was used over in the UDTs. We had to come up with a lot of different, exotic stuff to stock those shelves and racks. So to get the Team everything it needed, I took my paperwork over to ComUDU (Commander, Underwater Demolition Unit) and the both of us traveled back up to Washington to visit with bureaus up there.

We talked to every one of the heads of the different codes and we came back with an allowance list for the SEALs. The UDTs had been hard enough to explain to these guys; the concept of the SEALs was beyond them. The different bureau people had never heard of unconventional warfare, counterinsurgency, guerrilla warfare, or marine sabotage. And all of those things were parts of our mission statement. Those conventional Regular Navy sailors were all still out in the fleet firing fourteen- and sixteen-inch guns at sea. That was the Navy to those people. They preferred conventional warfare, like the WWII battles in which the sixteen-inch guns slammed between battleships and the Marines would move in to take and hold the beach.

In unconventional warfare, you would go in, hit a target, and run. Or slip in quietly and overrun an area and secure it. The training for unconventional warfare is very different from a normal training routine, and so Roy Boehm had to set up a cross-training program. We would be assigned to different elements that would be going to different training sites, such as Fort Bragg and the Army Special Forces School there.

With the Army Special Forces, we trained in foreign weapons, reconnaissance, sneaky-pete work, and specialized training. Our communications people went to the Special Forces communications courses. Our corpsmen went through some of the SF medics training, where they learned the more advanced field surgery techniques and so on. And we all went through the HALO (High Altitude, Low Opening) parachute training.

That kind of training prepared us to conduct some of our unconventional operations and marine sabotage. At that time we had only one type of submersible craft. And like the UDTs, we used them to attack ships at anchor, slipping up on them and attaching limpet mines to their hulls. That was the training and that was the job. And we needed the tools to complete that mission. Getting most of those tools was my assignment.

Roy Boehm came up with some real exotic pieces of hardware he wanted for the SEALs. Instead of going through the normal ordnance channels, which would have turned him down anyway, he went out and bought AR-15 rifles, enough to outfit both SEAL Team One and Two. We had the funds, he mostly had the authority, and he certainly had the attitude to just get what he needed to get the job done.

One of the strangest pieces of equipment Roy wanted was thirty or forty crossbows. In spite of the fact that we were trying to build a modern unit in 1962, Roy wanted crossbows. And he had some suggestions for sources in his request. The manufacturer was in England and supposedly they made the best crossbow then on the market. It wasn't my place to ask questions. They just told me what they wanted and I went out and got it.

So I submitted the crossbow request to the Navy purchasing office. That began a week or a week-and-a-half runaround. Jut because I wouldn't ask questions didn't mean that anyone else wouldn't. They wanted to know why we needed the crossbows and I would answer that we were still in a classified state, had a Priority 2 for equipment, which was pretty high in their ranking. This was what was on the allowance lists and we wanted them. About a month or so later forty crossbows and a whole bunch of arrows showed up at SEAL Team Two.

In spite of the exotic nature of much of what was wanted for the new SEAL Team, it all made sense to me. And that was because of my experience in underwater demolition. If there was a bastard outfit in the Navy, that's what the SEALs seemed like. No one without a real need to know, knew what we did, what we were, or why we needed what we needed. It was a never-ending argument every time the request went forward about another piece of equipment or parts and materials to keep what we did have going, going.

They wanted to know what, why, and where. And we could only tell them the barest essentials, if that, because of security reasons. Even the name "SEAL" couldn't be openly used on unclassified documents.

At the same time I was going through all of the work of preparing the allowance list and requisitioning gear, I had to get ready to do my own training to operate. Like all of the rest of the Team, I had to go to Fort Benning for Jump School; I had to make my dive qualifications, and every other element that was required to earn and maintain the SEAL job code.

Missions and deployments were something we all did. The officer or commander assigned a task would usually post an announcement on the bulletin board on the Team quarterdeck. The note was usually pretty simple; this is the trip, this is who's in charge, and then it would ask for volunteers. Every time, the list was filled up completely. So the officer in charge of that operation could pick the men he knew would best fit the job.

You didn't always like what you had to do, but you had to do it. For myself, I hated parachute jumping. I have no trouble saying I was scared every time I went out the door. But it was part of the job, so I did all of my training and kept up the jumps needed to remain qualified.

But the training you received in the Teams took over when you were doing a job. It didn't matter if you were scared, you would have been drilled often enough that whatever needed to be done, you did it automatically. But none of the SEALs were machines when they worked on a job. Everyone was a thinking, feeling man. The emotionless Hollywood lone-wolf type just didn't exist in the SEALs or UDTs.

There are men in the Teams who are extremely intelligent, and they have good common sense to go along with it. They are very good at making individual decisions when called on to do so. There are just no stereotypes in the Teams.

I met a guy who asked me if I had been a SEAL. When I told him yes, he looked at me puzzled.

"You don't look like a SEAL," he said.

"Well," I said back, "what's a SEAL supposed to look like?"

He didn't have an answer for that one. What he had been thinking of was the movie image of a huge, muscled guy coming up from the water with a black bandana around his head and a blazing machine gun in each hand. That's not a SEAL, that's just ridiculous.

Underneath all of the equipment, camouflage paint, weapons, and ammunition is a dedicated, committed warrior. Well trained, he knows exactly what to do to get the mission done. And he will carry that mission out. That attitude goes everywhere in the Teams, from the highest-ranking officer to the most junior seaman. Whatever the mission calls for, they will do it.

The men I worked with I could depend on for anything. Putting your life in your Teammate's hands was common. And he would do the same with you. When you had a Teammate next to you, you knew you would be all right. And he knew the same thing. There was no fear with your Teammates beside you.

The SEALs are a group unlike any other in the world that I know of. There's a bond between the men that you can't explain. It stems from the Underwater Demolition Teams of World War II who went in to the beach with no weapons at all except for a K-Bar knife. Then it came on up to the SEAL Teams. The difference in the kind of warfare and missions conducted just grew. From just underwater reconnaissance and beach blowing of obstacles to going in to the jungle, swimming up the rivers and streams of Vietnam, and going ashore to seek out the VC. Hit them first rather than let them ambush you.

Regular forces had to go in to an area, dig in, and wait. They secured an area and pacified it. The SEALs would slip into an area and seek out the enemy, and either capture the leadership or just wipe them out.

The UDTs and the SEALs were very much the same; the only real difference between the two units was their mission statement. Both units started from the same beginnings and went through the same basic training. When a UDT man came over to the SEALs, that's when he received the additional specific training called for by the type of missions SEALs did. By the 1980s, the missions of the SEALs and the UDTs were recognized as being so close that it was a duplication of effort. So the names changed and the UDTs became the SEAL Teams.

The man who joins this kind of unit has a high level of commitment to what he is doing. The willpower has to be there so that the individual will never give up, never ever give up . . . never.

■ Chapter 27

LEADERS AND LOSSES IN THE TEAMS

For a long time there was no career path for officers who had gone through UDT training and wanted to remain in the Teams. A career path meant the opportunity to make rank and move up in positions. But there were very few higher-ranking slots in the Teams, especially in the 1950s and into the 1960s.

Officers who wanted to move ahead in rank much past lieutenant often had to return to the regular Fleet Navy to pull their time on board ships and in staff positions. And there was a stigma that went along with having been a "frogman" in the regular Navy, especially among those who didn't understand the UDTs' mission. Not surprisingly, in some circles, volunteering for training and an assignment to a UDT was considered a career killer.

The Fleet Navy was also ignorant of the dangers that the men of Navy Special Warfare faced every day. Even without enemy activity, training and practicing for operations was often dangerous, sometimes even deadly.

Captain Thomas N. Tarbox, USNR (Ret.)

The first time I learned of the UDTs, I believe, was when I saw the movie The Frogmen *starring Richard Widmark. To me, it was just another movie at the time. Although I swam quite a bit most of my life and was very good in the water, I didn't give the UDTs another thought until I was in OCS.*

While I was at Officers Candidate School for the Navy, I think the student body was shown a short presentation on the UDTs. At that time I was a frustrated naval aviator more than anything else; I was just too short. There wasn't any way I was going to get any taller in time to fly the Navy's planes, so I had to look to other avenues for my time in the service. In OCS, your choices were small ships, big ships, or something other. No one wanted to be on a big ship, and a lot of people wanted to be on the small ships. So I decided to give the UDTs a try.

In January 1958, I began training at Little Creek, Virginia, with class 19. The fact that we were a winter class was in my favor. My home had been in Montana and Colorado; I could not have stood that swampwater summer so common in Virginia. Busting ice off my pants or cracking through the ice to get to the mud was okay for a young lad from Montana.

Training was everything that could be expected—a lot of harassment, a whole lot of physical training, and we learned a great deal about demolitions. But that last only happened after we had gone down to Puerto Rico.

At that time the heavy demolition training for a winter class was done down in Puerto Rico. A summer class was trained right there at

Little Creek. It turned out to be pretty awesome; I still can't believe the number of windows we broke along the beach.

It didn't appear that the instructors were any harder on those of us who were officers than they were on any other student in the class. They might have had greater expectations of us. It's tough to go into a Team as an officer when you're the same as any other trainee. It takes about a year and a half for an officer to start to know more about what you are doing than the men around you. That knowledge comes from working at a different level, from being aware of the op plans and specific orders which the men under you are not.

The UDT naked warrior slips up on a beach to attach a demolition charge to a concrete tetrahedron obstacle. Outside of his bag of explosives, he is armed only with a knife at his hip. It is from these beginnings that the lavishly equipped and thoroughly trained SEALs of today come from.

U.S. Navy

But before I could get to the Teams, I had to complete UDTR training. The hardest part of training for me was the deep, soft sand. Not being a great runner at the best of times didn't help me, but after a few hundred yards of running in the sand, my leg muscles would start to knot up. After that, just putting one leg in front of the other was about all I could do.

In spite of the trouble with the sand, at no time during training did I give much thought to quitting. Sometimes I feared that they might throw me out. And at that time the instructors could do that very easily. But I never thought of quitting the course. You develop kind of a love/hate relationship with the instructors, or maybe more of a hate/hate one. But I figured that if they could make it, so could I.

What got me through training was probably just looking at the instructors. And I just didn't see any reason to quit. As a fresh-cut ensign just out of OCS, you have no incentive to quit. If you did drop the course, the Navy might just have a worse place they could send you.

Even though I never considered quitting training, graduation day was still pretty good. We had our picture taken with an admiral and we knew were going to the Teams. But I had a little different situation—I was going to immediately leave for a Med (Mediterranean) tour. The reason was that the officer-in-charge of that deployment was Jim Wilson.

Jim Wilson had come down to our UDTR class right after we had gotten back from Puerto Rico. We still had a few weeks to go in training, but Jim came down to shop around the new officers and pick an assistant OIC (Officer in Charge). He picked me, and he did so for a very good reason. He figured we could wear each other's clothes since both of us were about the same size.

When you go to the Med in the summertime at the exalted rank of ensign, you use up a lot of white uniforms. You're assigned as boat officer, beach officer, import officer of the day—all those nasty jobs fall upon an ensign's shoulders. And you have to do them all in whites. Jim figured if we could wear each other's clothes, it might put us ahead of the pack. And he turned out to be right. While one officer was working with the platoon, the other could be standing duty in clean white, whether the clothes were his or not.

Officers had a real problem in the UDTs at that time, as there was no career path. You couldn't be promoted past a relatively low rank without leaving the Teams. So I left the service after my time was up and went back to college. In early 1962, I had already received a letter from the Navy trying to get me to come back into the Teams. Not only were the SEAL Teams being formed up at that time, they were also forming UDT 22. But I still couldn't see any future in it, so I turned the Navy down.

Then I received a letter from a friend of mine who was still in the Teams. Steve Young wrote to tell me about this new Team that was being created. He told me there was something called the SEALs coming along, and he thought the name meant Sink Enemy And Leave. But it looked like it might be something exciting up on the horizon.

Still being in the Navy Reserves, I spent my two weeks active duty at Little Creek. Sure enough, they had something called a SEAL

Team. I figured that if I played my cards right and was lucky, I might be able to make a career of it and still make some rank. I did and it worked.

Arriving at SEAL Team Two on 27 August 1962, I was not a plankowner of the new Team. But I became the executive officer (XO) fairly quickly. When I first returned to the active Navy I had said that I wanted to go to the SEAL Team. They told me that wasn't going to happen because at that time I would have been senior to the then XO, Roy Boehm. So instead, I was sent over to UDT 22 and told that I might be able to go over to SEAL Team Two on my next duty rotation.

In between the time that I was accepted back into the Teams and my actual arrival, Roy Boehm had ticked off enough people that he had to go someplace else for a while. So I was able to go into SEAL Team Two as their new XO. Within two years I succeeded John Callahan and became the Team's commanding officer.

Because I had been a reserve officer, the Bureau of Personnel asked me if I would like to extend my active duty time. I said that I would, but that I would like to have SEAL Team Two. So I was assigned and started spending my time at SEAL Team Two.

Those first few years we were spending a lot of our time doing new things, things the UDTs never did. It was kind of funny in a way because many of the men in the new SEAL Team had been very conservative operators while in UDT. Every time something new came along at UDT, these same guys would say how it had been tried before and didn't work then, so it wouldn't work now. In the SEAL Team, the same people were willing to try anything.

That first year at SEAL Team Two was full of new experiences, not all of them good. While on a training exercise in Turkey, we lost Lieutenant (jg) William Painter in a diving accident. Ensign Painter had been a plankowner of the Team, coming in to the Team directly from his training class. He was the officer-in-charge of a detachment sent to Turkey from SEAL Team Two in early 1963. During a diving exercise, Painter put on a rig and went into the Bosporus by himself, which was a big no-no, and never came up. As far as I know, his body has never been found.

We were very sorry to lose him. But to go down without a swim buddy was anathema to us—you just don't do that. He broke the rule and proved why it was a rule. It was our first loss, made worse for having been the result of a mistake.

By 1964, I was a lieutenant, and I had been a lieutenant while I was the XO. That year I became the commanding officer of SEAL Team Two. It sounded a lot more impressive than it looked at the time. I was in the same office, with the same people, and I don't think I even changed desks. There was a formal change of command, and the ceremony which the Navy calls for is pretty awesome, but other than that, it wasn't that big a change.

We lost another man from SEAL Team Two in May 1965 in a parachuting accident. Mel Melochick was one of the guys conducting a rehearsal for Sea Week, a big festival we have in Norfolk every year with shows and everything for the families. The SEAL jumpers were practicing over Willowby Bay, a little arm of Chesapeake Bay that's enclosed by Naval Air Station, Norfolk. About five jumpers bailed out of the aircraft on a water jump.

The jumpers did some maneuvering in the air and then Melochick pulled his rig (released his chute). I don't know if he waved off or not, but when you pull your rig and your canopy opens, you stop in the air in relation to everything around you. Jerry Todd, who was the jumper above Mel, couldn't maneuver out of the way in time and he crashed through Mel's canopy.

Melochick was probably killed instantly from the crushed vertebrae in his neck. That he was dead when he hit the water is fairly certain. Jerry survived the crash with a broken arm and I think a broken leg as well. But he recovered and had a full career afterward.

Joe DiMartino obtained a DC-3, a Navy C-46, to take us from NAS Norfolk to near Pottstown, Pennsylvania, where we took Mel's body home for burial. There was a full military funeral, with an Army firing squad and the presentation of the flag. His mother was very distraught, as were most of Mel's relatives. When the ceremony was over, we all left for the local American Legion hall and started drinking and having a party. I think if you have to go, it's a good thing to have your Teammates celebrate your life afterward.

The accident taught us that in parachuting, it is always important to give a wave-off, move your arms so that everyone around and above you knows you're going to open your parachute. We also learned how the press reacts to such a death. The guys had been talking in the airplane prior to the jump. And they didn't get wild, but their joking around was reported in the press later. From the journalism class I took in college, I knew how the press works and how anything you say can work against you, and I explained this to the men. And that no matter how the guy, or girl, acts, the media people are there on business and they aren't your friends.

Another thing I did in SEAL Team Two was get to be the first SEAL CO to send his men into a contingency, an active combat situation, when I dispatched a SEAL detachment to the Dominican Republic for the crisis there in 1965. At that time the Team was organized into assault groups, what would be called platoons now. And several assault groups were sent down to take part in the U.S. aid action there.

Sending my men into harm's way was a difficult part of the job. The Dominican Republic thing was much like many of the contingencies have been since. You couldn't tell the enemy from the friendlies. And we were obviously being Yankees in a place where not too many of the people liked us. There was a lot of sniping activity in the capital, Ciudad Trujillo. Our guys were out in the weeds more, but the actual combat turned out to be pretty light.

The incident was just one of those things that turned out to be like Vietnam and a lot of other places, though it hardly lasted as long as Vietnam. It was, however, the forerunner of Vietnam. The SEALs did some hairy things, but they did them very well and everyone got home safely.

A little less than a year after the Dominican Republic action, I left SEAL Team Two. It was August 1966 and I went up to the Defense Intelligence School. From that school, I went on to Okinawa and duties there. I never did get back to the UDTs or the SEALs. SEAL Team Two *was my last experience with an active Team. I spent time in staff positions within Special Warfare and was the later CO of BUD/S. But nothing was ever quite the same as those early years at SEAL Team Two.*

■ Chapter 28

THE CREATION OF THE NAVY SEALS

The serious development of the U.S. military's ability to combat the worldwide increase in Communist-supported guerrilla warfare began in the late 1950s during the Eisenhower administration. Development of these capabilities was slow and consisted of little more than studies and discussions among high-level military officers, politicians, and political appointees. It was not until the 1960s and the Kennedy administration that the development of these capabilities was pushed forward. Under President Kennedy, the military received the stimulus necessary to actively create unconventional warfare units.

Op-003/rer
Op-00 Memo 00242-01
3 May 1961
SECRET
MEMORANDUM FOR OP-01
Subj: Guerrilla Warfare

1. We should have a record of all naval personnel, particularly officers, who have been specially trained in guerrilla warfare, UDT, psychological warfare, and what the Army calls

"Special Forces Training." We should get more people below the age of thirty-five trained in this field.

2. Training is of course one of the key factors in guerrilla warfare. We will need such things as training pamphlets on this subject. We should take a look at the Army pamphlets. We should send people through other Service schools as well as our own survival courses and probably set up courses at the amphibious schools.

3. I know this is going to be difficult, but we are going to have to take over such operations as river patrol in the Saigon Delta, in the Mekong River, and other areas. Our people will have to know thoroughly how to live and fight under guerrilla conditions.

4. Will you please give me a list of equipment that has been developed such as silent motors, etc., along with things that we might need now? It might be beneficial to look at the Army's list of equipments.

Arleigh Burke

[The above is one of the first official documents produced by the CNO's office during the earliest development of the SEAL Teams]

On 11 July 1960, Admiral Arleigh Burke, the Chief of Naval Operations, directed Deputy CNO (Fleet ops and readiness) Admiral Wallace Beakley to study possible contributions by the Navy to unconventional warfare. Admiral Beakley responded to the CNO's directive by August 12 and included his suggestion that, because of their extensive training in small-unit actions of this type, the Navy's Underwater Demolition Teams and Marine reconnaissance units were the logical organizations for expanding the Navy's capability in unconventional warfare.

Four weeks after Admiral Beakley's response to the CNO, the Unconventional Activities Working Group was established within the Office of the CNO under the Deputy Chief of Naval Operations (plans and policy). The group was to consider "naval unconventional activity methods, techniques, and concepts which may be employed effectively against Sino-Soviet interests under conditions of cold war." This group was later succeeded by the Unconventional Activities Committee, which turned in the final report.

The year 1961 brought a large number of changes for the world in general and the United States military in particular. President Eisenhower was replaced by a new, young President who thought differently than others had and had experienced war in a very up-close and personal way. There was also a serious threat to world peace in the form of the Soviet Union, which was aggressively seeking to export its style of Communism to the rest of the world.

On 6 January 1961, Nikita Khrushchev, the premier of the Soviet Union, publicly announced that his country would "support just wars of liberation and popular uprisings . . . wholeheartedly and without reservations." The developing struggle in Vietnam was mentioned as an example of such a just war. A few weeks later, on 29 January, John F. Kennedy became the thirty-fifth President of the United States. At the age of forty-three he was also the youngest person ever to hold that office.

Admiral Burke maintained his advocacy of unconventional warfare in a response to Admiral John Sides (CINCPACFLT). In correspondence, Admiral Burke stated that unconventional warfare did constitute a proper mission for the Navy. In another memo issued in early February, he again suggested that the Navy "do as much as we can in guerrilla warfare . . . even if it is not our primary business." Burke proposed emphasizing UDT groups, escape and survival training, and the creation of a nucleus of young naval officers trained by the Army in guerrilla warfare. At that time the Army Special Forces at Fort Bragg were the only experienced guerrilla warfare group in the U.S. military.

President Kennedy met with the Joint Chiefs of Staff on 23 February. The President stressed the importance of guerrilla and counterguerrilla warfare responses to Communist actions. He wanted present capabilities increased and new counterguerrilla warfare concepts established and put into place as quickly as was practicable. On March 10, Rear Admiral William Gentner Jr., the director of the Strategic Plans Division, approved the preliminary recommendations of the Unconventional Activities Committee. The recommendations were to involve the Navy more directly in the lower levels (direct action) of counterguerrilla actions.

Specific proposals of the group included the recommendation that new units be established, one for the Atlantic and another for the Pacific command. The proposed units would be known by the acronym SEAL, "a contraction of SEA, AIR, LAND . . . indicating an all-around, universal capability." Initially, the units would consist of 20 to 24 officers and 50 to 75 men. Each detachment would have a three-faceted mission:

1. develop a specialized Navy capability in guerrilla/counterguerrilla operations to include training of selected personnel in a wide variety of skills

A slide from an originally classified briefing series showing one of the primary missions of the U.S. Navy SEALS.

U.S. Navy

2. development of doctrinal tactics, and

3. development of special support equipment

It was during that March 10 meeting that the name SEALs was used for the first time. The acronym was coined in Admiral Gentner's office. It is not known if the term originated with the admiral himself or one of his staff.

President Kennedy continued a CIA-run operation against the Communist government of Cuba that had begun during the Eisenhower administration. The CIA had been arming and training Cuban exiles to return to Cuba and lead a revolt to oust Fidel Castro. This would have removed a major Soviet-backed Communist threat from U.S. shores and Caribbean waters. Some of the personnel the CIA used as trainers had been recruited from UDT 21. From 17 to 19 April 1961, the Bay of Pigs operation took place as Cuban expatriates tried to take back their country from Fidel Castro and his Communist regime. Without proper support from U.S. military and clandestine forces, the Cuban invaders were stopped almost at the shoreline of the Bay of Pigs. The invasion was a complete failure.

Secretary of Defense McNamara met with the Joint Chiefs of Staff and civilian heads of the military services on 21 April, only a few days after the Bay of Pigs debacle. The meeting was to discuss the implications of the Cuban situation. During the meeting, McNamara suggested that "what is required is a new idea on counteraggression [guerrilla warfare] of the type we are seeing around the world."

Within a day or two of this statement, President Kennedy directed General Taylor of the Army to head the Cuban Study Group, which included Admiral Burke, Attorney General Robert Kennedy, and CIA Director Allen Dulles. The objective of the group was to determine what lessons were to be learned from the Bay of Pigs fiasco. Additionally, the group was to explore ways the United States could strengthen its capabilities in military, paramilitary, guerrilla, and antiguerrilla activities without going on to an active war standing.

By the end of April, the CNO's office had begun to seriously consider the direct participation of the Navy in guerrilla and counterguerrilla warfare and the creation of units specially trained and suited to that type of conflict. The first week of May, Admiral Burke issued a directive calling for an increase in the training of naval personnel in guerrilla warfare. The directive also announced an appraisal of the Navy's equipment to determine what would be suited to operations to be conducted in the swamps and rivers of South Vietnam.

In mid-May, Admiral Beakley reiterated the 10 March proposal by the Strategic Plans Division that the Special Operations Teams (SEALs) be established as separate components of the Atlantic and Pacific UDT commands. The SEAL mission statement was enlarged to include greater emphasis on conducting actual combat operations rather than training and support for them. Admiral Arleigh Burke decided to retire from active duty in the summer of 1961 prior to the implementation of his idea for the SEAL teams. His successor as CNO, Admiral George Anderson Jr., was not the proponent of unconventional warfare that Admiral Burke had been.

On 1 August 1961, Admiral George Anderson Jr. was sworn in as the new Chief of Naval Operations. He replaced Admiral Arleigh Burke, who had held the office for six years. By the end of August, Admiral Anderson was questioning the creation of the new SEAL Teams. Studying the plan for their creation with the intention of curtailing the program, Admiral Anderson felt that the manning requirements (20 officers and 100 men total) for the new Teams could not be immediately met. Encouragement was given by the CNO's office to "enhance and augment present naval support capabilities in the area of paramilitary operations by developing the existing capabilities within the Underwater Demolition Teams for demolition, sabotage and other clandestine activities. . . ."

In the fall of 1961, tensions between the Soviets and the United States increased rapidly with the Berlin Crisis in East Germany. The building of the Berlin Wall and additional actions by the Soviets and the Soviet-backed East German government distracted the Kennedy administration from Southeast Asia. This too retarded the establishment of the Navy SEAL teams.

During that time, specialized training for naval officers in unconventional warfare was not being well implemented. At the end of October, only four Navy officers, two from Underwater Demolition Team 21, were attending courses in unconventional warfare at the Army's Special Warfare Center at Fort Bragg. The push to create the SEAL Teams was now getting more emphasis from the CNO's office. On 13 November, a letter was written at the CNO's office outlining the size and organization of the two proposed SEAL Teams. A month later, on 11 December 1961, Admiral George W. Anderson Jr. signed CNO Speedletter Serial # 697P30. The letter activated SEAL Teams One and Two and UDT 22 on 1 January 1962. The document also contained the intended mission statement for the SEALs as well as a description of their organization, command, and logistical support.

Captain William Henry Hamilton Jr., USN (Ret.)

Just toward the end of World War II, I joined the Navy as a midshipman by virtue of going to the US Naval Academy. I heard about the UDTs after I had been on active duty for some years. Since I had been a naval aviator who had flown some of the service's earlier jets as well as having served aboard a number of ships, my career leaned toward the more active duties when I could manage it. It was suggested to me that the UDTs might be a good idea. So I volunteered in Little Creek, Virginia, and was accepted into the program.

But I didn't start training with the East Coast UDTs in Little Creek. Instead, the Navy ordered me to Coronado. Arriving there, I was able to join my training class in the early winter of 1953 and we graduated in July of that year after a long five months of hard work. Being a little older than the average trainee, I was all of twenty-four or twenty-five and a lieutenant (junior grade) when I went through UDTR.

That week of training that everyone speaks of, Hell Week, isn't any fun for anyone. But it's something everyone must go through to reach the Teams. The instructors wouldn't throw you out of training if you couldn't meet the standards. Instead, they seemed to leave it up to the individual. If you found that you couldn't do what they wanted you to do, you had two options. You could either drop out and quit. Or you could try to continue on, but in some cases the people who tried to stay on had some physical disability that kept them from making the grade. It was rare that someone was just thrown out.

For myself, I never considered quitting. There was no other thought in my mind but to complete the course. When I graduated from training, the Team I was assigned to had already left on a Far East deployment. So I was ordered to meet with the Team in Japan and caught up with them at Camp McGill. There, I reported aboard UDT 5, which later became UDT 13.

It was mid-1953 when I was first assigned as the platoon leader of Platoon One. Later I became the operations officer after UDT 5 had become UDT 13. In Japan, we were training our people to do underwater work and further explosives work. In general, our men were trained to do most any job that no one else in the Navy wanted to do.

The Korean War was not technically over. But the fighting had diminished to the point that nothing was going on actively any more. The truce had only been signed on 27 July 1953, so active combat in Korea was still a very recent memory for many.

Just before I left to go over to Japan and join UDT 5, I had met Commander Doug Fane, the commanding officer of Underwater Demolition Unit 1, the command element controlling the West Coast UDTs. The only first impression you could have of Doug Fane was that he was a very difficult, very hard-nosed, and dynamic person. If you didn't see him that way, you were missing the point. He was a very tough guy.

Later I had a great deal more involvement with Doug Fane when I was ordered from UDT 13 to become the chief staff officer to the Commander, Underwater Demolition Unit One (COMUDU1)—at the time Commander Fane. That position wasn't one I had asked for, but then the Navy doesn't often ask its personnel what they want to do.

My dealings with Fane always left me with the impression that I had to try harder to get along with him. He had some attitudes about regular Navy officers that didn't include me. So I did my best to get along with him and we both somehow succeeded well enough.

About nine o'clock on a Wednesday night one time Commander Fane invited me to go along with him to Tijuana and have a drink or two. It struck me that maybe I had been wrong in my opinion of him and that he was much more of a nice guy than I thought he was. After a night in TJ, having more than a few drinks, we eventually returned to the States and went to his house in Coronado. At the house we had more of a real disagreement than we ever had in our time together. It was my holding my own with him that night that made us close friends. We had finally gotten over any problems there were between us. But it had taken a real frogman's night together to do it.

Without question, Doug Fane was a real leader in the Teams. In my opinion, he's the only reason that the UDTs continued to exist after World War II. Even though there were a lot of other people who had a great deal to do with keeping the Teams going, he had the most to do with it. It's ridiculous for anyone to think that the Teams would be where they are today, and that includes their evolution into the SEAL Teams, without Doug Fane. He was the reason all that growth started in the first place right after World War II.

Largely because of Commander Fane, the UDT ended up with financial and operational support from the fleet that other units, such as the Scouts and Raiders of WWII, did not receive. It was through Fane's work that the UDTs developed and flourished while other units just disappeared at the end of World War II.

Doug Fane and I had many conversations about what should happen to the UDTs down the road. We discussed what we both should do to help the UDT become better known and better able to serve the Navy. We didn't discuss any specific new unit and we certainly didn't talk about a possible SEAL Team, as that term hadn't even been coined yet. But Fane thought we should have something further than what the UDT was doing in the later 1950s, and I certainly agreed with him. As things developed, and I make no claims to originating the term, the SEAL Teams came about to fit much of what Doug Fane and I had envisioned.

What one really has to remember is that Doug Fane was the man who really kept things going when there were fewer than 200 active

UDT men in the whole of the Navy. And he is the guy who triggered me to make the moves that I made when President Kennedy made his speeches in the early 1960s.

President Kennedy made a speech on 1 June 1961 recommending that the armed forces of the United States have a greater paramilitary and counterguerrilla warfare capability. The President made that speech while I was the commanding officer of UDT 21 and we were stationed on Saint Thomas in the Virgin Islands. I had heard about the speech and it struck me that this was precisely what Commander Fane and I had been talking about years earlier.

So I took it upon myself to begin putting together a letter to Admiral Arleigh Burke, the Chief of Naval Operations, proposing that the Navy create an organization like what the President was suggesting. Admiral Burke was an avid supporter of swimming and underwater work for the Navy. Of course, he was also very much a supporter of driving destroyers around for the Navy as well in conventional operations.

Going ahead with my letter, I kept in mind that if the Army was going to do something, the Navy might be able to work with them to do what we wanted to do. That proved to be true. The Army Special Forces people that I had been working with before in Key West at the Navy's Underwater Swimmer School, where I had been the executive officer, proved to be as supportive as they could be, and we in turn were supportive of them.

While we were in Saint Thomas, I had started to draft my letter to the CNO. By the time UDT 21 had returned to its base in Little Creek, I had the letter pretty well in the shape I wanted it to be in. One of the men in the Team, Charlie Watson, helped me revise a part of it before I submitted it. The letter was addressed to the Chief of Naval Operations via the commander of the Amphibious Force of the Atlantic Fleet and also via the commander of the Atlantic Fleet.

The letter went first to the three-star admiral who was the Amphibious Force commander, then it continued on to the four-star admiral who was the Atlantic Fleet commander. It went through their offices and in each case they called me and asked if I had written it. When I answered that I had, I was told to come over to their offices and write their endorsements. So that was precisely what I did in both cases. I wrote their endorsements and then the paperwork went on to Admiral Burke.

Now I found myself being approached by a captain from the Office of Naval Operations. He informed me that I was going to be ordered to the Pentagon. That wasn't something that I had asked for, nor was it something that I was that anxious to be doing. But I was going to be ordered to the Pentagon and they were going to tell me to start building the SEAL Teams.

You aren't given any options in this Navy, you do what the man tells you to do. And that was what I did. The first time I heard the word SEALs was from that captain who told me I was moving. That term had been invented in the Pentagon and I had nothing to do with its creation.

When I arrived in Washington, D.C., and the Pentagon, I was assigned as part of a small organization called OP343E. When I first reported in, I was given a copy of a letter written by Admiral Don Griffin to the Vice Chief of Naval Operations, Admiral Claude Ricketts. Admiral Griffin had been the commander of the Destroyer Navy at that point, as well as a supporter of the UDT concept. He wrote this letter to Admiral Ricketts saying that he thought we should go ahead and do this, that the Navy should build the SEAL Teams.

In the margin of the letter he received from Admiral Griffin, Admiral Ricketts wrote a notation to go ahead and build the SEAL Teams, recommission UDT 22, and to keep him posted about what was going on. That was the letter that I finally received and that I had volumes of copies of to show around. Anytime I would run into a destroyer sailor who complained that he didn't have any money or support to give for our project, I would just show him the letter and tell him that this was what your boss said you were going to do.

It was amazing, but after that letter, I had no trouble getting the money I needed to do the job. For the building and commissioning of two SEAL Teams and the recommissioning of UDT 22, I was given $4.2 million to work with.

That was around July 1961. I was given until December 1961, six months, to build the two SEAL Teams. What I found was that I was able to put them together by the eleventh of December, 1961. They were authorized at that time but then were not commissioned until 8 January 1962.

In those six months I had to build the SEAL Teams, I found the job was anything but easy. And everyone I had to work with wasn't necessarily on my team. I found people in the Pacific Fleet who thought that they wanted to do the job their way. And that was not the way that I wanted things done. And I found people in the Office of the Chief of Naval Personnel who wanted to do things differently from how I wanted them to be done. What I did find was that the biggest support I had was from Admiral Griffin. When I ran into a difficult situation, I remembered what he had told me at the very beginning of the project.

"Bill," Admiral Griffin said to me, "come and see me if you have problems that you can't handle."

At the time I was all of a lieutenant commander and he was a three-star admiral. All I could do was say, "Aye aye, sir" and continue on. So when I had a problem that I couldn't handle, I would go and see Admiral Griffin. There wasn't a lot of time to meet because of the admiral's schedule and delays were not something that could be easily afforded. After I explained the situation, Admiral Griffin would pick up his phone and call the "offending" party. Suddenly things would be straightened out, and it was all due to his phone call.

When I reported to the Chief of Naval Operations' office, I found that there was a letter that had been written by Admiral Griffin to Admiral Ricketts, who was then the Vice Chief of Naval Operations. Admiral Ricketts had told Admiral Griffin to go ahead and build the SEAL Teams and recommission UDT 22. What this told me was that I had an awful lot of things to do and not much time to do them. Therefore, I should get all the help I could.

So I drove down to Fort Bragg in order to get together again with my Army Special Forces friends whom I had trained to scuba-dive in Key West some years before. They could help me in putting together the new Navy units. They allowed me access to their documents regarding unconventional and counterguerrilla warfare.

While at Fort Bragg, I asked for all of the manuals and training paraphernalia, everything that I could use to build a SEAL Team. And I made it clear to them that I wasn't competing with the Army. Instead, I wanted to take everything that they had learned in building the Army organization, add to that the things that applied to the Navy, and go ahead and build the SEAL Teams.

The Army guys were terrific. They came through and gave me everything I could possibly have imagined wanting. And it was largely because of what they did that the job I had was done in the short six months that I knew I had.

In the Navy in those days, I wasn't able to control totally who would be coming aboard the new SEAL Teams. The Office of the Chief of Naval Personnel determined which officers would go to the Teams. I couldn't control that situation, though I did have a lot of input. Lieutenant John Callahan, who would be the first commanding officer of SEAL Team Two, was one of the officers that they found. One of the men that I found was Lieutenant Roy Boehm.

Lieutenant Boehm at that time was with UDT 21 and I had been the commanding officer of that Team. So I just picked up the phone and called him.

"Roy," I said, "let's get this thing going here. You've got a lot to do down there and we don't have a lot of time."

"Aye aye, sir," was what he said, "whatever you want, I'll do it." And he did.

It was only a few days after I turned in some of the paperwork to personnel and they gave me Dave Del Guidice and John Callahan to be the commanding officers of SEAL Teams One and Two respectively that I called Roy Boehm. I didn't know Callahan or Del Guidice personally, but I had known Roy Boehm and I knew I could count on him.

Roy Boehm is one of the finest people I have ever known. He is an ex–destroyer sailor and he knows what's going on. If you have a problem that you can't solve easily, you go to Roy and he'll solve it.

It was Boehm who had something to say to President Kennedy

---

when there was a problem with the weapons we were using after the SEAL Teams were up and running. As I remember, Roy told the President that he could line up a dozen of his people with any other weapon and he would line up a dozen of his people (SEALs) with this weapon (the AR-15) and we'll beat you to death. And apparently President Kennedy respected that.

Roy Boehm was, and is, a very unique person. He's a guy you can really count on. And that is what I needed then. To create a SEAL Team, you would be starting out with people who were Underwater-Demolition-Team-trained. In order to become SEALs, they would have to be further trained. And we had no way of knowing at the beginning who would be the best one from the UDT to become a SEAL with the additional training. There were no guidelines and certainly no experience I had to draw on.

So I couldn't speak for either of the two lieutenants who would be the commanding officers of the Teams. But I knew that once we put the program together, the system we built would be able to determine who could hack and who could not.

After that first authorizing letter, I wrote everything that was officially written about the SEAL Teams, including their mission statement. I started the Teams, put the people together, and got the mission rolling. The Navy has a booklet that tells a commanding officer what he's supposed to do. The SEALs had such booklets, called Naval Warfare pamphlets, which I wrote, and which described precisely what everybody was supposed to do in the Team.

So Callahan, Roy Boehm, and all of the new officers had this information to draw on. The information for the mission statement came from my conversations with Doug Fane, my Army friends, and whatever else I could think up myself. There was input, but not influence, from the Army Special Forces. And I wanted to take advantage of everything they could offer us. But we would be a Navy unit and we had to put Navy things in our mission. And we did just that.

So with complete confidence, I can say that I started the SEAL Teams for all practical purposes. There are others who will say that they would have happened anyway as a natural evolution. Well, I'm

Four modern-day SEALs rise up from the water, ready to move in silently and complete their mission.

U.S. Navy

sorry about what they might say. They didn't make the Teams as a unit; I did.

Later I became the Chief of Maritime for the Central Intelligence Agency. This meant I ran the CIA's Navy worldwide. I should emphasize that I went to the CIA well after the Bay of Pigs fiasco; I was not there when they made that mistake. But after the Bay of Pigs, I was invited to join the CIA and I went in as their number three guy in their maritime structure. After a few months I had become the number-one guy when I took the position as chief.

There were three wars going on at the same time when I took the position. There was the war in Vietnam, the war in Cuba, and the war in Africa. We didn't win the war in Vietnam, and the war with Cuba turned into what I call a Mexican standoff. But we did win our war in Africa against the Soviets.

Off and on, the SEAL Teams worked with the CIA in various areas. But I came along into the Agency well after that. They were my creation, but I never worked in the field with them.

When I received the order to start the SEAL Teams, first and foremost I felt proud and honored in being chosen, even though I hadn't asked for it. And I feel I was being honored because of the Navy in effect saying to me, we feel you are the best guy to start the SEAL Teams. That's an honor and a responsibility.

I wanted to do the best I could with the assignment. And I think that I did do that. The SEALs have proven themselves because of the beginning that I was able to give them. For all of what the Teams have done that is good, I am very proud of them. And you have to recognize that every-

Jumping with one of today's steerable parachutes, this SEAL is able to fly his rig over long distances and land with great accuracy. His equipment is a long way from the improvised parachutes and rigs used by the UDTs and SEALs in the late 1950s and early 1960s.

U.S. Navy

thing doesn't work all of the time. They have made mistakes and they have learned from them and been made stronger because of them.

The SEALs have become one of the most elite forces in the history of the United States military. And I am very proud of my part in their creation. Almost never in the history of the Navy has someone come along with an idea, and it wasn't totally my idea, been authorized to go ahead develop that idea into an existing capability, and then lived to see that capability become so well recognized and approved of. I had that honor.

The Trident was developed after I had been involved with developing the SEAL Teams. But I am authorized to wear it and I proudly do on my uniform. Some people in the Navy, especially the aviators and the submarine sailors, consider the device a little too ostentatious. Personally, I think they're right—it is a bit large—but it's what we

A squad of SEAL trainees conduct field operations as part of their land warfare training. From the lessons the SEALs learned in Vietnam come many of the techniques and skills taught to the SEALs today.

have. The men of the Teams wear the Trident proudly, as they should. It is a proud thing to have.

The term SEAL is an acronym; it means SEa, Air, and Land. I don't find that it means anything different to me than UDT did. There is a brotherhood, and a very stong one, that goes with having been in the UDTs or the SEALs.

Chapter 29

THE COMMISSIONING AND MISSION OF THE SEALS

On 27 December 1961, Rear Admiral Allan Reed issued "SEAL Teams in Naval Special Warfare," Naval Warfare Information Publication 29-1 (NWIP 29-1). Based on the experience gained in South Vietnam and elsewhere during 1961, the report was the basic SEAL directive for operations during most of the Vietnam War.

The following is a declassified excerpt from the still-classified Naval Warfare Information Publication. This forty-plus page document listed for the first time the capabilities of the new SEAL Teams and their mission statement.

The SEAL Mission Profile (NWIP 29-1)

(1) *Primary:* To develop a specialized capability to conduct operations for military, political, or economic purposes within an area occupied by the enemy for sabotage, demolition, and other clandestine activities conducted in and around restricted waters, rivers, and canals, and to conduct training of selected U.S., allied and indigenous personnel in a wide variety of skills for use in naval clandestine operations in hostile environments.

(2) *Secondary:* To develop doctrine and tactics for SEAL operations and to develop support equipment, including special craft for use in these operations.

(3) *Tasks:* Tasks may be overt or covert in nature.

(a) Destructive tasks—These tasks include clandestine attacks on enemy shipping, demolition raids in harbors and other enemy installations within reach; destruction of supply lines in maritime areas by destruction of bridges, railway lines, roads, canals, and so forth; and the delivery of special weapons (SADM) to exact locations in restricted waters, rivers or canals.

(b) Support tasks—The support tasks of SEAL Teams include protecting friendly supply lines, assisting or participating in the landing and support of guerrilla and partisan forces, and assisting or participating in the landing and recovery of agents, other special forces, downed aviators, escapees and so forth.

(c) Additional Tasks:

  1. Conduct reconnaissance, surveillance, and intelligence collection missions as directed.
  2. In friendly areas train U.S. and indigenous personnel in such operations as directed.
  3. Develop equipment to support special operations.
  4. Develop the capability for small boat operations, including the use of native types.

1 January 1962 is the official date of the commissioning of SEAL Teams One and Two. On 8 January, SEAL Team One, at NAB Coronado, California, and SEAL Team Two, at NAB Little Creek, Virginia, mustered for the first time at 1300 hours local time. The official commissioning date for the two Teams was eight days earlier, but there were no main actions until the first muster. This has caused some confusion as to the actual date of the SEALs commissioning. The date of 1 January is the official paperwork date. The 8 January date was the practical day that work actually began.

SEAL Team One was placed under the command of Lieutenant David Del Guidice and took its personnel as volunteers from UDTs 11 and 12. Lieutenant John F. Callahan was put in command of SEAL Team Two, which took the majority of its personnel from the ranks of

UDT 21. Thirty-seven men and officers of the initial complement for SEAL Team Two were at the 1300 muster on 8 January. The balance of the ten officers and fifty enlisted men would arrive over the next several months as they completed training or were released from previous commands.

Lieutenant Roy Boehm was the officer-in-charge of SEAL Team Two prior to its commissioning and was responsible for selecting the initial complement of men and setting up their training and equipment. He was given the assignment to make the first SEAL Team and has earned the name "First SEAL."

Lieutenant Commander Roy Boehm, USN (Ret.)

Back in 1962, I was the officer-in-charge of SEAL Team Two, waiting for someone senior enough to be the commanding officer of the team; this turned out to be Lieutenant John Callahan. He came in and relieved me, taking the position of CO while I moved to the XO's slot.

It was the actions of Lieutenant Commander Bill Hamilton, who was the commander of UDT 21 at the time, that got the SEALs started. He wore two hats, being the commander of Underwater Demolition Units, Atlantic Fleet, at the same time. Both gave him a hands-on role as a Team leader and put him in a position to see more of the strategic picture.

We were in Saint Thomas in the Virgin Islands with UDT 21 at the time and I was the Team's operations officer, acting as Hamilton's second-in-command during advanced UDT training. He ordered me to organize and give him a commando outfit, a group of men that would go anyplace, at any time, in any way, and do any thing. I asked Commander Hamilton to give me a line of guidance for the unit. His answer to me was, "When you're called upon to do anything, and you're not ready to do it, then you've failed."

That was a pretty wide scope. So I started to assemble a group from the men within UDT 21. They were sent out to different types of training, as I wasn't sure of where were going at that particular time. I had read books by Che Guevara, Mao Tse-tung, Sun-tzu, Admiral Mil-

ton Miles, and others for much of my life. And I knew the Underwater Demolition Team had so much more potential than our country was using.

In those days (the late fifties, very early sixties) we were restricted to the berm line on the beach. That mark was as far as we could go as underwater demolitioneers. From the berm line on belonged to the Marine Corps. That was a rule violated a bit more than observed pretty much continuously. Still, in the Teams, we had all of this talent going to waste. To make more use of it, I had been pushing for just such an opportunity to break all of the rules. Bill Hamilton's wonderful order for that group of "anywhere, anytime" commandos freed me.

This was what I started out to do. Well before the SEALs were begun, requests for surgical type precise operations were sent down to us from the "up-there" types. These requests were to perform certain of these missions on a very covert basis.

At that time each operation could be choreographed, trained for, and built up on just the single mission itself, whether it took two, three, five, or seven men. That commando group I thought would be nothing more than just a special group. Bill Hamilton was going to be the skipper and I was going to be his exec. This was well prior to the commissioning of the SEAL Teams.

We found out that we were working for the President of the United States. Since he was our commander-in-chief, all of us in the military were officially working for him already; now we'd just be a little more under his direct control. Our special team was for specific surgical strikes and was assembled on a mission-by-mission basis. We were a "dirty dozen" well prior to any book or movie.

The cadre of men in UDT 21 from among whom I would choose a mission team were always adding to their skills because of the schools they were being sent to. There were men who knew how to hot-wire cars, crack safes, and get in and out of buildings without being noticed. This raised more than a few eyebrows around the base, but it added to our mission capabilities.

Men were sent to Jump School for training. Prior to the commissioning of the SEAL Teams, I was trying to get all of my men airborne-qualified. After the SEALs were a functioning unit, the airborne quali-fication could just be made mandatory for them.

Some of the missions we did from the special group at UDT 21 in-cluded training some people who came out of Panama City, Florida. The Cubans were watching that area fairly closely, as a number of ex-patriates were training there. We taught the people assigned to us demolitions, how to take out generators, some of the tricks that we had in our repertoire.

This group was going to act as a training cadre for their fellow ex-patriates in techniques that would help them retake their country from the Communists. Whatever other arrangements had been made for these individuals wasn't something I was privy to. My job and that of my men was to teach them the mechanics of operating.

When I first put together my operating group, I didn't know how many people I could get from UDT 21. The Underwater Demolition Team at that time only had about 115 personnel in the ranks. These men were spread out all over Europe, South America, and the Caribbean Islands. With using my special group as the reason, I was able to get about 80 percent of the Team special training of one kind or another. It was when it came time to commission the SEAL Team that the manning issue became very critical.

Prior to the official commissioning of the SEALs, I had been told to prepare for a much smaller group than was finally created. Origi-nally, I was told to come up with a group of about twenty or thirty men. To make that number, I figured I couldn't go wrong by trying to arrange additional training for all of UDT 21. About the time that the SEAL Team finally did go into commission, I was so relieved and happy that the original group of people I had put together as a spe-cial group at UDT 21 had been used extensively. When I heard that the SEAL Teams would contain ten officers and fifty enlisted men each, and one Team to each coast, I couldn't have been happier: we needed all of the help we could get.

There were some problems with filling out the ranks of SEAL Team Two. On the West Coast at Coronado, where SEAL Team One would be, they had the men from UDT 11, 12, and 13 to draw from. They could fill their Team without hurting their parent units. At Little Creek, we had UDT 21, just 115 men to be our qualified manpower pool. If I had taken 10 officers and 50 enlisted men to fill out the SEAL ranks, I would have gutted our parent Team. I was far too good a sailor to do that.

So I did have my fifty all earmarked, but I couldn't take them all immediately. They had to finish the operations they were already on in order to shoulder our responsibility to the Atlantic Fleet. There were a few rules I had to break or bend seriously to get some of the men I needed. To build the SEAL Team, I had a Presidential Priority, just as Admiral Rickover had had to build the Nuclear Navy. If you're nothing but a lieutenant junior grade, but you have the same priority as an admiral's unit, why not use it? I needed the best storekeeper chief in the United States Navy and that was James "Hoot" Andrews. So I stole him from Admiral Rickover's high-priority nuclear submarine project.

To be the keel of the new SEAL Team, I had to have a good master-at-arms who was also an operator. To fill that job I had Rudy Boesch over in UDT 21. I had first met Rudy back when I was a first-class bosun's mate and he was a third class. All I saw over the years was Rudy getting better and better. He stayed longer in the Teams that anyone else ever has. At the time that Rudy finally retired in 1988, there was only one commanding officer at SEAL Team Two who hadn't had him as their master-at-arms.

Not everyone was available for some time after the SEAL Team was commissioned. Some openings in the ranks were filled with a small group of fresh graduates from the most recent UDTR class at Little Creek. Others I just waited for. There was Robert "The Eagle" Gallagher. When I first met the Eagle Gallagher, he looked at me and said, "Boehm, I'm going to be better than you ever thought of being." And this was when he was fresh out of boot camp and I was his instructor in UDTR. He didn't give up easily and was one tremendous man. If I had to list the people who fit the image of the true warrior, in the Teams or elsewhere, I would have to put Gallagher at the top of the list.

There was no way I was going to take too many men from the ranks of UDT 21 and risk destroying that Team as a functional entity for a while. That Team was the wellspring whence we came. It was also going to be the support group we were going to need to build and polish the SEAL concept of commandos.

It is interesting to note that at the time the SEALs went into commission, I strongly protested the difference between them and the UDT. As far as I was concerned, we should all be SEALs and receive the same training to conduct the same mission. For myself, I could see no good reason for there being a difference. It took the United States Navy from 1962 to 1983 to realize that I was right. In 1983, the UDTs were all decommissioned and made into SEAL Teams. We can be a little slow sometimes and many times it seems we have to learn the same lessons over and over.

There were still more than a few difficulties in getting the SEALs up and running even after the men had been chosen and were on their way. The equipment we needed in order to operate was a constant problem. The Army had just recently adopted the M-14 rifle, an improved version of the M-1 Garand that the U.S. forces had carried since just before WWII. The weapon was large, heavy, had a thousand-yard range, and was just far more than we needed. The M-1 carbine was a lot less than I wanted. What I needed for the new Team was a weapon that was light, had a 500-yard maximum range, and was lethal. We were going to operate up close, move fast, and if we got into a fight, make it a quick, savage one.

To fill my needs I opted for the new AR-15 rifle, which had not been adopted by BuWeps (Bureau of Weapons). It fired a small, fast bullet that destroyed its target through hydraulic shock. Short version: it was a deadly bullet if it hit you. The small, light 5.56mm rounds fired by the AR-15 let you carry a full third more ammunition than an equivalent weight of 7.62mm ammunition for the M-14. This gave me more rounds per unit of weight, something we needed to consider for the fast, long-range operations I might have to ask my men to conduct.

The AR-15 was what we wanted, and O'Connor, who was the head of BuWeps at that time, told me I didn't need it. Besides, the weapon wasn't in the supply system then. I suppose I can't really blame the bureaucrats for the way they did their jobs, though I still do; we were so secret an organization that I couldn't explain to them the kinds of missions we were actually going to do. They just weren't in on the secrecy involved with our Teams.

A small group of us from SEAL Team Two had watched a demonstration of the AR-15 at the Cooper-McDonald facility near Baltimore, Maryland. The weapon looked like what I wanted for the Team. I was given several to examine, so we ran them through the mill. One was frozen in a block of ice in an icehouse. Another was thrown into the Chesapeake Bay and allowed to sit in the surf, locked and loaded with a magazine and ammunition. Within my group of people, we tested and examined the weapons extensively.

The results of our testing were submitted to BuWeps. They ignored both our tests and further requests. When I went up there to face them down on the question of the AR-15, they said that we were not a recognized testing facility and that we didn't need it. But I was determined to get my men what they needed, as judged by an operator and not a bureaucrat.

So to outfit the SEALs with the best weapon available at that time, I used the open purchase allowance I had available, money I could just spend to buy equipment, and bought the AR-15. This deal was basically done on a handshake with the Cooper-McDonald people from whom I bought the weapons. And this was also what led to one of my formal board of inquiries leading to a possible court-martial.

Before dealing with those consequences, I had taken my storekeeper along with me to Cooper-McDonald and bought the weapons I wanted. SEAL Team One, commanded by Dave Del Guidice, had told me that whatever I did for my Team they wanted done for themselves. So I ordered 132 brand-new AR-15 rifles with spare parts, accessories, and ammunition. The magic number came from the needs of two SEAL Teams of 60 men each and a 10 percent spare rate.

Another weapon I had trouble getting for my SEALs was the specific sidearm I wanted. We needed the capability of taking out some of the "hands-across-the-sea" outboard motors our State Department had been handing out to developing countries. The VC had received a number of these motors for their sampans by simply taking them. The bullet from a .357 Magnum would crack the block of such a motor, so that's what I wanted.

The weapon I asked for was the Smith & Wesson Model-19 Combat Magnum. Some gun enthusiast someplace along the line decided we could have the Smith & Wesson Model-15 Combat Masterpiece, a .38 Special revolver. He had fired the Model 19 on the range, but someone had put .38 Specials in it to make the recoil easier. He figured there was no difference, so gave us the cheaper weapon.

It seemed that all of our procurement fit into this kind of reasoning somewhere along the line. If they hadn't used it before, we didn't need it. Another example of this was when we ordered parachutes for the SEALs. The chute we needed had to be able to support a combat-laden man and have a steerable capability. The only such parachute on the market at that time was the HALO rig made and patented by the Pioneer Parachute Company. It was a beautiful rig and even had a safety feature, a barometric release, that made it even better for our purposes. The barometric release opened the chute automatically when it reached a set altitude even if the jumper was unconscious.

We couldn't get the parachutes we wanted; again, the proper bureaus said we didn't need them, they hadn't been accepted, they didn't like them, they were too expensive. . . . So instead, my crew modified the parachutes we did have, cutting out sections of canopy and sealing the nylon back up with soldering irons. These worked, made what we needed, and had the steerable capability we needed.

Modifying the parachutes was a no-no in two ways. First off, we were using salvage parachutes because they were what we could get. Second, we were doing unauthorized modifications to salvaged chutes. This, and a few other parachute-related difficulties I had, led to another formal board of inquiry investigation pending a court-martial.

Another weapons-oriented situation involved my wanting something we could use to take somebody out silently. I wanted to be as sneaky as I could be and I didn't bother trying to follow Hoyle's rules. You can't play by the rules when you're the only person reading the book. The kind of enemy we would be fighting would be sneaky, underhanded, and fight as dirty as he could. So we had to be better at that than he was.

First, we tried to get some silencers, but those were very hard to come by. The people who had them didn't want to admit it and they certainly didn't want to give them up. But there were some drawbacks with using a silencer on a weapon: it left that smell of gunpowder in the air and could be noticed. But we still wanted a silent way to take out a sentry now and then, so I investigated modern crossbows. England put out the best sporting crossbow, according to my research. So with my Presidential Priority, we again drove the supply people into fits by ordering crossbows.

We did get the bows and my people practiced with them. They were getting pretty good with the bows and were able to target in on the right spot so that a sentry wouldn't make any noise. This was going fine and they were kept sealed up in our armory. Then someone brought in an outside inspection team and they looked at our armory.

We shouldn't have had to pass a regulation inspection since we weren't doing regulation things. But the Navy had a problem with that, so we had an inspection. Some supply officer came into our armory, found out we had crossbows, and looked them up to see what they were. He had no idea about what we were doing. Hoot Andrews was leading the guy around when he found the crossbows and apparently thought they were against some Geneva Convention or other agreement. They weren't, but he couldn't be convinced of this.

The name of the game for us was do the mission and make sure *everyone has a round-trip. Anything that made it more likely that all of my men would come home after an operation was fine by me. But this officer was convinced the bows were illegal and took them away. Another case of a little knowledge along with some authority being a bad thing.*

Finally, the higher-ups had a whole series of charges they wanted to lay at my feet. It seemed that getting the job done wasn't in their vocabulary if it went outside a very limited viewpoint. It looked like I was going to face a series of courts-martial, but at least my men had what they needed for the most part.

There were always risks that had to be taken to achieve real results. My problems seemed petty compared with what my men and I might have to face out in the field.

As soon as the SEAL Team was in commission, I started losing people. Some men were being lost to assignments with the Agency, others were getting overseas assignments. H. R. Williams went over to Southeast Asia and became the head of the Junk Force in Vietnam for a while to see what was needed over there. The cold war was rolling right along and Cuba was coming to heat things up a bit.

We did a recon of Cuba and I led the Team in. It was a group of SEALs and UDT men. Myself, J. C. Tipton as my swim buddy, and H. R. "Lump-lump" Williams made up part of the recon Team that came from SEAL Team Two. The other half of the team was taken from the ranks of UDT 21 and included George Walsh, Chief Schmidt, and Gene Tinnin. What I was trying to tell the Navy was that a mix of UDT and SEALs could work very well and that there shouldn't be a difference between the Teams. My team went in to Cuba, launching from the submarine Threadfin *for an underwater swim in.*

The people up in Navy supply had done their best to sabotage the mission before it began, and that was with them working on our side. I had ordered the German Draeger closed-circuit breathing rigs for our mission. The rigs were completely silent, released no bubbles into the water, and were very dependable. Some bureaucratic problems with the head of Bureau of Ships ended up giving me the rig that he felt was suitable. The time constraints of our operation forced me to go ahead with what we had for the operation. And it almost cost me some of my men.

The rigs we were given lasted long enough for us to lock out of the submarine. Almost as soon as we hit the water, one of my men's rig flooded out, the rebreathing bag taking on water. In a rebreather, a closed-circuit system, a mixture of caustic chemicals called Baralyme chemically scrubs the CO_2 from the air you breathe. Getting this chemical wet causes what we call a "caustic cocktail." The diver ends up sucking in something like wet lye into his lungs. This does not make for a safe situation.

While we were dealing with one of our team strangling on chemicals, to complicate matters, two Cuban Komar-class missile boats came into the area at high speed. The boats appeared to know that we had been launched from the submarine. Perhaps our secrecy somewhere up the line hadn't been everything that it could have been.

As the boats came out to us, we had to dive under them. As the Cuban patrol boats passed over us, all I could imagine were the series of events occurring on them that would result in our all being killed. I could see the Cubans taking out grenades, pulling the pins, the grenades arcing though the air, striking the water, sinking to our level, the fuses burning down. . . .

George Walsh's rig was completely flooded out by this time. The situation was more than tense. An explosion in the water would cave our rigs in, bust our eardrums, and generally work us over more than if we had been in a heavyweight prizefight. And that was if the blast wasn't close to us. Then the Komars continued on their way. They may have been a lot more interested in the sub than us, or they might have just been passing by.

Now all I had to deal with was being off a hostile foreign coast with at least one of my team having severe troubles with his breathing rig. It was a very good thing that I didn't lose anyone on that operation. I just might have had to make a visit and look someone up at BuShips.

Our intelligence for the operation listed an obstruction in the wa-

---

ter that caused the current to eddy back against the normal flow. That wasn't quite the way the situation was, so we had to swim against the current all of the way in. We reconned about two miles of beach and charted it in case there had to be a U.S. invasion of Cuba itself. Going back out, we had trouble with that same obstruction in the water. It made the water too shallow for the submarine to come in and pick us up.

H. R. Williams spoke to me and asked what would we do if they didn't come in and pick us up? I told him not to worry, that I had the situation all figured out. We would just swim out to sea and drown. That made my team a little bit angry and they threw a bit more into their kicks as we swam out past the obstruction. We had a line stretched between the two groups of us to catch the buoy line the submarine was supposedly trailing.

When we reached deep enough water, there was that submarine with her gallant crew and their very cool commanding officer. They had avoided the Komars and were as close in as they dared to be to pick us up. We snagged onto their buoy line and had located the boat underwater.

The only problem now was the same one we had started with. The 'lungs we had were pretty much crapped out, flooded, not working, in general everything I thought they would be. You can only lock three men into the escape trunk at a time, and all six of my men had followed the buoy line down to the forward escape trunk. Now I had to signal three of them to go back up to the conning tower while the other three of us went into the trunk.

Ducking into a flooded escape trunk is like going into a bucket underwater that's only half-full of air. You duck under the hatch coaming and then you can stand up in an air bubble while you shut the hatch behind you, blow out the water, and open the hatch in the deck that lets you into the sub itself. There's also an intercom at the top of the trunk that lets you communicate with the interior of the sub.

As soon as I ducked into the trunk, I was on the intercom to the captain. He told me to move as quickly as I could, that the Komars were making another sweep back. I told him I had men on his conning tower and it was going to take time to clear both groups through the trunk. He understood the situation and knew what I had meant when I told him the ball was now in his court. He surfaced the sub enough to clear the conning tower and pulled my men in. As soon as I was told they were aboard, we started locking in through the trunk. And the boat was diving as we were clearing out the water.

We all returned to the United States and came out with the information we had been sent in to get. It would remain to be seen if the landing site we had been sent in to recon was really secret to the Cubans. Those Komar missile boats had been Johnnies-on-the-spot waiting for us when we were in the area.

President Kennedy came down to Little Creek to inspect the SEALs and see what the unit he had wanted built looked like and what our capabilities were. I wanted to show him just how good we were, so I built a sand-charged "bomb" with a flashbulb and timer. The bomb was concealed where President Kennedy would be. I later set off the "charge" and told the Secret Service what had been done and how. They weren't too happy about it, but it did show that we could slip past almost anyone.

Vice President Johnson was a gun enthusiast and he got with just the right man in my team—A. D. Clark, who also was a firearms expert. Clark had been one of the men who had helped me test and evaluate the AR-15 rifle. Vice President Johnson was talking to A. D. about the selection of our weapons that were spread out for viewing. They got to talking about the AR-15 rifle, which was still very rare at that time.

A. D. Clark picked up the AR-15. "Now, you take this," he said. "This is the weapon that we want and this is what my boss got me."

"Well, what's the problem?" the Vice President asked.

"My boss is getting a court-martial for buying them for us."

Vice President Johnson went and got President Kennedy's naval aide, who in turn got the President. President Kennedy went over and examined the weapons, speaking to A. D. Clark and looking at what we were doing.

Shortly after that visit, Admiral Edmund B. Taylor, who was the commander of the Fifth Naval District and out of my chain of command, contacted me. Admiral Taylor was a personal friend of President Kennedy from his days as a senator. Admiral Taylor called me up and asked me if I had a civilian suit. After I told him I did have one, which hadn't been worn very much, he told me to get my suit and meet him at the naval air station.

President John F. Kennedy inspects men from SEAL Team Two. In spite of the existence of the SEAL Teams being a secret at this time, the presidential visit had a large number of cameramen record the event. President Kennedy is examining the semi-closed circuit Mark VI breathing rig worn by Louis A. "Hoss" Kucinski on the right.

UDT-SEAL Museum

It doesn't really matter if an admiral is in your direct chain of command or not; when one asks a lieutenant to meet him somewhere, the lieutenant shows up. When I asked Admiral Taylor where we were going, he told me I couldn't ask. When I asked him who we were going to see—I already had my suspicions—he again told me I could not ask that either. So I said, "Aye aye, sir," and climbed on board the aircraft.

The flight to Washington, D.C., wasn't a long one. The drive from the air station to the Blair House, right across the street from the White House, wasn't a very long one either. Sitting at that house, waiting for whatever heel was going to land on me and grind me into the dirt, that was a long one. Then President Kennedy came in.

I was so startled to see the President walk into the room that I blurted out probably one of the most stupid things I ever said in my life. "I didn't vote for you, Mr. President."

It only took a moment for me to realize just how dumb that sounded, so I quickly tried to save face by saying, "But I'm willing to die for you."

It wasn't that I really wanted to do that either. But he was graceful about it. He asked me if I knew what a Presidential Priority was. I told him that I did and how it was supposed to allow me to gather the materials and men I needed to do the job that was assigned to me. And I may have also mentioned something about being stonewalled by bureaucrats and so-called experts.

At that time I had five formal boards of investigation hanging over me. I felt there was no way I was even going to get out of the Navy with an honorable discharge, let alone continue my career.

The President then said something I found unusual at the time. He said, "Roy, you'll make your number."

What he had meant was that I would make my promotion to lieutenant commander later. And my five formal boards of investigation went away as well.

Someone could probably have put together the SEALs a lot more smoothly than I did. But the problem was that we had immediate missions that had to be performed, and we had equipment that wouldn't do the job. The only way I could get the materials for my people, to ensure that they would do their missions as a round-trip and not one-way, was to turn up the heat. After doing that, I couldn't complain about the heat.

There were a lot of people without whose work there wouldn't have been a SEAL Team. Bill Hamilton organized the paperwork and took a concept and made it a reality. I took that reality and give it manpower and equipment.

There was a time when I called the Team together during the Cuban Missile Crisis. I needed fifteen people to prepare to jump in to Cuba on a possible mission. Our skipper, John Callahan, was coordinating the Cuban effort from both SEAL Team One and Two. So I was running the Team while John was coordinating the entire naval unconventional warfare mission. So I called the Team together and asked them all for fifteen volunteers. Then I said I really needed only thirteen volunteers. My swim buddy, Lump-lump Williams, was going in with me and that made two of us.

When I asked for the thirteen volunteers to step forward, the *whole of SEAL Team Two took one step forward. That was probably one of the highest honors I have ever been paid.*

What could I say to them but, "I'm in charge of the dumbest bunch of people I have ever met in my entire life."

I already had their names because I had a hunch that they would all step forward, and they all did.

■ Chapter 30

THE FIRST CO

Though Roy Boehm was the first officer-in-charge of SEAL Team Two, he was not the first commanding officer. That position was assigned to Lieutenant John Callahan. Like so many of his counterparts in the UDTs, Callahan had no idea who or what the SEALs were. Given all the work involved to qualify to join the UDTs, transferring out of them into a new and unknown unit did not hold a lot of appeal.

But orders are what a sailor follows and John Callahan moved his family from the West Coast to the East Coast. After arriving at the new SEAL Team's headquarters, greeting the men, and then leaving for training and meetings with higher command, Lieutenant Callahan still had to learn just what this new SEAL Team of his was all about.

Lieutenant John F. Callahan, USN (Ret.)

Officially, SEAL Team One is the older of the two Teams by twelve minutes. There was a document that had to be signed and sent to the Chief of Naval Operations' office stating that the command was manned and ready. The receipt of that document was the official be-

The artwork approved to be the unit patch by Lieutenant John F. Callahan, the first commanding officer of SEAL Team Two. The seal is superimposed over the number 2 to signify the Team. Under the seal is a pair of swim fins bracketing an open parachute. Above the crest of the parachute is the oval of a swimmer's face mask while below is a stylized M3A1 submachine gun.

ginning of the team. David Del Guidice beat me to the CNO's office with his paperwork by twelve minutes. But that was okay; we got all of the publicity.

Back in November 1961, I was just returning to the United States after a nine-month detachment in WestPac (West Pacific). I arrived in time to see my wife and, for the first time, my three-month-old child. Then I was informed that it was fine for me to see my family, but that the admiral would like to see me at three o'clock. So much for coming home.

When I arrived at the admiral's office, he told me that he had a set of orders for me and that I would be proceeding to Little Creek, Virginia, to form and commission Navy SEAL Team Two. My first question was, "What's a SEAL Team?"

The admiral explained the acronym to me. Then I said that I really didn't want to leave UDT. He informed me that eventually all UDTs would become SEALs and then said that I would still be in the (Special Warfare) community. He finished by telling me that the orders were very impressive and that I should be very happy to take them. "Yes, sir, Admiral," I said. "I'm ready to go."

My wife was from La Jolla in Southern California, and her question was, "What's Virginia Beach like?"

"It's just like La Jolla," I told her. I paid for that last remark for years. But we were a Navy family and moving was part of the package. One thing that didn't go with me to the East Coast were any people from the West Coast UDTs. Upon arrival at Little Creek, I was immediately informed that I couldn't take any of the people from UDTs 11, 12, or 13 for my new Team. Everyone for SEAL Team Two had to come from the East Coast, and that meant UDT 21.

Names were run by me as possible people for SEAL Team Two, and I didn't know a one of them. So I told the people running the personnel pool that I would like the source of the men split. Part of the officer core I wanted to be mustangs, who had a lot of experience in the Navy and the Team prior to receiving their commission. The rest of the officers could be ensigns, fresh new officers who would work and learn. The men were to be the same way, a core of very experienced Navy UDT men and the balance fresh new people who could learn from the others.

A mustang officer was someone who had gone into the Navy as an enlisted man and then specialized in his rate. After spending time in his rate, developing rank and learning his skills, some men would put in for and receive their commission as an ensign. In another program, these men would become warrant officers and remain in their field. But the mustang officer would be a fully commissioned officer and he could expect to go on to be a lieutenant or lieutenant (jg) fairly easily, depending on how much time he had left that he could spend in the service. These men would broaden themselves to become a complete officer rather than stay in a single discipline. These men had a tremendous background in skills and knowledge.

The young officers who were fresh graduates were very gung ho. The world was theirs and they wanted to take it on. That was also what we wanted because it gave the Team its heart and a lot of life. But this enthusiasm could be tempered by the experienced mustang officers. They were also in a position to teach the new ensigns, who had to learn more and more as things went on. So I looked at my mustangs as teachers who could spread their wealth of knowledge throughout the Team.

There was some consideration made for my family and I was able to spend the holidays, Christmas and such, with them prior to the move. So I arrived at Little Creek the first week of January 1962. Arrangements had been made ahead of time to house the new SEAL Team and some buildings, Quonset huts and such, had been made available for us on the base. The structures had to be cleaned up and reconditioned a bit before we could use them. So I asked that some of the personnel who were going into the new SEAL Team be detached from their UDT and assigned to our area to help get things ready. At that time, Roy Boehm, Joe DiMartino, and about ten or twelve men went over to what would be the SEAL compound. The buildings we were assigned hadn't been used in some time, so there was plenty of work to do.

Then I arrived and we started to put some things together. I have always tried to be an up-front man, but when I sent that message to the CNO saying we were manned and ready, I had no idea what we might be ready for. We had a few dozen K-Bar knives between the bunch of us, didn't have an armory, and there was already some yelling from the UDT since many of the guys had brought their fins and gear from UDT and those had to be replaced.

During those early days in the Team, we were fortunate in that a lot of our enlisted men who came over from UDT were more senior than you normally saw in a commissioning crew. During my first three days at the Team, I didn't really talk to anyone except Rudy Boesch, SEAL Team Two's master-at-arms. I knew him by reputation and also knew that the UDT really hated to lose him. But they sent him and I was very glad to have his experience. I got to know him as he did me. Rudy soon learned what I was willing to put up with and what I wouldn't. That gave him the guidance he needed to work with the enlisted men. That was a fantastic relationship.

There we sat in the middle of the base at Little Creek, Virginia, calling ourselves SEALs. None of us really knew what a SEAL was yet; we hadn't done anything to build up the name. At that time the biggest thing that we were sure of was that we were going to get parachute training. The UDTs still weren't sure they would all receive parachute training. That was one of the reasons some of the guys volunteered for the new SEAL Team: it was the only way they were sure to get parachute training.

Initially, the new Team had come about and was thrust on the

Amphibious Base without a lot of prior discussion. We didn't have our financing fully organized yet and there wasn't anything in the base's budget for the SEALs. So the base would take some money from Special Services, a little money from the Seabees, and some from other organizations to build us up. We were very close to being McHale's Navy at that time. We were secret and no one could talk to us. Not that they'd have learned much; very few people in the Team knew anything about what we would be actually doing. There were a few missions that were going to start very soon, but little beyond that.

Everything that came down to us at the SEAL Team followed a single channel of communications. But there were several different people feeding the channel. Someone had planned out what we would be getting into in the way of small boats and riverine warfare. Another guy was talking about HALO operations, but it wasn't the same person. Another guy was talking about the special delivery units for the submarines. But none of these people seemed to be talking to each other. All of these things were coming at us from different areas. There wasn't a single man at the top looking at everything and funneling us directions with some kind of priority.

The equipment we had at the very beginning was almost a bad joke. We didn't have much of anything in the way of gear. Guys were going into civilian stores and buying their own gear, even their own handguns. I never really wanted to know the full story, but Roy Boehm went out with some of the men and came back with AR-15 rifles. Later enough AR-15s came in to equip the whole Team and SEAL Team One as well. Those were the first AR-15s in the Navy. The Army wasn't going to see the M-16 for several years yet. And Roy just bought them through an account he had available. Then the ammo was made available.

There was one big thing that we were sure of—schooling. Everyone had to go to school. That put us in very different areas of the country at any one time. I think that Joe DiMartino, Roy Boehm, Chief Boesch, and I passed each other every few months and said hello, asked who was around, and if anyone new had shown up. This was because we were being sent everywhere.

They sent me to the Royal Canadian Air Force Survival School in Edmonton, Alberta. Then I was sent to the Army's Jungle Warfare School in Panama. Then it was off to the Marine Corps Escape and Evasion School in Pickle Meadows, California. And I was sent to a Code School in San Francisco. All of these things were four and five weeks long and you were away for all of them. I would come home, my wife would do my laundry, and I would go into the base for a few days. So everyone was cross-training.

The Marine School at Pickle Meadows, California, was one of the real eye-openers of training. It was unbelievably effective. First off, we took a bus out of Reno, Nevada, up into the mountains to where the school was located. You were tired when you finally got there and the instructors told us just to throw our equipment into our rooms and that they would give us an orientation speech.

Just a few minutes into the speech, the doors flew open and guys stormed in wearing Soviet uniforms. They gathered us all up as prisoners and stacked us in the back of a truck like cordwood. Then they drove off, traveling for hours over back trails, kicking up dust, and winding and turning through rough roads. Then they took us from the truck, stripped us of our belts, shoelaces, and whatever else we had with us, and threw us into compartments.

They had different-size compartments they put us in depending on what they wanted to do. When they wanted to talk to you, they had this one container that was about the size of a coffin. They would put you in there and pile heavy rocks on top of the box and just let you go for a few minutes, only you didn't know how long the wait would be. Another of their devices was a big pipe in the ground full of water.

There was a wire mesh above the pipe that they closed once they slipped you into the water. The water was about up to your chin. All of a sudden they would throw a whole bucket of water into the pipe and you would crash your head into the mesh trying to rise above it. The water would cover your head, but what you didn't know was that there were a number of holes all around the pipe that drained the water away in something like 30 seconds.

They would ask you questions and dump water in on you. This was great training. All of their techniques had been taken from people who had faced it firsthand in prison camps in the Soviet Union and North Korea. They gave us about a day and a half or more of the prison camp treatment, then we were "released" and had half a day off. Then the classroom work started and the instructors showed us what we had done wrong.

Those of us from the Teams knew nothing, or very little at most, about how prisoners had been interrogated during the Korean War. There were simple tricks that had been used. If it was cold and you asked for a blanket, you first had to sign for it. This was not anything unusual for someone who was in the service—you signed for everything. The next day they showed the propaganda documents about how we had signed confessions about the atrocities we had committed. That wasn't what had happened, but they showed us how it could be made to look that way.

So after three days of classroom training, they took us up into the hills in groups of four and chased us. We could come in every morning and they would give the group of four people a couple of hot dogs and a cup of rice. We had lucked out because of some maneuvers that had been staged in the training area. One of the men with me was a SEAL corpsman and we found two boxes of C rations that had been buried by the troops. Checking the dates on the boxes, we saw that they were fine. So we sat up there for two days eating regular Army chow, so that wasn't too bad.

The lesson I learned during that school was if you were captured and they were going to kill you, they would have already done it. Nothing was worse than dying, so just take the abuse you were going to get. Don't fight it, don't make a big deal, do nothing. The only way to beat the system at all was to do nothing.

No one back at the Team ever said, "What do you do if you get captured?" And that was simply because everyone said it didn't matter how many they were fighting, they were not going to be captured. And the question never had to be answered. No SEAL was ever taken, alive or dead. It would have been a huge propaganda coup if a SEAL had been taken in Vietnam or wherever. He would have been paraded through villages and shown off. There were rewards placed on a SEAL's head in Vietnam, and it was never collected. What every man in the Teams knew was that you never gave up, and you never left anyone behind. It didn't matter who you were, what your rate or rank was, everyone knew that. Everyone was important, and everyone was a Team player.

But we still had a lot to learn about being a SEAL. That first year at SEAL Team Two, I don't think that anyone could tell you anything about what happened at SEAL Team Two as a whole. No one was around long enough to find out. Then we started to sit down and find out more about where we were going. People started to plan more about what would happen with us operationally.

One day I received orders for four officers and twenty-eight men who were going to arrive. Two of the officers were senior to me and I thought I was going to be replaced. Finally, I received a phone call from Lieutenant Knight, who was one of the officers. He asked if he could come over and meet with me and I quickly agreed. This sounded like a chance to find out just what was going on. Then Lieutenant Knight arrived and the first thing he asked me was, "Why am I here?"

Now it was time for a call to Washington. When I got through to higher command, they told me the situation was highly classified and that I would have to go up to D.C. for a meeting. So I flew up to D.C. and was told that I would be receiving boats within the next two weeks. Two of the boats would be PT boats that were being taken out of mothballs in Philadelphia and reactivated. Another two boats would be brand-new craft coming in from Norway. The enlisted men and officers were going to be my boat crews.

The boats were late in coming, so I found things for the extra men to do. They were a little bummed out because we made them do calisthenics right along with us every day. Some of those men had been on ships for years, so it was a good idea to try to condition them and get things ready.

Finally, the boats arrived, and they came with a package that contained information about riverine warfare. That made sense. We were

Navy divers and combat swimmers. What was going to be used in the rivers and shallow waters? You could tell that at that time they were thinking about Southeastern Asia. We weren't really going full bore in Vietnam yet, that was still some years away. But you could tell that was the direction things were pointing.

These boats did not have torpedo tubes, so we were not a part of the regular Navy and were not going to attack large ships. Instead, these boats were going to be used to move people in and out of areas, make quick raids along coasts and up rivers. Everything on the boats was geared toward making as much speed as possible. What we did was discuss which weapons would go on them, where they would go, and why. How could explosives be safely stored on them? Could you take along a limited amount of diving gear if you needed it for an op?

We made a lot of mistakes initially. The diving gear question was reexamined and it was asked what it would be used for in the first place. Those boats were for running and fast striking, not supporting an underwater operation. Everything was trial and error, since there was nothing written up on how these boats would fight.

We finally came up with the information to write up the manual for using these boats. A Commander Clay gave me a great book compiled by the IRA, of all people. Another book I used was on guerrilla warfare and it was from the CIA for dropping into Cuba. The works of Che Guevara were used. All of these things pointed at the jungle as a place to fight.

We started to get more information from the Army Special Forces. We had a lot of people who wanted to fight in the jungle, but no one really knew how to do it. How was a patrol conducted? How many people did you need in one? What were their jobs, their equipment, their support? All of these questions had to be answered and we had to obtain the equipment we needed to conduct the operations once we had the answers.

We tried to take a look at each situation and get the best people the new Team had on it. Joe DiMartino was told to take a look at the dive locker. He was not only to make note of what we had on hand but also to take a look around in the industry and see what else might be available. We started to work with the Emerson as our new rebreather rather than the old system which had been in-house at UDT for a while.

Another officer was a lieutenant (jg) who had also been a mustang and a gunner's mate when he came up through the ranks. He was asked what we were looking at in the way of weapons. One man was very experienced with parachutes, so he was asked to make his recommendations.

The guys in the armory were told that they weren't just to polish equipment. They had to come up with whatever weapons we were going to need. What were we going to do with them? And where were we going to get them? We had to study foreign weapons, since we might have to use them.

That sort of thing got a lot of people thinking in the Teams. You could see the enthusiasm build up during those first few years. Everyone had something to contribute, and it wasn't things that had just been passed on by others who had learned about them years before. Assigning the men projects that they had to research stretched them and made them learn more than they would have learned any other way. And we started learning more about what we were going to do and where we were going to go.

It was very tough in the beginning in part because some of the other services saw us encroaching on their mission. The Army Special Forces helped us, but wondered if we were going to take some operations away from them. Marine Force Recon felt the beach and hinterland was their territory and now this new Navy unit (us) was taking that away. That's the way it was and that was the way it was going to be.

The regular Navy had gotten behind the SEAL concept for one reason: money was being sent to Special Warfare units. The Army had the Special Forces, the Air Force had the Air Commandos, and the Navy didn't have anything. What they had was the UDT, which they now made into a Special Warfare unit. That meant we would be getting special funding, and in the next year the money came from Special Warfare.

In the early years there was a lot of rivalry between the SEALs and the UDT. It was like brother against brother. That took its toll along the way and we had to work hard and quick to repair the break.

The backbone of the UDTs, the SEALs, the Scouts and Raiders, or whoever is the individual. It was high-quality individuals put together that made the Team. We were worried about the training units. Would they be able to maintain the quality of their graduates and increase the numbers to fill the new Teams?

The training units always had pressure on them from outside the community to ease up, change things, make a quota in the number of graduates. That was one of the things that we felt we could not give in on, no matter what else we did. That pressure never went away. My last year and a half in the service, I ran BUD/S training in Coronado. It was a continual battle against outside forces who tried to change the way we did training.

Noncommunity people wanted to know what made some trainees quit and if we could talk them into coming back. As far as I was concerned, I didn't want to talk them into coming back. They had quit, they didn't want the program, and that was enough.

That constant pressure to change training was a much bigger concern than the rivalry between the UDTs and the SEALs. As far as the rivalry went, in a short period of time, as we worked together more, it became a benefit. The competition drew the best from both sides. But there were some jealousies that also came up.

We had started with nothing at the SEAL Team. But then all of the money and all the new toys started to arrive. Now the UDT didn't have everything and they were feeling left behind. Now they were borrowing from us and we were happy to share. I like to kid Richard Marcinko about the time he came to me while he was a third class at UDT 21. And he was in the UDT parachute locker, only they really didn't have much in the way of parachutes compared to us. So we would take many UDTs with us when we went jumping. Again, this was for a building up of the individuals who made both Teams.

Now we started to build up our supply of equipment and increase the skills we needed to operate. The boats were developing in application and people were brought in to do that job. Now the whole Special Warfare unit began to take shape. The boats would take us in and out, and we wouldn't have to worry about that. That freed up men in the Teams, and qualified personnel were in short supply to begin with.

Then we started building a staff, and that took a lot of the paperwork burden off those of us in command. Dave Del Guidice and I were the commanders of SEAL Teams One and Two, but were just lieutenants. My knowledge of office procedures was limited. I had never really been behind a desk during my time in UDT. The second month I was at SEAL Team Two, they assigned me a first-class yeoman. That was the best thing that happened to me. Not only did he know procedures, he could type. Everyone wanted a report on what the new SEAL Team could do, what we were learning, and when we could do whatever. We could not operate and do all of the paperwork. Now it was starting to get done.

President Kennedy had a lot of influence on the creation of the SEALs, even if not directly. He wanted a force that could fight the wars that he could see coming up, not the major land battles where tanks slugged in out on the plains, but the little guerrilla fights that could bleed a country dry and make it fall. During the president's visit to Little Creek, I had the privilege of talking to him for twenty minutes about the Teams and what we were to do. An unheard of amount of time in his schedule. But he had an enthusiasm for what we were and what we were going to do. That came in part from his own Navy background in PT boats during WWII.

President Kennedy knew what a small group of determined men could do. And he wanted that capability for his armed forces. Why were the first two commanding officers of the SEAL Teams lieutenants? Because he did not want the new units to be led by men who had been brainwashed by the traditional Navy. If full commanders had been put in charge like the Navy wanted originally, it would have been a, "We're going to do it this way because this is the way we do it on a destroyer or cruiser or whatever."

Del Guidice and I used to kid each other that what was wanted was *a couple of dummies who could just stand up there and take it. I hadn't been involved in any of the creation and planning of the new SEAL Teams. But I was open to new ideas and new things, so that was why I was put in charge of SEAL Team Two. And the same general thing is what led Dave Del Guidice to be put in charge of SEAL Team One. If things had been done any other way, the SEALs could have been just another unit. And they never were.*

■ Chapter 31

SKILLS

The men who filled the ranks of the first SEAL Teams were chosen for a variety of reasons. All were competent operators and most had long proven themselves in the UDTs. Others had already received training that the rest of their teammates would receive at formal schools. And some had skills they could teach to their Teammates. Among the plankowners of the SEAL Teams were a number of individuals who possessed all of the above characteristics.

Leonard "Lenny" Waugh, Senior Electronics Chief, USN (Ret.)

As a plankowner of SEAL Team Two, I was one of the original crew to man the Team, handpicked by Roy Boehm from the ranks of UDT 21 back in 1962. Rudy Boesch and I were both over in Europe on a deployment when the orders came out for us to report to SEAL Team Two. We were flown back to Norfolk and were met at the airport by Harry Beal. He was the one who told us that we were no longer frogmen, we were SEALs. I had always wanted to be a frogman; now I'm a SEAL.

It was the next day, January 8, 1962, that we found out what the SEALs were. We mustered at UDT 21 and were moved over to this little place that had been set aside for SEAL Team Two. I was impressed to be there, but all we were told that first day was that SEAL stood for Sea, Air, and Land. And that was about all we could be told.

For myself, and a number of others, we wanted to know a little bit more about what we were going to do. We were told that we would be parachuting, and that pleased me because I like jumping. Then we were told that we would be working underwater. That also pleased me since I liked diving. It sounded like my kind of thing, but I still had no idea what we were going to do.

I had joined the Navy back in 1951. By 1954, I had volunteered for the UDT and went through training with class thirteen. We started in August 1954 and graduated that December. My classmates included Roy Boehm, Jake Rhinebolt, Bill Sutherland, Bill Bruhmuller, and a number of others who stayed with the Teams. My class had a very good retention rate, our guys mostly stayed with the Teams throughout their Navy career. I stayed with the UDT from 1954 until 1962, when I was moved over to the SEAL Team.

When the first class of frogmen went to Jump School down in Fort Benning, I was in Europe on a deployment. But I was back in time to get to Jump School with the second group from UDT. From the moment of my first jump, I knew this was something I liked.

We came back from Jump School in November 1958, and within a month or so I was the first frog on the East Coast to make a free fall. We knew nothing about how to do it; I had bought a parachute and just strapped it to my back. In fact, I had to wear two harnesses to jump. The reserve chute wouldn't fit on my parachute harness, so I had to wear a second one just to hold the reserve chute.

After that first free fall, everyone in the Team seemed to get the bug and we all started parachuting. It may have been my parachuting skills that helped get me picked for the first SEAL Team, but I was also a brown belt in judo, an electronics technician, and maybe some other things that may have gotten me picked, or at least pushed me in the new Team's direction.

Later I was one of the first two SEALs to go to the Air Force's Judo School in Nevada along with Jim Wilson. We were both to feel out how that school was set up and whether it would be a good place to send the SEALs. I felt the Air Force had done a fine job in their training and we both recommended the school. The first martial art studied at SEAL Team Two was judo. There was a Marine who came down to our training and taught judo to the UDTR students. After several of us received our belts, we started teaching the art to our Teammates. But the Air Force course was our first organized martial art training school.

It wasn't very long after the SEALs had been commissioned that I was sent over to Vietnam. Bill Burbank and I were sent to the West Coast to join with a SEAL Team One detachment and we went to Vietnam in early 1962. That detachment was MTT (Mobile Training Team) 10-62. I had no idea what we were going to do over there. The mission turned out to be training Vietnamese naval personnel. But I loved the country very much and came back from the deployment with a Vietnamese bride.

Personally, I thought we were doing a bang-up job over there. We were in Da Nang teaching their personnel to do underwater work, demolitions, and sneaking and peeking. Eventually, our training helped develop the Vietnamese Junk Force, their Biet Hai. Later the West Coast SEALs helped train and set up the Vietnamese LDNN, their Lien Doc Nguoi Nhia—"soldiers who fight under the sea"—the South Vietnamese version of the SEALs.

Five years later, in January 1967, I returned to Vietnam with SEAL Team Two's Third platoon. Larry Bailey was our platoon leader and I was with him in first squad. Bob Gormley was the assistant platoon leader and he had second squad. Second platoon from SEAL Team Two also deployed with us, with a fresh young ensign Richard Marcinko as assistant platoon leader.

Everyone from SEAL Team Two had wanted to go to combat in Vietnam with the first deployment. SEAL Team One had been in operation incountry for almost a full year before we arrived. I felt very good about coming back and being able to fight for my wife's coun-

try. We thought we were doing some good and were going to win the war against the VC.

This wasn't really my first combat in Vietnam. Back with the MTT in Da Nang, we had gone out on several ops with the Army Special Forces. They had wanted to see a little bit of us and we wanted the same of them. So we kind of cross-trained each other a bit.

But that first deployment was different. We knew we had the best group going from SEAL Team Two. We were all handpicked and enjoyed working with each other. What we called a crackerjack group.

We didn't win the war, though we did think we might at the very beginning. But the SEALs certainly carried their share of the load. We did well in the operations we did and left our mark on the Viet Cong.

■ Chapter 32

FIRST COMBAT

No matter how well trained, how experienced in other ways, or how old and mature, a SEAL or UDT man can never be certain about his reactions to combat until he has experienced it firsthand. That experience allows the operator to know and be certain of the confidence he can have in his training. He knows how to react and has proved it to himself.

During the first years of the SEALs' direct action involvement in the Vietnam War, combat veterans were few in number. Initial deployments could be nerve-racking when platoons finally went out on their first operations. To ease a new platoon into operating in Vietnam, members of a previous platoon that had been incountry for a while or were from a platoon rotating back to the States would introduce a new platoon into an operational area.

Breaking-in ops became a standard procedure for the SEALs throughout the Vietnam War. Experience could increase an operator's confidence in himself, his training, and his teammates. And actions during combat could draw out the finest in men.

Frank Toms, Boatswain's Mate Third Class

A brother of mine had been in the Navy before I joined. He left the service just as I finished high school. There wasn't a job I could find and so I decided to join the Navy, as he had done. My brother had told me that I would be bored to death in the Navy if I didn't get into something exciting like a UDT or SEAL Team. And that was where I first heard of them. It was my second or third week of boot camp in San Diego in 1964 when a person came around recruiting for UDT.

Sinking deep into the mud of Vietnam, this SEAL operator keeps his Stoner Mark 23 light machine gun well clear of the mud. Having just stepped off the insertion craft, this man has sunk to his hips in the thick, brown mud. It is situations like this that proved the value of the mud flats training during UDTR and BUD/S.

U.S. Navy

The person that I happened to interview with was Bud Jurick, who was well known to all of the instructors I was soon going to meet. Bud had been in just about every Special Warfare group the services had to offer. He had been a Marine, an Army Ranger, and looked like a Sergeant Rock from the comic books. He had this deep voice, square jaw, and immaculate appearance. He was impressive, and I took one look at him and thought I wanted to be one of those.

He tried his best to talk me out of volunteering for UDT training. I had done fairly well on my entrance exams and could have gone to an A School. But I was adamant and wanted to be a frogman.

My UDTR training was with class thirty-four, a winter class in Coronado. And of course, mine was the last hard class. At first the place scared me to death. I wasn't sure I could get through training, but I definitely knew I wanted to. Every day in training on the Amphibious Base—and this was back when we were training out of a Quonset hut on the eastern edge of the base itself—when we marched to chow we would see frogmen and SEALs in their starched fatigues. Later, when some of us were in the Teams, they would make us get dressed and stand there for the trainees to see us.

By far the hardest part of training for me was the last three weeks, which were spent on San Clemente Island. We went out there in a large landing craft with everything we would need for our stay. We lived in tents, had cold-water showers, and worked a lot. Those three weeks on San Clemente you use and practice everything that you've learned in training. For the past eighteen weeks, you had been training for San Clemente. And when you got to the island, you put it all together.

Every night we had a night problem. You would go to your briefing first. Then go and do the problem. And then return and do your debrief on the problem. And if you didn't do things right, you did the whole thing over again. In the three weeks we were there, we did every problem over again except one, and that was because it was daylight by the time we finished it.

Hell Week was rough. But you kind of go into automatic pilot during that week. I was fortunate enough to be in a very good boat crew. Everything was competition between the crews. A boat crew was seven people, and that moved over into SEAL Team with you since a squad was also seven people.

But during that week, we had races every night carrying and paddling our rubber boats. Everything was competition and mine was a good boat crew—that and we cheated a lot. But cheating was encouraged. We were going into an unconventional unit; unconventional thinking was something we were going to have to practice. But you didn't snivel about things when you got caught cheating during training either.

Winning Hell Week was worth it for my crew and me. We secured a half day before the rest of the class, and we didn't have to help clean everything up either. That week was tough and we did lose a lot of people. Other folks quit, but I was just too focused on the competition to think about quitting. It wasn't that difficult for me, though it was very hard just to stay up during that week. We were always falling down almost asleep. Guys would slip facedown into their food while eating.

And I thought about quitting—there was no shame in that. But it wasn't during Hell Week. Instead, it was at San Clemente Island. Whenever the instructors told us to hit the beach, of course we all did. And a buddy of mine and I were convinced that the instructors were going to kill us. And that was crazy, so we were going to quit right there. Then the instructors told us to hit the beach and we jumped right in along with everyone else.

The cold was miserable. I was from Texas and had seen blue northerns before. But I'd only seen the ocean once before joining the Navy. And that was the Gulf of Mexico, which is nothing like the big, blue, cold Pacific.

The last day of training was wonderful. It's very hard to put into words what it feels like to graduate from UDT training. All of these people that we'd seen during our training, all of these impressive frogmen and SEALs—and you always knew the SEALs because the UDT wore a patch on their sleeves—these people all made an impression on us.

And then there were the instructors. For twenty-one weeks they had been trying to kill you. And then at graduation, they put their arm around you and said, "Welcome aboard." For me, it was just incredible. It had seemed such a lofty goal, and I was sure I would be struck down by lightning or something before I graduated. But there I was standing with my class that last day. My brother was extremely proud of me.

After graduation, I was assigned to UDT 11. At that time there were UDT 11 and 12 on the West Coast, and UDT 21 and 22 on the East Coast. SEAL Team One was in Coronado and SEAL Team Two in Little Creek. Basically, we had the odd numbers and they had the even ones.

But once I was at UDT 11, I couldn't wait to make a deployment to the Philippines. That first trip was great, especially for a youngster from Texas. It was just incredible to go to the Philippines, do the diving there in the tropical waters, and meet the girls in Olangopo town. We even got to go to Vietnam and practice a bit of what we had learned.

Our Vietnam deployment was the hardest I worked in my life. We were stationed in Da Nang, but were going someplace up and down the coast every day to do beach surveys. Frequently, we would be out on an APD for up to two weeks reconning beaches. We would be in the water from 8:00 in the morning to 5:00 or 6:00 at night. Just swimming and taking depth soundings was the basic job, along every inch of landable beach in Vietnam.

More often than not, at the end of the day, we couldn't take a freshwater shower because the ship only made enough fresh water for the crew. It seemed the UDTs were always extra baggage aboard the APDs. That was the toughest I ever worked. And it wasn't due to any enemy action. We just didn't see a lot of that in the UDTs at that time. It was because we reconned more shoreline than I care to think about.

After I did that first deployment with UDT, I was able to go over to SEAL Team One. It was 1966 and they were stepping up the SEAL commitment to the Vietnam War. SEAL Team One had the only combat deployments to Vietnam that year. SEAL Team Two wouldn't be in-country with platoons until early 1967. They needed people for the SEAL Team and I was torn between volunteering and staying with UDT. I didn't have to worry about things much since I was one of the guys soon drafted into the SEAL Team.

They came up with a list of names that was posted that basically said we need you in SEAL Team One. So as much as I would have liked to go back to Olongapo and further adventures with UDT 11, being invited into the SEAL Team was quite an honor.

So I went into SEAL Team One in 1966. After arriving in the Team we all had to first complete SEAL cadre training and then get put into a platoon. We were one of the earliest full platoons to go over to Vietnam. Previously, the detachments that were sent over were as groups of SEALs. All of us were pretty much in our regular Team platoon as we went through cadre training. There were no veterans of Vietnam in our platoon, just fifteen very green rookie SEALs.

So we just had to kind of step out into the waters of combat in Vietnam. And that first stepping out, our first operation, was terrible. The SEALs who had been over there before us took us to a fairly secure area for our "break-in" op. Being rookies, we didn't know a secure area from anything else. So we had about a five-hundred-yard patrol that took us all day to conduct. We were positive that there was a VC behind every tree.

After you had been over to Vietnam and been on a number of operations, you started to learn about what was, and wasn't, there around you. By the end of our six-month tour, we knew that there were certain parts of the jungle you could run through. And there were other parts where you had better get down on all fours and crawl.

It was kind of tough breaking in to combat. But that was our job and we did it. The first combat engagement we were involved in could easily be described as total confusion. Until you have been in a SEAL seven-man fire team and heard all of the noise when we initiate an ambush, you can't believe anything can be that loud. Personally, I always tried to think of what it would be like to be the other guys, and I think I would have been just as terrified as they looked.

Frequently—like 99 percent of the time—we saw the expression on their faces because we always tried to take prisoners. There was a saying in the Team that dead men wouldn't talk. So we wanted them alive. Where we were operating in the Rung Sat Special Zone, prisoners were very valuable.

We always tried to take prisoners rather than just kill the enemy. If there are two expressions in Vietnamese that I will never forget, they are dung lai, which means "stop," and lai dey, which means "come here." So we always said those words, unless of course they were pointing a gun at us. Even when we initiated an ambush, we tried to start it with those words first.

More often than not, the VC would be terrified looking up and seeing seven people with green and black face paint on. And that would be if they could see us at all, since we were always well camouflaged. Most of the time they would dive into the water and all hell would break loose as we opened fire. The blast of fire and noise would just seem to be total confusion. Your job during an ambush was to cover your sector of fire and just empty your weapon at whatever target was there. And that would usually be the time when the VC's heads would come bobbing up in the water. I often felt sorry for them, especially during that first operation of ours. We operated at night and used a lot of tracers, so seven men with automatic weapons would put out a lot of noise, muzzle flashes, and streaks of red light zipping through the air.

What stands out most in my mind about that first tour is how we matured and operated before we left Vietnam. Most of the SEALs I knew wanted to stay over there and just not go back to Coronado. Even some of those who went back quickly tired of the regimen and wanted to join with the first platoon they could find that was going to Vietnam.

But during that first six-month tour, the platoon all grew as a team. And I stress that word Team because I think that's where the SEALs and UDTs have excelled. Other Special Operations units gradually incorporate the team concept into their actions. But with us, it was drilled into you from the first day of training. You were part of a Team and you always did what was best for the Team. The very few people we had in the unit who really didn't know the meaning of fear stood out a bit for the rest of us. I personally knew the meaning of fear, and I have no trouble saying so. But you put seven of us together, and we forget the word.

During that first tour, my platoon, Kilo Platoon, had been ambushed badly by the VC. It was 7 April 1967 and we were going back up the river to Nha Be and our home base when we started taking some fire from the shoreline in the Rung Sat. That was pretty much what we had been looking for, so we turned the boat around and headed into the fire, giving them all we had from the weapons we carried and that were mounted on the boat. As luck would have it, they dropped a mortar round right into the boat.

When the mortar shell went off, I and my closest friend, Jan Halderman, were manning one of the forward .50-caliber machine guns. The blast knocked us both away from the gun. Jan was down on the deck, hurt pretty badly in the neck. I was down there with him trying to get a pressure bandage out to put on his wound. Then I felt something running down my eyes, reached up, and found out it was blood. So I panicked a little bit myself. First I got Jan taken care of, then I was trying to get somebody to look at my head.

I thought maybe I had been wounded pretty badly in the head. I could see my helmet lying on the deck and there was a big hole in it. The corpsman or one of my other Teammates just kind of told me to shut up, that there were other people who were really hurt in the boat. Later I found out that Lieutenant Dan Mann was killed along with Don Boston, who had gone through class thirty-four with me, and Ron Neil.

That was one of the SEAL Teams' worst single losses due to enemy fire during the Vietnam War. Not only were three men killed, but a large number were wounded as well. In fact, I'm not sure anyone on the boat escaped some kind of injury. Mine was pretty light, though my helmet didn't look like this was so. I spent one night in the hospital, then got up and hitchhiked back to the base.

The Stoner machine gun was the SEALs' weapon of choice in Vietnam. It was a belt-fed small machine gun that fired the same round of ammunition as the M-16 rifle. It carried a 150-round belt and could put out its ammunition at 850 rounds per minute on the average. Each squad tried to have at least two Stoners with it on every mission.

On my second tour, we were going in on an ambush, transporting in an LCPL. We had probably an hour or so to go to get to our landing site and I was doing what a lot of combat men do in such a situation. I was asleep. You get up about 1 A.M. to prep yourself and your gear. Then get on board the transport going in to the insertion point. I just always liked to grab a little extra sleep before insertion time.

Since I had experience in that part of Vietnam, I was helping to break in a new platoon. Three other guys from my platoon were help-

---

ing as well. We were going in on a predawn ambush. My fire team was in the front of the LCPL, which is a small cabin maybe eight by fifteen feet. There were eight of us in the cabin and one of the guys, Walter Pope, had stacked his Stoner right next to where he was sitting on the deck.

We must have hit the wake of a sampan or some other wave. But the motion knocked Walter's Stoner over; it hit the deck and the retaining pin fell out of the action. The retaining pin holds the bottom trigger mechanism to the weapon, letting the trigger and sear hold the bolt in the cocked position. When the weapon opens up, there's nothing to keep the bolt from going forward and the weapon just starts firing uncontrollably.

From what the doctors tell me, I was immediately hit by six to ten rounds from that Stoner. What was later explained to me was that Walter Pope grabbed up his weapon and pulled it to his chest to try to control it. And that has to be so since there were eight of us in the front of that boat and only Walter and I were hit. The six to ten rounds that hit me were bad, but Walter took over forty rounds when he pulled the gun into himself. He died instantly and I passed out.

Before I slipped away, I cried out, "Ambush!" When that sudden firing woke me up, I fully believed we were being ambushed by the VC. Only later did I realize what had happened. If it hadn't been for Walter pulling that weapon into himself, I don't see how any of us in that cabin could have escaped. He sacrificed himself for his Teammates.

In spite of our losses, the SEALs were very successful in their operations in Vietnam. We operated in small groups and could move very quietly through the night. We could sneak up on a position, or just hide in the darkness, and wait until the enemy practically came within arm's reach. And the VC weren't expecting us, they weren't listening for us. And we could get close enough to kill them with a knife, and we did.

The SEALs of today should know the debt they have to the Teammates who came before them. The men like Roy Boehm, who started the Teams, and others who opened the way in Vietnam. We all come *from frogman stock, so there's a big debt to those men from before the SEALs, back to World War II, who started it all.*

I was one of the men lucky enough to have been in the Teams during the Vietnam War, during which the SEALs made their name known. But the men who came before then are the ones who made me. And the SEALs of today were made by those of us back then.

Even when we didn't have a separate insignia to wear, people on a Navy base knew who a SEAL was. Today it's the same man, but he also has the Trident he can wear. But all of the SEALs are the same underneath. We are all tough. You put seven of us together and we're a Team. Those guys are my brothers. You put seven of us together and nobody can whip us.

■ Chapter 33

THE JOB

In the SEAL Teams and the UDTs, men were often asked to volunteer for some very unusual assignments. A single operator with a long career in Navy Special Warfare could find himself in a number of unusual situations. It is to the SEALs' credit that all missions and assignments were considered and no worthwhile idea was left unacted upon.

The kinds of missions and assignments that were offered to the Teams include learning an esoteric skill, qualifying on an unusual piece of hardware, or participating in a scientific study or experiment. All of these were conducted at one time or another in the Teams.

One thing that is always a constant in the Teams is the level of trust between Teammates. Each man knows the others can be depended on completely. When one man cannot complete a job, others will join in until the job is finished. It is their sense of brotherhood that causes many men in the SEALs and the UDTs to risk everything for a Teammate. Though these men are patriotic to the extreme, they do not always accept the hardships and do the difficult for their country, or even the Navy or their families. But they always do it for each other.

There is a bond between partners in the Teams that is hard to explain to the outsider. Even when that partner isn't human. . . .

Bill Bruhmuller, Master Chief Boatswain's Mate, USN (Ret.)

A strange set of happenings led me into the UDTs and then SEAL Team Two. When I came into the Navy in January 1953, the Korean War was still going on and I wanted to be active and do my part like so many of my peers did. At that time I only thought the Navy owned things like battleships, aircraft carriers, destroyers, and submarines. I didn't know anything about the Amphibious Force or the minesweeping force.

As luck would have it, I did not get my requested assignment aboard a battleship. Instead, I ended up in what was called a receiving station in Charleston, South Carolina. For about 15 months all I did was the general work assigned to new untrained sailors in the Navy. Mess duty in the galley and all the other jobs the low man on the totem pole does. It didn't take too long for me to notice the guys being transferred from the jobs that I was doing onto the little wooden minesweepers. During my Charleston tour, I had the occasion to ride one of these minesweepers and I quickly became satisfied that it was not what I wanted to do.

Fortunately, the plan of the day came out prior to my getting orders to the minesweeping fleet and it had a request out on it for volunteers for underwater demolition training. I didn't know anything about UDT but thought it sounded good and that I should check it out. One of the first requirements for UDT was that you had to pass a swimming test. That didn't sound like any problem for me; I had always been a good swimmer.

Going over to the testing area, I took the PT test and swimming test, passed them, and thought this was going to be a piece of cake. Then I talked to several of the older guys who had been around awhile. All they could tell me about UDT was that going to UDT was crazy and that I didn't know what I was doing. But they would never tell me what UDT was all about.

My orders came in and I was on my way to Little Creek and UDT training. This was what I had wanted, to go to a Navy school. My parents had always told me that the Navy had the finest schools of all of the services and to get into as many of them as I could.

Arriving in Norfolk on a Sunday, I had to take a taxi down to Little Creek, which was basically all farmland in those days. Dropped off at the main gate, I had to walk a couple of miles with my seabag on my shoulder, down to a building where I checked in with a guy. He told me to grab a bunk and that they would get with me in the morning. I stayed in that building for three days without hearing from anybody. Finally, I started searching around and found out where I really was supposed to be. There was a receiving station that was a holding billet for a couple of weeks until the next training class started.

Then training started and I got the surprise of my life. I was waiting for my little copy of the curriculum and the class agenda, and my book and pencil. That was not what I received. What I did get was a boot in the fanny, a couple of sharp words, and the orders to fall in smartly.

The class was something like 138 people at the start. Within a matter of weeks we were down to 60 men, then 50, then 40, and the class size continued to drop. Hell Week was the third week of training then. Fortunately for me, just a class or two prior to my training, Hell Week had been the first week of training. If I had gotten off of that taxi, stepped onto that base, and gone right into Hell Week, it would have really been a shocker. Three weeks later was enough of a stunner.

There really wasn't any preparation, at least not enough to get you ready for that intense training. That was probably what caused a lot of people to drop the program: they weren't physically prepared. Being eighteen years old and in fairly good shape worked in my favor, so running, push-ups, and such didn't bother me as much as they could have. And as training went on I got better and better.

But Hell Week was the real eye-opener as far as sitting in a classroom and learning things from an instructor standing on a platform was concerned. But I was going to learn a lot from the group of instructors who were running around beside me, booting me in the pants and yelling and screaming at me, belittling me, and doing everything they possibly could to make me want to go away.

Now I was in the position of still not wanting to get aboard that minesweeper, and seeing what the Amphibious Forces had in the way of ships. LSTs, AKAs, APAs, and other landing ships I also certainly didn't want to go aboard. So the only option I had was to try to stick this training out and see where it led. I am very glad I did this. It set up the rest of my Navy career, for which I am extremely thankful.

My class was class thirteen and there were 21 of us standing there that last day at graduation, seven officers and 14 enlisted men. Along the way, 117 people had quit, so that made us a very proud and select few. In those days we had two Teams, UDT 21 and 22 on the East Coast, and UDTs 1, 3, and 5 on the West Coast. Each coast ran its own training then and the graduates stayed in their respective areas.

My fellow graduates and I were given the option of UDT 21 or 22, and I selected 22. Several of the people I had come to know during training were at Team 22 and that's why I selected it. My class was almost split in half between Teams 21 and 22.

There's no question, of course, that the East Coast had the harder training. Now, before my West Coast Teammates start sniping at me, I should really say that both coasts had equally hard training. The quality of graduates from either program stands on its own. The whole objective of UDTR, and later BUD/S, training was to try to get the student to graduation mentally prepared for whatever his career in Special Warfare might hold for him. Neither coast had the option of relaxing its standards when it came to training. This resulted in fit, prepared men who had gone through the hardest training available in the U.S. military. This level of fitness also resulted in some strange assignments for UDT operators.

In 1957, the United States still hadn't gotten into space proper. We had launched gondolas from balloons and rocket planes had gotten men up to 150,000 feet or so, but a man hadn't really gone into space yet. There was a difference of opinion between scientists as to what kind of person, from a technical and physical perspective, it would take to get into space and survive the trip. The scientific people felt that the person would have to be superior technically because there was so much involved in the instrumentation and all the other factors involved in going into space. The other, much smaller group felt that the individual had to be a physically superior specimen to do the job and have the best chance of returning safely.

There was an Air Force Captain McGuire who was able to convince the powers that be to let him go out and find the best physical specimens he could. That captain received permission to basically shop through the services for men. He ended up coming to the Underwater Demolition Teams at Little Creek, where twelve men were selected for the program.

The twelve of us who were chosen were transferred to Wright-Patterson Air Force Base in Ohio, initially for two weeks. We went up to the base in groups of four to a cordoned-off, secure area. From 6:00 in the morning to 6:00 in the evening, we worked, doing just as many tests as the scientist could possibly do.

For example, we sat in a heat chamber at 140 degrees for three hours. They wanted to see our reactions—would we remain stable, get antsy, or just what the exposure to heat would do to the human mind and body. They had a series of serums they injected into us and then a scientist would sit there and talk to you for probably about 60 seconds. He would tell you your mouth was getting watery and then your whole body would seem to turn red and you felt that you were burning up inside. Then they would immediately stick your feet into a pan of ice water. It was our reactions to sudden extremes that many of the tests were examining.

The cordoned-off section of the base prepared for us had its own barracks and private mess hall. There were MPs guarding the roads so no traffic or anything else could come near us. We were not to be disturbed at all. You take four UDT sailors who are used to a lot harder schedule than 6:00 to 6:00 and park them on an Air Force base: they will become a little bored. There was not that much of a physical demand put on us, certainly nothing compared with our initial training. So for the first week we pretty much adhered to their rules. By the second week the TV, which really wasn't all that great in those days, wore thin fast.

We would get up and maybe go for a little run in the mornings, something the guys would mostly just do on their own. By the second week we decided to venture out a bit and see what town was like. All we had with us was one Navy white dress uniform and the rest of our clothes were our regular green UDT fatigues. Since we didn't have a car, we would have to hitchhike into town anyway, so why not wear the white uniform? It would be easier to get a ride, since people in those days would readily pick up a serviceman.

There wasn't a real big problem for us to get past the guards at the base and around our building. We hit the road and started thumbing our way into town. We discovered an amazing number of young ladies who wanted to give young sailors a ride. This turned out to be a pretty good exercise for us. We would dance and have a few drinks, just a generally good social evening, and probably get back to the barracks around 1 or 2 A.M.

It was quite evident to Dr. McGuire that something was different about us the next morning. The procedure was, if you were going to make a high-altitude run in the pressure chamber, you had to pre-breathe pure oxygen before the test. So they put a flight suit helmet on you and you breathed oxygen for a couple of hours to take all the nitrogen out of your system. Having your head in that helmet put you in a closed, tight compartment with little noise surrounding you. And the several hours of just breathing was pretty boring, and the extra sleep didn't sound too bad after the longish night before.

The scientists were not used to having their test subjects react as we did. The tight helmets often caused claustrophobia. To us, it wasn't much different than wearing a face mask on a dive. We just went to sleep. And when they woke us up, we would tell them to leave us alone. It was when we went into the test chamber that things changed a little bit.

When we were all wired up to record our reactions, the doctor would look at his readouts and ask us what we had done the night before. He would ask us if we had gone out on the town the night before and we would just tell him we watched a little TV and went to bed. But that we woke up about midnight and just couldn't get back to sleep.

There wasn't much question that he knew what was going on. When he asked us if we had been drinking, we could easily tell him that there wasn't anyplace in our limited area where we could go drinking. And that we were staying religiously dedicated to the program. It was to his credit that he never tried to discourage what was going on. He knew what we were doing. But the combination of our daily activity and our nightly escapades made answering his questions even better.

There wasn't much question that we were fit enough to take on the doctor's daily physical activity. And our enthusiasm for our nighttime activities gave him an end result that was even more than he had expected. And the results were rewarding for us as well. You knew that you were doing something worthwhile. As well as learning things about yourself that you probably never would have otherwise gotten the chance to learn.

We were "flying" in the big centrifuge, all of us pulling about eleven Gs. One of the guys, Tom McAlllister, passed out. And the reason Tom passed out was that he was too relaxed. That sounds unusual, but normal anxiety can keep some of the muscles twitching more, keep the blood moving better, and push more of it up to your head. Full relaxation will let the blood drain from your head and you'll just pass out.

Even though we were high-level physical specimens, it didn't prove necessary to be like us to go into space. The recent space flight by John Glenn helps prove that. He's a kind of national hero who has taken care of himself over the years. His attitude is so positive that there didn't seem to be anything bad that could happen to him on his space shuttle flight. And it's a great example for those people in the population who are reaching sixty and seventy years old. It shows there may be some life in the old body yet.

And being one of the people who helped to literally open the door on the manned space program feels pretty good. And I'm sure the other individuals who were up there with me feel equally good about it. The small part we played was one of the stepping-stones for what we are doing today. It's nice to know you were a contributor to that. And what seems particularly fitting is that Captain Bill Shepherd is going to be the first commander of the space station, and Bill Shepherd was also a SEAL. So the group of us back then helped pave the way for Bill, and I let him know it every time I see him. But that's just friendly in-house harassment.

It was only a few years later that I had another first adventure in the UDTs. Prior to the commissioning of SEAL Team Two, there were some indications that I was going to be selected by this new special organization. Nobody would tell you what its members were going to do, what the mission was, or even how big the units were going to be. We didn't even know if it was going to be located at Little Creek. No information was coming out on the new Team. All that was told to some of us was that after the first of the year (1962) we were going to be assigned to this new unit. You did have the option of refusing the assignment. But any guy in the Team, if you give him the chance to try something new or something that's going to be a challenge, he's going to be very reluctant to turn it down. So I certainly wanted to take the new assignment on, and that was the only way I could learn about what it was going to be.

The original group was only about ten people. Roy Boehm was our

Navy SEALs

officer-in-charge and we had yet to be officially formed up, but we were getting close to it. We met in a little office over in UDT and stood around wondering what we were supposed to do. So we tried to at least look busy, really just kind of fake it through the day until commissioning came through. When Rudy Boesch came out during a muster on January 8 and read the names of the members in the new Team, we were all excited to have been selected. By that formation, we had some twenty-five guys and that number soon jumped up to fifty.

There was still a lot of anticipation about what we were going to do. And that was the big question, what was our mission? All we could find out was that we were going to be an unconventional warfare unit. That kind of set your mind to working. That assignment meant we would have to be sneaky, and we would have to be trained in a lot of other special areas that we hadn't studied for our UDT mission.

Bill Bruhmuller during a SEAL demonstration at St. Thomas in the U.S. Virgin Islands in 1964. He is wearing a Rolex watch as well as a Mk 1 Mod 0 compass on his left wrist. In his left hand is the transducer for the AN/PQC-1 UTEL underwater telephone hanging from his right hip. His breathing rig is the closed-circuit Draeger Model LT. Lund II.

Richard Brozack Collection

Roy Boehm, being the crusty old gentleman that he is, knew that if the Navy was going to start an organization like this, the best way to keep its members strong and get them ready for what might be coming was to get them trained in whatever and wherever they possibly could. So he arranged schools all over the country. This was when we really got our interface with the Army Special Forces down at Fort Bragg. A lot of the young SEALs today don't realize this, but if it hadn't been for Special Forces, I'm not sure we would have gotten off of dead center as easily as we did. We owe a lot of thanks to them. And I don't hesitate to convey that to the young lads in the Teams today.

Some of the materials we trained with over the years involved some really exotic hardware. And eventually, a few of us worked with the most exotic piece of hardware there was. The weapon was called the SADM—Small Atomic Demolition Munition. It was a nuclear weapon that could be delivered by a couple of people to an objective area. The SADM could be swum in submerged, towed by a swimmer pair, or parachuted in. Both individuals were trained on setting up and arming the device. Then they were to exfiltrate and there would be a nuclear blast.

As I recall, the bomb was maybe a maximum of three feet long and probably between twenty-four and thirty inches in diameter. This was after it had been taken out of its large, sealed packaging of course. When I was selected to participate in training on the activation of the device, and we were given the briefing on what it was and its capability, it really scared the hell out of me. There was a really great potential here for a massive screwup.

I just thought that things go wrong sometimes. But if this one went wrong, I wouldn't be around to know about it. I think I had kind of mixed emotions about working with the SADM. One thing was that I wasn't afraid to get involved with the thing. But I was very afraid to make a mistake with it. This was something really highly technical. It wasn't like another explosive charge or demolition technique, nothing of that nature. This was something that could cause massive destruction. So I was just very concerned that I might do something wrong so that it wouldn't explode, wouldn't do its job. What it could do to me didn't really enter my thoughts. I had to learn how to handle it, and to do that properly.

Prior to SEAL Team Two's direct involvement in Vietnam, I had watched the news clips of the war and what had been going on in that country. In a number of the clips, I saw Marines and Air Force personnel going on patrol, and there were dogs in the scene. So I had the idea that maybe there was a mission involving dogs with the SEALs. By this time we pretty well knew we would be doing pa-

trolling, ambushing, and things of this nature. A dog offered something beyond what the human was capable of, and that was their senses of hearing and smell. If that was going to be an advantage to us, to help us in our missions, I felt that we should examine its feasibility.

Silver, one of SEAL Team Two's German shepherd Scout Dogs demonstrates the view an unwary Viet Cong could expect to see.

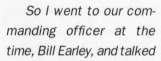

So I went to our commanding officer at the time, Bill Earley, and talked to him about the idea. He agreed that if I could get a dog and get the training needed, we would give the idea a try. There wasn't enough time before I was scheduled to deploy to Vietnam to go to the formal military dog school at Fort Benning. So if I could get some basic training from the Norfolk police force, Bill agreed to back my suggestion.

There were only about ten weeks before I was to deploy. I called the Norfolk police, the K9 force; Bob Bouchard was their training officer at the time. After explaining my idea to him, I asked if there was any possibility of coming up with a dog. He wasn't quite sure if he could do that, but he promised to call me back inside of twenty-four hours with some kind of an answer.

Fortunately, Officer Bouchard called me back and said that someone had just donated a dog we could have. After talking the situation over with his command, he had found out that the idea was okay with the police if the Navy would release me for the standard six-week K9 police training. That was okay with everyone involved and I went out for the training.

The dog was a big German shepherd named Prince and we went through training very well. The police had attack training, search

---

training, and things of that nature that still looked like they would fit our mission. There isn't a lot of difference between a house and a hooch as far as searching goes. So I saw some value in all of the training. There was the opportunity to fire on the range with the dog lying beside you to see if the animal had any problems with the loud noise. Prince had no anxieties about the firing and that was another plus for him since I wouldn't have time to worry about the dog once the shooting started.

Prince was an exceptional dog and he learned very quickly. On graduation day, he graduated number one in his class and I think I came in number two. But we became very close and we deployed to Vietnam together. What I hadn't known was that we would be deploying to the Mekong Delta area of South Vietnam. That is a very muddy area.

During the dry season, everything was fine. The dog would go with us on patrols and we could use him very well. When we set up an ambush I could have the dog lying right beside me. He knew when something was coming down the trail or canal well before any of us. You could tell by the way his ears moved, and the way he would look in a particular direction and his nose would go up in the air. He gave us the early warning system that was so valuable in the performance of our jobs. We would know what direction something was coming from and surprise tended to be on our side.

We used the dog on patrols and hooch searches as well. Prince found several weapons caches in hooches just because of the smell. I did have him out on a patrol one day when his searching abilities became something of a bother. During our training together at the police K9 unit, we always trained for a length of time together and then took a break. Just like a human, the break allows the dog to relax and come down from what he was doing. The dog remains in a work profile until you tell him that you're going on a break. You just change your voice and tell him, "Take a break!"

Now, this is play time, and Prince would wander off to do dog things. He would never go very far and would always immediately return when called. So there I was, just kind of sitting there, leaning up against a tree, and Prince came back and dropped some toy he had found right between my legs. It was a hand grenade.

That scared me to death. He just backed up and looked at me. In his mind, he had just found a ball and he wanted me to throw it so he could chase it. So I took it away and said, "No!" He went away, and came back with another one. Again, he dropped it between my legs and I took it away again. He did this three times and dropped all three grenades between my legs.

Something was going to blow eventually if I didn't find out where the dog was getting the grenades. So I followed Prince and found where he had uncovered a fairly large weapons cache. He was pulling out the hand grenades and bringing them to me, thinking they were balls.

Prince was later awarded a Purple Heart for his actions while we were on a standard patrolling operation one day. We were looking for some North Vietnamese who had supposedly infiltrated down into the delta. We ran into a small ambush while patrolling. It was quite surprising that he didn't pick up on it before the ambush was triggered. Prince was acting strange, but he didn't do the normal alert indicating that someone was to the right, left, or directly in front. I think this might have been because the enemy had been there for some time.

They initiated the ambush and there were a lot of hand grenades being thrown back and forth. Prince didn't get shot or hit with a grenade. I think it was a 40mm grenade that went off very close to us that hit him with some fragmentation in his side. That wasn't enough to stop him during the action and he was later awarded the Purple Heart.

In this deployment, Prince and I were part of the first SEAL Team Two platoons deployed to Vietnam. People have different impressions of what it's like to go into combat. I was in the Dominican Republic operation some years earlier and some people consider that to have been active combat. But when you get into a country like Vietnam where the fighting is really very serious, you have thoughts about what you may run into and how big a force you may have to fight.

The SEALs sometimes operated in three-man or six-man groups,

Chief William Bruhmuller and Prince after their first tour in Vietnam. Prince is wearing the Purple Heart he received for being wounded during an ambush in Vietnam. The action took place during the first SEAL Team Two combat deployments of the Vietnam War.

depending on the mission. We all had the inherent confidence in ourselves and our abilities that we could handle most anything that was tossed at us. But when it comes right down to seeing a mass of people firing at you, and you have to shoot them before they kill you, there are some anxieties you are going to have. I can still remember the first guy I ever shot. It was in a river. And I swear I can still see him today. There was probably a fraction of a second of hesitation on my part before I pulled the trigger. There was still that quick reaction in my mind where I wondered if there was something else I could do besides kill this guy. My common sense won out before he was able to open fire.

Once you have passed through that first incident, you realize that this is the job that you have been trained to do. And you try to do your job to the very best of your ability. Every SEAL I know, or at least the very great majority of them, develops a mind-set that; regardless of how horrendous the situation might be and what the end picture looks like, they all possess the ability to do what they have to. That's probably the reason why the majority of the SEALs who served in combat in Vietnam don't have the flashbacks and things that so many of the other military forces have had.

These were young kids who fought in that war. And these were horrendous experiences to many of them. To see body parts flying around and battle taking place can be quite shattering to someone who places a value on human life. And seeing how fast that life can be taken away will affect many people. So in order to maintain the peace of your own mind, just do your job and forget about it. And I think everyone possesses that ability.

■ Chapter 34

THE TESTING GROUND

The Vietnam War was to prove to be the crucible that would test the SEAL Team concept. All that had gone before with the UDTs, the actions in Korea, WWII, the Scouts and Raiders, and finally the NCDUs on Normandy Beach laid the groundwork for the SEALs. Vietnam would prove what they had become, the finest unconventional fighting force of the United States military.

Every skill the SEALs had would be tested to the utmost in the rivers, streams, and canals of a small country at the outermost edge of the Southeast Asian mainland. They would soon prove worthy of the legend that grew up around their actions during seven years of active combat.

And the story of the SEALs was just beginning.

The Trident

The only outward sign of a uniformed Navy man being a SEAL, besides his high level of fitness and air of cool assuredness, is the Navy Special Warfare Breast Insignia he wears on the left breast of his uniform. The Trident, as it is called by the men who wear it, can be properly worn only by an individual who has completed the Basic Underwater Demolition/SEAL (BUD/S) course of instruction or the earlier Underwater Demolition Team Replacement (UDTR) course and a six-month probationary tour with a SEAL Team.

Receiving their Trident is a significant moment for all of the men of the SEAL Teams. Some of these men can put their feelings into

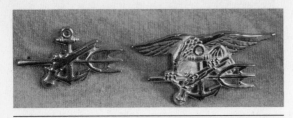

The UDT breast insignia on the left and the Naval Special Warfare uniform breast insignia on the right. The UDT insignia was only issued for a few years before it was decided that both the UDTs and the SEALs would wear the same uniform device.

Kevin Dockery

words, while others have a hard time expressing their emotion at such an event. And a very few others can describe the Trident in very proper SEAL terms understandable to all members of the Teams.

Barry W. Enoch, Chief Gunner's Mate, USN (Ret.)

When we first became SEALs, we were given our Tridents. The Tridents for enlisted men were silver at that time and the ones for officers and chiefs were gold, to match our uniforms. Later on, the gold Trident became standard for all Navy SEALs and Navy SEALs only.

The Trident itself is a breast insignia. The lower part of it displays an anchor, indicating the branch of service, the United States Navy. Neptune's scepter—trident spear—is crossed with the anchor, indicating that we work from and under the sea. There's a half-cocked pistol, an old flintlock type, showing that we're always at the ready. But to me the most important part of it is the American eagle, which stands watch over the anchor, standing on the trident and holding the pistol.

The American eagle was se-

The U.S. Navy's UDT Combat Swimmer.

U.S. Navy

lected because of his keen eyesight. He's a bird of prey that flies higher than any other bird. The stronger the winds and higher the air currents, the better he likes it. He selects a mate for life and he builds his home and returns to it each year. That nest he rebuilds each year.

And he feeds his mate while she's on her nest. When the young are hatched out, he helps feed them. He's one of the only birds that helps teach his young to fly when they're ready to leave the nest.

You'll find the American eagle in a lot of places. You'll find him on the President's Seal. You'll find him on guard over the Ten Commandments behind the Supreme Court. And you'll find the American eagle at the top of a flagstaff and on an officer's hat device.

In all of these places, you'll find the eagle standing tall and proud.

Today's Navy SEALs proudly carry forward the traditions laid down before them in the deserts of the Middle East, the swamps of Vietnam, the frozen wastes of Korea, and the beaches of the Pacific and Atlantic Oceans.

Andre Dallau

But only on the Trident does he bow his head. And when I think back on the men in combat, the ones who are always standing on the edge . . . the ones who have been wounded, and the ones who have died . . . I think I can understand why he bows his head.

And that's what the Trident means to me.

Index

Metzel, Jeffrey C., 26, 27
Mine clearance, 217, 223–224
Minisubs, 44–45
Mission of Navy SEALs, 176, 265, 275–276, 277, 284
Mistakes of Tarawa Atoll ("Terrible Tarawa"), 59, 68, 187
Mobile Training Team (MTT), 319, 320
Montgomery, Sir Bernard, 31
Moreell, Ben, 13
Motivation Week. *See* Hell Week
MTT (Mobile Training Team), 319, 320
MU (Maritime Unit), 123
Mustang officers, 307

Naked Warrior, The (Fane), 177
Namur invasion, 61
Naval Combat Demolition Units (NCDUs), 23–58. *See also* Kauffman, Draper
    Admiralty Islands invasion, 51–52
    Amphibious Training Base (FL), 16, 33
    assignments, 47–58
    atomic bomb, feelings about, 57
    Biak landings, 38
    cast and recovery system, 54
    closed-circuit rebreathing rigs, 56
    cold-water training, 43
    DUKW vehicles, 24
    elimination event for, 35–36
    enemy fire, 42, 54–55
    England assignments, 48
    Ernest J. King, 8, 25, 26
    fear, 41–42
    Frank Kaine "MacArthur's Frogman," 8, 36–47, 50
    frogmen, 42
    grouper fish feast, 40–41, 52–53
    Hell Week, 35–36, 50, 65
    Japan occupation, 41–42
    jobs of, 51, 53
    John F. Kennedy and, 45
    Kiska invasion, 48
    Landing Craft, Personnel, Large (LCPLs), 29, 31
    Leyte Gulf operation, 38–39, 53
    Los Negros operation, 39–41
    mental discipline for, 54, 57, 79
    minisubs, 44–45
    mission evolution, 46–47
    missions of, 175
    Naval Demolition Unit #1 (NDU), 28–47
    Navy Bomb and Mine Disposal School, 27, 28, 29
    obstacle clearance, 25–26
    officers versus enlisted, 49, 57
    Operation HUSKY, 28, 30–31
    physical fitness for, 50, 64

    reconnaissance of beaches and offshore waters, 37–38
    Robert P. Marshall, Jr., 32–33
    Scouts and Raiders (S&Rs) and, 171
    Seabees and, 28–31
    selection process for boat crews, 65–66
    Sicily target, 24–25, 28
    Southwestern Pacific assignments, 48
    swimming emphasis, 36
    teamwork importance, 34–35, 41–42, 54, 80
    training experiences, 49–50, 63–65, 78–79, 81–82
    Underwater Demolition Teams (UDTs) versus, 43–44, 46
    William L. Dawson, 48–58
Naval Demolition Unit #1 (NDU), 28–47
Naval Underwater Demolition Training and Experimental Base (HI), 60
Naval Warfare Information Publication excerpt, 289–290
Navy Bomb and Mine Disposal School, 27, 28, 29
Navy Demolition Unit, 20–22
Navy in Scouts and Raiders (S&Rs), 17, 18
Navy SEALs commissioning, 289–305. *See also* Callahan, John; Navy SEALs creation
    A. D. Clark, 302–303
    airborne qualification, 293
    Allan Reed, 289
    AR-15 rifle, 295–297, 302–303
    Bill Hamilton, 291, 292, 304
    bureaucrats' uncooperation, 296, 297, 298, 299, 304
    "caustic cocktail," 300
    crossbows, 262–263, 298–299
    Cuba reconnaissance, 299–302
    Cuban Missile Crisis, 304–305
    date of commissioning, 290
    David Del Guidice, 284, 290, 296, 306, 316, 317
    Draeger closed-circuit breathing rigs, 299–300
    Edmund B. Taylor, 303
    George Walsh, 299, 300
    guidance for unit ("anywhere, anytime"), 291, 292
    H. R. Williams ("Lump-lump"), 299, 301, 304
    James "Hoot" Andrews, 256–265, 294
    John F. Callahan, 290–291, 304
    John F. Kennedy inspection, 302, 303–304
    Lyndon Johnson, 302
    Magnum Model-19, 297
    Naval Warfare Information Publication excerpt, 289–290
    Presidential Priority, 294, 298, 304
    Robert "The Eagle" Gallagher, 294–295
    Rudy Boesch, 179–183, 294, 308

Normandy and Southern France (*cont.*)
    "Jeeter's Skeeters," 86
    Joint Army Navy Experiment Test (JANET)
      board, 80, 88
    Landing Craft, Mechanized (LCMs), 80
    Landing Craft, Tank (Rockets) (LCT(R)), 83
    Landing Craft, Vehicle, Personnel (LCVPs),
      82–83
    Landing Ship, Tank (LSTs), 81
    largest amphibious operation, 76
    Myron F. Walsh, 77–89
    Omaha Beach, 76–77, 145
    Operation DRAGOON, 77
    Scouts and Raiders (S&Rs), 79, 169
    shell hole-to-hole movement, 84–85
    Tellermines, 86, 88
    unexploded ordinance, 86, 88
    Utah Beach, 76, 77, 84
North Africa. *See* Operation TORCH
Northern Attack Group, 19, 20

OCI (Office of Coordinator of Information), 122
Office of Coordinator of Information (OCI), 122
Office of Strategic Services (OSS), 122–128
    Arthur Choat Jr., 124
    cast and recovery system, 125
    Charles Q. Lewis, 124–128
    double-loop snare, 125
    espionage, 123
    Iwo Jima invasion, 125–126
    Kerama Islands operation, 127
    Lambertsen Amphibious Respiratory Unit
      (LARU), 123, 148
    Landing Craft, Personnel, Large (LCPLs), 126
    Landing Craft, Personnel, Ramped (LCPRs),
      125
    Maritime Unit (MU), 123
    Office of Coordinator of Information (OCI),
      122
    Okinawa operation, 127
    Operation TORCH (North Africa), 22
    others' view of, 123
    swim fins, 123–124
    Underwater Demolition Teams (UDTs) and,
      123–124
    William J. "Wild Bill" Donovan, 122
Office staff for Navy SEALs first CO, 316
Officers versus enlisted
    Naval Combat Demolition Units (NCDUs),
      49, 57
    Underwater Demolition Teams (UDTs), 131,
      159, 239, 267
Okinawa invasion, 113–118
Okinawa operation, 127
Olsen, Norman H., 43, 187–188
Omaha Beach, 76–77, 90–91, 145
OP343E organization, 282
Operating Platoons, 104–105

Operation CORONET, 157, 183
Operation DRAGOON, 77, 169
Operation FISHNET, 223
Operation FLINTLOCK, 61–62
Operation FORAGER, 63, 70
Operation GALVANIC, 58
Operation HIGH JUMP, 95
Operation HUSKY, 28, 30–31, 248
Operation NEPTUNE, 90
Operation OLYMPIC, 183
Operation OVERLORD, 90
Operation TORCH (North Africa), 18–23
    Central Attack Group, 19
    Fedala target, 19
    first major amphibious landing, 19
    Frederick A. Henney, 21
    Henry K. Hewitt, 19
    Higgins boat, 21, 22
    James W. Darroch, 20
    Lloyd Peddicord, 21
    Mahdia/Port Lyautey target, 19, 20, 21–23
    Mark Starkweather, 20, 22
    Navy Demolition Unit, 20–22
    net/cable cutting team, 20–22
    Northern Attack Group, 19, 20
    Office of Strategic Services, 22
    recognition of, 20
    Safi target, 19
    Scouts and Raiders (S&Rs), 18, 19–20
    Southern Attack Group, 19
    Western Naval Task Force (Task Force 34), 19
Operation WATCHTOWER, 10–11
"Operational Plan 712H—Advanced Base
    Operations in Micronesia," 7
Orange plans, 7
OSS. *See* Office of Strategic Services
Others' view
    of Navy SEALs, 264
    of Office of Strategic Services (OSS), 123
    of Underwater Demolition Teams (UDTs),
      112, 116, 231–232

Painter, William, 269
Parachuting
    accident, 270–271
    Gap Assault Team (GAT), 96
    Navy SEALs skills, 287, 297–298, 318
Patton, George S., Jr., 18, 30–31
Pearl Harbor attack, 5
Peddicord, Lloyd, 17, 21
Peleliu, 104, 113, 118, 147
Perkins, William B., Jr., 147
Philippines, 113, 324
Phonies, recognizing, 241
Physical fitness
    for Naval Combat Demolition Units (NCDUs),
      50, 64
    for Navy SEALs, 102, 167

Kevin Dockery has been a soldier in the President's Guard under Presidents Nixon and Ford, a grade-school teacher, radio broadcaster, gunsmith, and historian. He even spent time in Iraq and Kuwait during Desert Storm as what he refers to as a "corporate mercenary." As a noted military historian, he has written a number of books detailing the history of the Navy SEALs and the lives of the men who lived that history. He has also written a number of firearms reference books, some of which are considered unique in the field. Presently living in southeastern Michigan, Mr. Dockery follows his hobbies of raising Rottweilers, blacksmithing, and knife and sword making.